the real thing

BROWN'S IRON BITTERS

CURES
MALARIA
DYSPEPSIA
& FEMALE
INFIRMITIES

ALDEN & CO. LITH. BALTE

THE BEST TONIC.

the real thing

performance, hysteria, & advertising

MADY SCHUTZMAN

WESLEYAN UNIVERSITY PRESS

Published by University Press of New England

Hanover & London

WESLEYAN UNIVERSITY PRESS

Published by University Press of New England

Hanover, NH 03755

© 1999 by Mady Schutzman

Printed in the United States of America

5 4 3 2 1

CIP data appear at the end of the book

For

ANNA, 1894–

&

AMANDA, 1990–

Contents

Figures

Preface

In writing this book I faced two particular methodological challenges. The first was how to simulate the culture of popular advertising iconography—a crytopographic and self-referential semiotic environment—while simultaneously critiquing this culture. The first draft of this book contained more than 250 ad images, an attempt to replicate the disconcerting barrage of images we consume daily. I wanted readers to experience the disjunctive polyglot of meanings, associations, and contradictions that characterizes image consumption. I did not want the more rational, discursive logic of the written text to engulf the more ambiguous logic of the visual text. Although only 65 of the 250 images prevail here, the reading remains inspired by visual logic; the criticism refuses linear, historical dissection; and the tension between sensorial and rational knowledge is intended to mimic the daily tension of regulating reality.

The second, and related challenge, was to write criticism that spoke *through*, and not just *about*, hysteria. Earlier drafts of this text dramatically reflected the hysteria that it explicates: the authorial voice was more polyvalent, juxtaposing autobiographical anecdotes, feminist theory, medical case studies, original (parodic) advertisements, hysterical rants, correspondences with advertisers, and metawriting. I wanted to convey and incite, through my textual strategy, the vertigo of hysteria's ever-shifting symptomology. It is by way of an embodiment, or performance, of hysteria, that I envision a viable critique of hysteria.

But in the attempt to provide a more "consumable" critique in keeping with biddings of academic marketability, much of this earlier vertigo was tempered. In the name of "readability," I meet you here, in these pages, in a more temperate invocation of hysteria and advertising culture than my own critique deems imperative. I worry that a significant point has been obscured: normativeness is *not* the language through which hysteria, or any "cultural pathology," will be transposed into a language of critical intervention. I worry that in the face of a more straightforward narrative, you will mistake this book as a history.

I have, nonetheless, granted the subject of this story—hysteria—opportunities to speak for itself, so that readers may become attuned to its desires, frequencies, and warnings. Although we may try desperately not to listen, hysteria is not going away. I invite readers to enjoy whatever "confusion" they might encounter as the delirium that results from a critique that is intimate with its delirious subject. I ask that readers consider that the absence of a map is a challenge to study the darkness, so to speak, without reaching prematurely for a flashlight.

Acknowledgments

I was very fortunate to study at the Department of Performance Studies, Tisch School of the Arts, New York City, under the concurrent influence of Mick Taussig and Peggy Phelan. Mick taught me where spirit and power conspire, how language both kills and heals, and how the everyday is riddled with terror. I am particularly thankful for his embodiment of these paradoxes. Peggy launched my love affair with theory; she guided me to that remarkable place in my own writing that hung precipitously between passion and articulation; she forged a path in my thinking wherein pleasure and pain, love and resistance, living and loss, are not mutually exclusive. I thank Peggy also for her patience, innumerable readings and insights, and for following me so generously through every symptom and nervous dysfunction a writer could suffer.

I am grateful to Joe Roach who read this text in its early stages while serving as acting chair of performance studies and offered support beyond the call of duty, even after departing from Tisch School of the Arts. I am indebted as well to the encouragement of faculty members Phillip Zarrilli, Richard Schechner, and Barbara Kirshenblatt-Gimblett. My colleagues at New York University stood by me in the researching, conceptualizing, drafting, redrafting, presenting, and re-presenting of this work. I want particularly to thank Jan Cohen-Cruz, Rebecca Schneider, Leslie Satin, Jon McKenzie, Robert Sember, Navtej Johar, and Deborah Mutnick.

My writing of this manuscript was enriched by a 1994 Mellon-Pugh postdoctoral fellowship at California Institute of the Arts, and by my subsequent full-time position at CalArts. I thank the School of Critical Studies for providing me with time, funds, and encouragement toward preparation of the manuscript. Particular thanks goes to Dick Hebdige, dean of critical studies, for valuing the literary endeavors of the faculty and accommodating the mercurial demands of finishing a book; to Cathi Love and Lisa Pedersen for an uncountable number of small favors; and to Beverly O'Neill, provost, for approving several requests for Faculty Development Grants. I am grateful to Liz Barrett for her suave and reliable research on hundreds of ad images, to Teena Apeles for tracking down the trade cards, to Ken Ehrlich for bibliographic research, and to Amy Jones and Dina Pielaet who so generously offered their services at Greyzone and so endearingly tried to convince me that the task of reproducing images would be fun. I thank all the agents, artists, managers, and legal departments who granted permission to reprint images. I credit *Vogue* as the original source of the image "Special Effects."

I would not have sat down and sent out more than two hundred letters requesting permission to reproduce the ads without the knowledge, humor, and confidence of Stuart Carroll from Volunteer Lawyers for the Arts, Los Angeles.

The last year of writing this book was particularly challenging. I was experiencing radical shifts in my relationship to language that I did not know how to integrate into a text that was nearly complete. Gwyn Erwin made it possible for me to proceed without compromising my most current thinking. I cannot thank her enough for her close readings, copious notes, and heartening words. Rebecca Schneider read the book cover to cover at least twice and has been an indispensable critic, editor, and fan of this work for years. Friends and colleagues read chapters and inspired me with their invaluable comments: Jon Wagner (for everything from Yellowstone to Paris, the Moustache to Mulligans), Sande Cohen (who kept me laughing with his delirious tactlessness), Roberta Cantow, Eve Luckring, Connie Samaras, and Linda Kintz. I owe much of my sanity and resilience to Jane Lazar, Eve Luckring, and Susan Harris for simply being there, again and again.

Several years ago my mother sent me a card featuring a disarrayed woman scribbling madly in a book. The accompanying text read, "Pretty slow day here." And inside: "Just sitting around drawing stretch marks on magazine fashion models." My family may or may not understand exactly what it is I do, or why I do it, but they have never asked that I do anything else. Thank you, family, for your ceaseless confidence in me.

Suzanna Tamminen saw me "perform" one of the chapters in this book as part of the *Medical Circus*—a multimedia show of words, slides, music, video, and installation art presented at the Performance Studies Conference at New York University in 1995. Thank you for appreciating what I presented that day amid the spectacle of helium-inflated latex gloves, crinolines made of plastic speculums that lit up like Christmas trees, and flying Day-Glo ping-pong balls signifying schizophrenic turmoil. I appreciate your meeting me in that hysterical moment and accompanying me through this entire process with such poise and steadfastness.

Finally, I am grateful to Tom Radko and the e-mail brigade—Jan Cohen-Cruz, Phillip Zarrilli, Amy Robinson, Charlotte Canning, Terri Kapsalis, Sande Cohen, Peggy Phelan, Jill Dolan, Jon McKenzie, and Rebecca Schneider—for helping this book survive February 1998.

M.S.

the real thing

Introduction

I. HOW TO ATTACK A WILD HUNGER

It could be any time of day, any place. The ground she slithers across appears suspended, ethereal. It's striated like a stormy sky, or a well of stairs, a cage, tiers of light and darkness betraying depth and clarity. She is scantily dressed and her body is striped like the space that surrounds her, holds her, threatens to forsake her. Her hands emerge out from the space toward me, fingers clawed and spread wide as if grasping, as if she knows she is on shaky ground. Her hair is mussed to appear like the mane of a feral animal. Beneath curled brows her eyes squint with rage, her lips are tightly gnarled as if restraining an overwhelming desire to bite. My own brows cramp in response, I detect my lower jaw receding just enough for my upper teeth to protrude like fangs, my nostrils to spread. Poised in defense, I sense we are kin. But the tiger markings sketched on her dimly lit face with black eyeliner strike me as absurdly unreal. I consciously relax my jaw and for a moment reclaim my civility. "You know when you're working hard and you begin to get really hungry?" she moans seductively. My stomach growls with sudden appetite. I turn the page, disgusted with my body's involuntary reaction, but I can't get away. Animal prints are in this year. Clothing, accessories, lampshades, bedspreads, gift-boxes, more women's bodies, all transformed into cheetahs and leopards. I turn back to the riveting stare of the tiger. Bold copy declares, "HOW TO ATTACK A WILD HUNGER." I want to know. In spite of her preposterous appearance, I notice that she is much thinner than I. "Think about what you're doing," she barks. I think I eat too much junk food. "Tear into a Tiger's Milk bar, all natural and packed with lots of good-for-you things. Because it's a jungle out there." I wrest my attention from the page and look around the room, seeking comfort in familiar things. But everything appears disconcertingly strange.

In the late 1800s, after a century of neurasthenia, fainting spells, and "the vapours," a new female malady was "discovered." Hysteria (from the Greek *hystero*, meaning womb) erupted in epidemic proportions across the body of women in England and the United States. It signaled, in ways often not heeded, a sickness ravaging not only woman's body but the social body.

Hysteria was in large part a silent scream of distress. The late nineteenth century was a time of radical change: industrial capitalism was expanding at a rapid pace, men were losing a sense of mastery in the workplace due to mechanization, women were entering the public sphere, a middle-class women's movement was flourishing, medical science was typologizing madness, and the advent of the ad agency standardized representations of gender. While opportunities for women increased, inequities of gender severely limited women's actual power within the public realm. Women protested through their corporeal bodies, expressing on a localized site that which was inexpressible on a public site. Hysterical symptoms were endless; they invented themselves as rapidly as the social body invented ways to displace societal power conflicts onto the female body as if they belonged to *her*. Hysteria in women was, and still is, a reflection of the male hysteria of dominant culture.[1] An investigation of hysteria's symptoms—particularly how and why they are performed—reveals the material reality that women cannot live.

In current late-capitalist consumer society, material realities are presented through the media, which masterly manipulates imagery to *disguise* the politics of power. First, media images represent the least privileged as mouthpieces of those who deny them power; second,

---

1. When referring in this text to "male hysteria," I am not talking about hysteria in men. Rather, I am referring to a set of (often unconscious) heteronormative social values that constitute a complex of institutional sexism and habitually gendered realms of cultural experience. I use "male hysteria" to identify a body of prevailing cultural fantasies regarding gender and the resultant practices by which reality is fabricated and sold.

they pretend that we all have equal access to power and freedom through our ability to consume. Women buy the illusions that sustain the power of those most invested in refusing their privileges to women. According to Judith Williamson (1986b),

> Women, the guardians of "personal life," become a kind of dumping ground for all the values society wants off its back but must be perceived to cherish: a function rather like a zoo, or nature reserve, whereby a culture can proudly proclaim its inclusion of precisely what it has excluded. . . . The repressed, instead of disappearing, is represented or replaced by a symptom or dream image. (106, 112)

Advertising epitomizes this paradoxical double-enunciation; it is a ubiquitous state art that barrages with incongruities and displacements through images that stereotype and idealize. The female body is represented as the dream image that disguises her own exclusion. In this book, I offer advertisements as the visible stuff that consumers mimic. Women mimic the overt solutions and looks that advertisements sell us. But the ideals sold to us are impossible to live, creating a hunger that keeps us unsatisfied and forever buying. We are both the hungry tiger and the commodity that supposedly appeases the hunger. We are hopelessly seeking the healthy candy bar in the "jungle out there." Through the consumption of advertising's "reality," consumers, particularly women, become hysterical: reality and representation blur, subject and object merge, the symptoms we act out masquerade for the social disease that causes them.

To study hysteria is to delve into the complexities of performance and mimicry:[2] through an embodiment of a sign, an image, an idea, there is a shift in meaning. As women reenact ad images that objectify them, they endow the images with a new subjectivity; women inevitably bring their individuated bodies and experiences to the stereotypical images or roles they play. The "new" performances are a combination of an immaterial image and a material body, a social agenda and a personal life, a repetition of the dictates of "femininity" and a defiance of them. They are informed by surgings of rebellion and discontent that are, in turn, appropriated in advertising imagery. The process is dialogic and ceaseless. The lived tension of hysteria is the result of ceaseless attempts to *refuse* the resolutions proffered by ad images.

2. See Taussig (1993) and Diamond (1989; 1997).

Advertising imagery prescribes how consumers are to appear and behave. Women attempt to swallow the "pills," but inside these "antidotes" are indigestible contradictions. What advertising prescribes, women regurgitate in rage, histrionics, amnesia, and paralysis.[3] These symptoms break out as the hysteric puts on current fashion with one hand, while trying to rip it off with the other. The irony is that these ambivalent performances of hysteria may teach us how to embody the duplicity of power while at the same time heal us of its toxic effects.

To utilize hysteria as a strategy of resistance or healing is possible only by becoming conscious of our hysterical performances. It is in the spirit of embracing the hysterics' insubordination and bringing it into critical consciousness that I engage this project.

2. PERFORMING AMNESIA

I was in a room of colleagues, all women. The woman conducting the workshop asked each of us to identify the first time we remembered performing. Coming from a family of frustrated comedians, at first, I remembered only a slew of unbearable moments as a spectator. My Uncle Eddie imitating Jerry Lewis and Buddy Hackett, my Aunt Sue reveling in her impersonations of Phyllis Diller and Gracie Allen, my dad's original knock-knock jokes that only he seemed to find funny. I scrolled back in time, perusing various locations for clues. Brighton Beach, P.S. 252, 1957. I was in second grade, standing among a group of children surrounding my teacher, a woman whose name escapes me but whose temperament does not. She was harsh and angular, dark, aloof. It was difficult to get her attention. I was not her favorite, but I desperately wanted to be. So I cleared my throat, over and over, each time louder and louder, hoping she would notice me, even if out of irritation. The workshop leader asked us to perform the memory. As I did, suddenly, and with an uncanny feeling of horror, I

3. I am aware here of the dangers of presenting a seemingly cohesive category of "woman" without regard to race, age, class, or sexual preference. Advertising, however, coagulates a cohesive category of "woman"; in spite of shifting faces of fashionable femininity, advertising offers (white, youthful, upper-class, and heterosexual) standardized bundles. My intention is to critique, not recapitulate, this coagulation. Image consumption of course differs for different women, and this book does not pretend to be a comprehensive reading of consumption across various demographic lines.

was thrust into a wave of memories, memories of my mother. There was no one's love I wanted more than hers, while my mother got all the love she needed being conspicuously emotional, sick, or worried to death. I remembered. My first performance, and many others to follow, was feigning illness.

Although no organic cause for hysteria was clinically proven, late nineteenth-century medical science believed that the roots of hysteria lay within woman's physical body. Treatment consisted of tissue biopsies, leechings, hysterectomies, and clitoridectomies. Freud revisioned hysteria as physical displacements or conversion reactions of psychosexual trauma rather than physiological essence. It wasn't until 1987 that the term *hysteria* was eliminated officially from use, even as its signs are still everywhere intact. Hysterical symptoms were classified in the American Psychiatric Association's *Diagnostic and Statistical Manual of Mental Disorders: DSM-III-R* (1987) as symptoms of other, more clinically substantiated mental illnesses.

Histrionic personality disorder, still referred to as "hysteria" in common parlance, is diagnosed by authorities on a basis of performative criteria. Sufferers, mostly women, are *perceived* to be overdramatic, vain, demanding, self-indulgent, reactive, shallow, and disingenuous. They are *perceived* to be incessantly drawing attention to themselves, overreacting to minor events, and displaying irrational tantrums. These performances—as well as symptoms that manifest as physical pain—continue to be perceived colloquially as signs of a woman's incapacity to negotiate conflict and incongruity, and not as signs of the conflicts and incongruities of the social body.

What is extraordinary to me about my realization of feigning illness is that in spite of investigating hysteria for more than six years, these memories were buried in my unconscious. In the desperate attempt to be seen and heard, I exhibited symptoms as if they were "real," as if they belonged to me. I did not remember them as performances because I did not experience them as performances. As a young girl, I perceived my mother's histrionic displays as something one could "put on" in exchange for attention and credibility. Women figure prominently in ad images: their bodies "put on" the credible illusions being sold. To the observer, women's subjectivities fuse with purchasable commodities. Advertising teaches women to "put on images" as if they were only clothes, and to *live* them as if they were real.

I am disquieted by the ease with which I (and many others) am complicit in rituals of submission. In realizing that my intellectual understanding does not liberate me, I turn to my body. I recognize, with reluctance, that one of the most unnegotiable aspects of malaise is shame; it appears too readily, does not respond to rational explanations, grips one's body as if no thought, no other sensation, could rent it away. In 1986, I came upon a *New York Times* book review article written by the Argentine writer Luisa Valenzuela. It was about national literacy campaigns following the overthrow of the military regime responsible for the eight-year Dirty War. Through these grassroots workshops, people were given the opportunity to put into words that which was impossible to articulate because of political repression. For years, Argentines struggled to represent in words the fear that did not go away even after overt danger had passed. They were grappling with issues of shame, powerlessness, rage, and their own internalized postures of the oppressors. Valenzuela posed several questions in her article: "After ten years of bloody censorship, does a nation remember how to write? Do people remember their own names when next-door neighbors had 'disappeared' and could not be mentioned again? How do people recognize the truth when what is now known as the complicity of silence has stifled them?" (Valenzuela 1986, 3). I wondered how women, how I, recognize the truth after centuries of censorship and complicity. How can our voices of resistance be *enhanced* by our intimacy with the dynamics of complicity?

In exploring hysteria and advertising as intimate bedfellows, I aim to expose how together they endow the female body with a signature that secures her absence while simultaneously blinding her awareness of the erasure. Herein lies the possibility of regaining vision, of investing our hysterical performances—politically, paradoxically— with the wisdom of critical sight. I do not imagine that this critical sight will mandate an ultimate termination of hysterical performances. Such a mandate is as impossible as escape from mediated culture itself. But with this realization comes the healing possible only when one abandons the search for cure.

We were instructed to work in small groups to create performances. We had only ten minutes to find tableux, gestures, phrases, sounds, movements, that together would somehow contain, or echo, elements from each participant's stories—stories of revelation. There were three of us, though it seemed there were a dozen, each story conjuring images, ghosts palpable and fleeting. As we tried to embody them the resistance was equally palpable: in my body, Joan's body, Peggy's body, I sensed that something ineffable was about to be tragically abbreviated. We were entering a kind of death space in order to give our experiences a manifest form for others to consider. Performance can do that. Performing revelation only intensified the foreboding sense of loss that I imagined would accompany embodiment.

The wisdom of hysteria works in mysterious ways. It wants to leave a mark precisely where it recognizes that nothing will remain after the act. We performed. Joan had directed us to swing our right arms over our hands and strike our left arms, as if cutting them off, in that inside tender place just below the bend of the elbow. Five times. It did not require undue force; as performance it required only the look of force. But within minutes of completing the gesture, a deep purple welt emerged that grew conspicuous and unsightly over the following days.

I took Joan's story, not even my own, into my body as a mark of an unspeakable violence. Unwittingly, I refused to perform without also surrendering, without consciousness, to an opportunity to create a physical sign that would remind me, remind others, that in our performance something bold, something brutal, would not be expressed. That in my wound was another story aching to be told simultaneously. In this wound is the revelation of hysteria itself—and the wisdom of its double-enunciation.

3. TALKING SYMPTOMS

In the pages that follow, I cite a myriad of hysterical symptoms. They range from definitive physical ailments (rashes, vision abnormalities, muscular pain, sexual dysfunction, speech impediments, nausea, and palpitation) to more dissociative forms (multiple personality, fugue states, amnesia, and hallucination). Similarly, I reference various definitions and explanations of hysteria, each nuanced differently, many in contradiction with one another. These definitions evoke the mutability associated with the hysterical enactment—a mutability that typifies the femininity invented in ad imagery. It is by virtue of this mutability that women, in attempting to fulfill what is expected of them—what is credible—are never capable of doing so. Mandates for sanctioned femininity change as rapidly as fashion. As women play these fashionable roles, changeability itself is marked by medical science as pathological. Somatic symptoms emerge, perhaps as did the wound on my arm, as signs that speak and contest the violence of being pathologized, misrecognized. Meanwhile, the political infrastructure that sustains the gender hierarchy remains relatively fixed.

Hysteria: the result of uncontrolled flow of female menstrual fluids (Veith 1963; Russett 1989; Shuttleworth 1990); the result of any control over the natural flow of female reproductive fluids (Veith 1963; Russett 1989; Shuttleworth 1990); a vacancy of consciousness in which an emerging idea meets with no resistance from any other idea (Möbius, in Abse 1982); possession by demonic forces; epidemic behavior characterized by faints, fits, trance states, hallucinations, and/or stupor (Fenton 1982); collective outbreaks of repressed tensions resulting from the displacement or camouflage of real conflicts (Sirois 1982); "biologically determined primitive patterns of behavior of survival value to the organism in response to threat" (Kretschmer, cited in Fenton 1982, 238); a distress signal (Sim 1982); a subversive demand to be seen and heard (Smith-Rosenberg 1972); a caricature of femininity (Chodoff 1982); a display of constant need for an audience in which "dramatic gestures vary with current fashions" (Sim 1982, 270); the incapacity of rational processes to monitor emotive drives; histrionic, puerile, attention-demanding, and manipulative behavior (Eysenck 1982; Woodruff 1982); physical conversion reactions that indicate unresolved Oedipal conflicts (Freud 1962); state of being trapped in the present (Chodoff 1982); state of "suffer[ing] mainly from reminiscences" (Breuer and Freud 1955, 7); incapacity to render an ordered history of one's life (Whitlock 1982); inability to distinguish between reality and illusion; lack of a core, thus an unsynthesized personality consisting of only a number of different exteriors (Jaspers 1963); "petrified anxiety" (Walter Benjamin, in Buci-Glucksmann 1987, 228); absence of the subject-object distance that allows for critical self-reflection; a disorder of doctor-patient relations (Slater 1982; Whitlock 1982); a riddle, particularly regarding sexual identity (Wajeman 1988).

Given the often incongruous definitions of hysteria (a list of symptoms would be equally long), Weir Mitchell, the famous late nineteenth-century American neurologist responsible for the diagnosis and treatment of Charlotte Perkins Gilman, characterized hysteria as "the nosological limbo of all unnamed female maladies" and renamed it "mysteria" (Mitchell, cited in Showalter 1985a, 130).

Of all the definitions of hysteria, there is one I found most enduring over time. It is also the one I adhere to most regularly when using the term throughout these pages: hysteria is the incapacity to differentiate between reality and illusion. In late-capitalist consumer culture, this same incapacity is propagated and manipulated by mass media. I suggest that this current "crisis of representation" be viewed as the hystericization of culture. Consequently, I posit that hysteria is a viable analytic for investigating contemporary postmodern conditions within which representations of reality—illusions—are the only reality.[4]

In taking this position a dilemma and a challenge immediately arise. In the last twenty years, critical theorists of popular culture tend to assume, broadly speaking, one or the other of the following postures: (1) a poststructuralist approach that celebrates the explicit surface, seeing artifice as most "telling"; (2) feminist readings that focus more often on what lies beneath the visible surface of things, on the material realities or techniques of manipulation that are being disguised. It is imperative to merge these equally significant critical approaches whose political strategies have not been successfully conjoined.

Those who practice poststructuralist writings/readings (such as Baudrillard 1990a, 1990b; Kroker 1989; Deleuze and Guattari 1988b) privilege fluid, polyphonic, and surface positionings in their analyses. Poststructuralist approaches are essential if we are to apprehend what we are experiencing. If we don't find ways to tune in to the language of cultural madness that we are investigating, then we can never heal. In diagnosing crises through prescribed codes and language, we cannot perceive the madness as anything but aberration and threat; the invaluable wisdom that it bears is destined to

4. In claiming that we all live in a contemporary state of consumer hysteria, I do not undermine or eradicate the particular struggles of women diagnosed with neurological disorders. Many cultural theorists have employed medical metaphors: Lasch (1979) with narcissism, Deleuze and Guattari (1983) with schizophrenia, Glass (1993) with multiple personality, Showalter (1997) with hysteria. While they have been criticized for collapsing actual illnesses into vacuous semiological tropes, I find their use of metaphor casts light on the pathological formulation of certain aspects of institutional culture; such is my intention as well.

be cured, or wiped out. Alternatively, a poststructuralist approach grants hysteria the opportunity to speak for itself. The problem is that those who embrace this critical methodology often neglect categories of gender and race and fail to identify who benefits from the "crisis of representation" they glorify. They read at times like overexcited junkies lost in the dream world of their own entrancing and sexist critique.

On the other hand, many female scholars, fearing that their voices will be lost again if not represented according to certain narrative conventions of coherency and viability, forge their critiques from either the launching pads of male master narratives or from a position rooted in identity politics.[5] For women to engage in intimacy with, or expression through, "pathological" conditions is to risk being labeled pathological again. The compulsion to challenge male scholars who engage in "experimental writing" without the same risks is strong. For all these reasons, women scholars generate a lot of reactive scholarship.

Many mass media critics writing during the last three decades—such as Marcuse (1964), Ewen (1976, 1988), Goffman (1979), Schudson (1984), Orvell (1989)—position themselves as immune to the effects of consumerism and mass technology. Many feminist critics, often more conscious of gender politics, similarly fail to implicate themselves in the seduction.[6] It is as if, by virtue of an assumed critical distance, scholars believe they have stepped outside the culture of representational politics, unlike the "masses" whom they

5. I recognize one reason that feminists engage with psychoanalysis is to unveil the "masculine" logic that Freudian discourse represents. The tendency toward coherence does not reflect an epistemological choice. Rather, it is in the face of potential eradication—in the very politicization of feminist and minority discourse by conventional authorities—that a more oppositional, rigid, and often essentializing counterforce is engendered. This counterforce explains, I believe, the political positioning within much antiracist work. Stallybrass and White (1986) discuss this in depth in their analysis of the carnivalesque.

6. Given the professional risks for women scholars who assume authorial voices of self-implication, I shall not disparage the works by feminist theorists who do not chose this textual approach. The most obvious exception, however, is Cixous and Clément (1975). See also Althusser (1971) and Foucault (1967). While they do not implicate themselves in their texts, they deserve citing here for recognizing that ideological transcendence is not a viable option.

portray as naively consuming advertisements without analytical reaction. I believe the general public to be aware of advertisement as hype. But awareness does not inoculate any of us from hysterical contagion. Advertisers may even welcome and profit from our apparent awareness of their spin. In recognizing that ads are superficial renditions of reality, consumers come to believe that advertisings' effects on us are also superficial. In believing we are above ads, perhaps we consume them with less resistance.

In this text, and in keeping with the very dictates of hysteria and advertising, I bring the agendas of poststructalism and material feminism into dialogue. Two misconceptions are juggled at all times: (1) the assumption that one can stand outside of culture, and (2) the assumption that one can be completely controlled by culture with no possibilities of agency.

5. STEALING THE TROPES

In studying advertising through the lens of hysteria, and vice versa, I identified five performative tropes: masquerade, ventriloquism, narrative, ritual, and magic. These are allied through the theme of duplicity. *Masquerade* suggests the relation between what is manifest and what is concealed, revealing the duplicity inherent in the construction of hysteria. *Ventriloquism* expresses the apparatus that operates behind the appropriation of voice, substitutes dummy for woman, and imposes the invisible presence of an ubiquitous authority. *Narrative* addresses language and symbolization itself, and how, in the cases of medical and media narratives, "woman" signifies and circulates male fears and fantasies. *Ritual* is the term I have chosen to address the hypnotic effects of repetition and mass reproduction, and the process through which women are initiated into appearances. *Magic* conveys the techniques that treat an abstraction as a concrete material object, transform material objects into magical and erotic powers, and create a religiosity that fosters obsessive consumerism.

These tropes are discussed in various configurations throughout the chapters that follow. They serve as performative links between the systems of advertising and of hysteria. I specify them, however, not merely to identify how hysteria and advertising use dramatic means to disable consumers, but also to identify the dramatic means that can be employed to reenable consumers. The tropes used to fool consumers are the same ones that women use to mimic and challenge the ads; what in one instance is used to dominate in another is used to resist. Hysterics masquerade the masquerade. In so doing they not only steal the tropes but the power they represent. It is through these tropes that our radical interventions are staged.

6. IMAGE-SPEAK

Advertising images "speak" to one another in codes that are visually consumed but not necessarily registered critically. The theories I purport in these pages are based, in part, on decades of images I didn't know I had internalized. Yet the very structure of this manuscript owes itself to an epiphany when the hundreds of ads "spoke" to me. One afternoon, I cathartically recognized underlying themes among a batch of unclassified ads strewn across my desk and floor, plastered on the walls, overflowing from drawers and file cabinets. I felt like Helen Keller realizing a sequence of hand signals meant "water," that another meant "book." Just as dramatically, I saw patterns and connections of otherwise floating signifiers forming several unforeseen families. The six largest groupings became "first drafts" of the six chapters that follow. These visual bundles remained the guiding principle for subsequent writing. At times their relation to one another leads the narrative; at other times, the written analysis leads.

I have limited the images to those from print advertising. First, still images most powerfully convey the arrested and engendered poses that hark back to the hysterical iconography of Jean-Martin Charcot, the French neurologist who, in the 1870s, employed medical photographers to capture his female patients in the midst of their hysterical attacks. Second, print ads visually break down the fast-moving, cinematic narratives of postmodern life into the bits that are edited together into the fictions we take as truth. These still frames can be scrutinized to bring to awareness the narrative strategies used to promote commercial interests and cultural pathology.

Photography is a functional and epistemological link between hysteria and advertising. Early medical photography was integral in manufacturing a typology of hysteria. Photography was employed as a scientific tool, a way both to capture nature and to evidence the existence of female disease. What medical photography captured, advertising marketed. Commercial photographers employ the same technology to institutionalize a visual repertoire of stereotypes of feminine beauty, desire, and character. In the realm of epistemology, the importance of photography is in its capacity to elicit and preserve a quality of the real, the original, in a way that is lost in a moving image. We can hold the photograph, touch it, alter it, place it within our physical space, move it around, engage with it as a tactile object. The photograph, as a form of representation, epitomizes the literally stilled-life. Barthes (1981) speaks of the photograph (in phenomenological terms) as having a greater power of authentication than any other form of representation; it "fills the sight with force" (91) and holds us in its unique claim to reality. This fusion of illusion and reality is analogous to the psychic fusion that characterizes hysterical symptomology.

For these reasons I juxtapose advertisements from magazines published in the 1990s against an investigation of hysteria and mass image-reproductive technology that begins in the late nineteenth century. I highlight contemporary images because our aim is to better understand contemporary gender politics and issues of sexual difference. However, I attend to the earlier historical period to enable a cross-historical reading and to *show* how advertising arrests history upon female bodies. That is, the surface appearances of flux and mutability that characterize hysterical performances are revealed as recurrent images of femininity within the consumer unconscious. Over the last century there have been significant changes in women's economic and political status. Advertisers express those changes in typologies, polls, name brands, trademarks, mug shots, and cover girls. Images from the late 1800s share not only pages but uncanny resemblances with those from the 1990s; historical change is reduced to seemingly ahistorical "looks" that manage fears of the unmanageable, of change.

7. PERFORMANCE, HYSTERIA, AND ADVERTISING

While much has been written about advertising technology, consumer capitalism, and medical science, few scholars interweave them as ideological conspirators in the invention and reproduction of gender. This goal influenced the structure of this book: *all* chapters address *all* the disciplines. There is no one discrete chapter on hysteria, another on advertising, or another on feminist approaches to gender construction; the work proceeds more as a montage than as a historical argument.[7] It is through the unfolding of the entire text that any one of the component parts will be fully understood. Each chapter, however, privileges a particular lens through which to read the convergent discourses and performative tropes. Definitions and symptomology of hysteria arise in each chapter as actual symptoms arise in the women they afflict—unexpectedly, repeatedly, inevitably.

In Chapter 1, "From Darwin to Barbie: in search of the female thing," I focus on the medical and social developments at the turn of the nineteenth century, the time when women increasingly entered the public sphere and hysteria reached epidemic proportions. As notions of mastery were threatened by mass reproduction, advertising and medical science marked the domains of production and the real as male, consumption and reproduction as female. Meanwhile, the advent of the advertising agency, employing photographic techniques to create an idealized femininity, fostered a rising crisis of authenticity.

In Chapter 2, "I look, therefore I have: photography as consumption," I discuss the conflation of photography, consumption, waste, and the female body. The simultaneous development of photographic technology and the medical practices of surgery and gynecology promoted an invasive and ravaging gaze. The by-products were tactile photographs and physical symptoms. I address the similarities between the two, which leads to a discussion of hysteria and photography as fundamentally surreal: something is concretized yet elusive, arrested but never fully captured.

In Chapter 3, "Arrested," I address Jean-Martin Charcot's iconography of hysteria and the influence of photography and medical science in creating typologies of madness. The chapter highlights portraits of Charcot's "leading ladies of hysteria" who performed their attacks for the Parisian medical community, often under hypnosis. I focus on the politics of repetition and the potential for transforming, through mimesis, the meaning of hysteria itself. In reviewing the motifs of precariousness and buffoonery that typify hysterical

7. While this text contains much historical information, I do not posit it as a history of either hysteria or advertising. Rather than seeking causal and/or linear meaning, I encourage readers to leap across discursive realms and historical times, appreciating both the durability and vertigo of hysterical iteration itself.

performances and ad imagery, I turn to the subversive qualities of the carnivalesque. Hysteria's ambivalence, grotesquery, and transgression are assessed as a return of the socially outlawed and psychologically repressed.

The language in which hysteria speaks determines whether it will be heard. In this regard, it is important to explore the language of early psychoanalysis. Rather than submitting psychoanalysis as a developmental or explanatory model for hysteria, however, I consider Freudian concepts as "bodies" of thought through which hysteria matured. In Chapter 4, "What does man want? the fetish and the anorexic," I discuss the language of the fetish, particularly the codependence between commodity and psychoanalytic fetishism. Commodity fetishism constructs the female body as capital, refuting the material reality both of women's lived exploitation and of the production of images per se. Psychoanalytic fetishism constructs the female body as phallus, refuting sexual difference. When commodity and psychoanalytic fetishism are employed in tandem, advertising constructs the hysterical body, which, like the fetish, projects both hyperpresence (or all-body) and vacancy (or no-body). Following a discussion of Freud's uncanny, I address performances of "the dark continent"—particularly how ad imagery intersects female sexuality, race, and the primitive. I parallel the hysterogenic private body to the capitalist public body, as both are plagued by binging and purging, and "resolved" in the paradox of inconspicuous consumption.

Chapter 5, "Eat my face: a ritual journey," traces women's initiation from the private to the public sphere as a sexualized ritual of submission into economic and psychic prostitution. I employ the metaphor of femininity as a "genital face," emphasizing cosmetic and erotic defacement as a displacement of male hysteria into the female body. Induction into public visibility for women requires that they capture the attitude of ownership while simultaneously conveying their status as sexual and economic property.

Throughout these chapters, I continually allude to the possibilities of embracing hysteria as a feminist strategy by consciously duplicating the duplicity it rails against. In Chapter 6, "Representation is dead, long live representation!" I explore the possibilities of hysteria, spectacle, and advertising itself as vehicles for aesthetic resistance. I pose ways in which the performative aspects of hysteria may be cultivated as forms of nonoppositional resistance—resistance intimate with what it resists. In spite of the seemingly onerous task of demystifying the politics of the "look machinery," it is the formidable power of popular revisionings, violations, and mimicry that keep the ad industry so desperately in business.

Hysteria is a valid—not sick, not invalid—site of resistance. Women use the roles they have put on to express their own subjectivity as well as to understand subjectivity as a social and ambivalent space. In concluding this book, I demonstrate why and how hysteria, as a visual spectacle, is a way both to critique cultural definitions of femininity and to advertise the masquerade of identity itself. If women can surrender to the instability of the hysterical performance while remaining vigilant to the inequities of lived experiences, then hysteria will shed a discerning light on real things.

From Darwin to Barbie
in search of the female thing

I

I. THE RISE OF REPRODUCTIVE CULTURE

Upper-class women of the late nineteenth century provided the prototype of sanctioned femininity. They displayed subdued emotion and unsullied tact, a practiced frailty, restricted mental activity, domestic privation, and a constriction of physical activity. One hundred years later, this prototype is still recognizable in popular imagery. In an Oscar de la Renta ad for perfume, the copy reads: "Experience the power of femininity." We see a woman collared in a tight necklace of delicate white flowers fashioned out of porcelain and beads, her head cropped from above luscious and pursed lips. Beneath this recurring image of female propriety, complex and contradictory cultural biddings are at work.

According to late nineteenth-century popular medical lore, it was necessary that women direct all their energies into reproductive functions, particularly into controlling the otherwise immoderate tendencies of these "savage" functions. Menstruation represented an excess that made the female patient overexcitable, nervous, and hypersensitive; mere possession and normal functioning of a womb deemed women hysterical. It was imperative, however, that nothing obstruct the free flow of menstruation, for any blockage to the female economy caused by mental or physical excitement, such as anger, fear, grief, or pleasure induced by reading, writing, and sex, resulted in pollution of her entire mental, emotional, and physiological economy (Shuttleworth 1990, 59). Obstruction of menstruation resulted in hysteria as well. Thus, on the one hand, women, by virtue of their uterine systems, were presumed to be biologically incapable of control, prisoners of their own bodies. On the other hand, they were expected to exercise more control than men, imposing restrictions upon themselves in both private and public. When women failed to control behavior in public—exposing the excessive desires, feelings, and needs that menstruation "naturally" bestowed upon them—then their immodest behavior was certification for madness. "*Womanhood itself is thus figured as a form of pathology: only when polluted and out of control (and thus not 'feminine') could females be socially accredited with the title of true 'woman'*" (Shuttleworth 1990, 62).

Ironically, while women were culturally mandated to concentrate on fertility, they were simultaneously denied sexual pleasure, identity, or subjectivity. Culturally defined femininity required suppression of naturally defined femininity. Medical science reconstructed gender to safeguard against their own dreadful interpretations of natural female processes.

Contemporary ads continue to relay this duplicity. A 1990s tobacco company, Liggett and Myers, markets the "original" woman we are to embrace: their ad copy for Eve cigarettes declares, "There is a little Eve in every woman." A pharmaceuticals company provides the cleansing antidote in its product, Summer's Eve hypoallergenic "feminine wash." Female functions apparently need to be checked just as nature itself, wild and inexplicable, needs to be checked lest it burst forth and envelop, with disastrous effect, the social body. This social body was undergoing tremendous change at the end of the nineteenth century; the female body became the site upon which these terrifying social changes were located. Her perceived "natural" disorder was appropriated as a metaphor for the state of disorder the whole social organism was experiencing.[1]

1. In a 1992 ad for Seabreeze, a woman, along with a swirling pool of oil, dirt, and makeup—the polluting superfluities of industrialism—is literally going down the drain. The female body is posited as commensurate with contamination and impurity. A foregrounded male lifeguard declares heroically, "Hang on! SEABREEZE TO THE RESCUE. It cleans deep . . ." It is his job to cleanse her in order to save the social environment from her surging infection.

According to Shuttleworth (1990), ideologies of gender differentiation at the turn of the twentieth century reflected the contemporaneous increase in the division of labor that accompanied industrial capitalism. *Man* was well established ideologically as the autonomous, rational actor in control of his own destiny. But *men* were mere cogs defined and controlled by the wider operations of the expanding social organism. As men adapted to industrialization, they adopted an ideology of self-will and mastery. Attributes of self-control and self-help were assigned to masculinity, while helplessness and submission to biological demands were aligned with femininity. This vision of female immaturity was promoted as an underlying force of decay undoing male control. In the *Atlantic Monthly* of that time, women and children were frequently portrayed as emotional and financial burdens. Ads for insurance policies were abundant. While copy did not always explicitly blame the irrational female body economy for augmented insurance policies, the iconography of the female body was associated with disorders that needed curing. An 1895 trade card advertised Root Beer as "the world's best blood purifier," restoring women to the desired state of "refinement and femininity" (Fox 1987, month of May, unpaginated). Modern-day "root beers"—douches and other products that freshen women's insides—fill store shelves, their ads tucked into the back pages of most popular magazines. A contemporary ad for Advil employs similarly gendered logic. The manufacturers, Whitehall Laboratories, are presented in written text as experts, while the accompanying visuals feature an enfeebled young woman suffering menstrual cramps. The juxtaposition suggests that Advil is the scientist's remedy for ailing womanhood itself.

The Advil ad insinuates the impossible yet characteristic double-bind of womanhood according to the credos of late nineteenth-century medical science: woman is cursed with a naturally polluted system, but if she acts in accordance with her "naturalness"—child-like, emotional, and unruly—she is unfeminine; in order to be feminine she must exhibit a cultivated, waste-free disposition. Sanctioned femininity is something of an unnatural state, a masquerade worn to disguise another femininity rooted in biological essentialism.

While upper-middle-class women paraded their husband's wealth in the marketplaces and served as models of cultured femininity, lower-class women, having less consumer potential, and thus immaterial to advertisers, were used as experimental fodder of medical science (Jordanova 1989). Their living bodies were frequently designated for exploratory surgery; their dead bodies were appropriated for dissection and autopsies. Along with African-Americans, poor white women were viewed by medical science as primitive brutes whose physicality represented an even less differentiated status along the evolutionary scale than their (not so evolved) wealthy sisters.[2] Many lower-class women at the turn of the century feigned fits of weakness, nervousness, or disgust, in hopes of a diagnosis of hysteria along with the attendant treatment: the rest cure, which would relieve them of their overwhelming domestic duties. Upper-class women feigned such hysterical symptoms as well, not to escape obligations, but as a protest against a prescribed and constricted femininity that was breeding illness. Denied access to the symbolic realm of spoken and written language, women relied upon the language of the body to convey a signal of distress, or what Smith-Rosenberg (1972) calls a "product and indictment of her culture" (678). On some level, probably unconscious, this signal was heard. Most likely, it provoked an internalized guilt harbored by the proprietors of power. To ward off any liability or sacrifice of power, medical authorities, influenced by the sexologists who were influenced by Darwin, regarded this language of the body as primitive and invalid.[3] The corporeal messages of hysteria bore a negative stigma. Simulation of hysterical symptoms provided further evidence that women had a natural propensity to malinger, lie, and manipulate. Rather than recognizing the *performances* of hysterical symptoms as dramatic appeals for recognition, somatic symptoms were repeatedly interpreted as proof of the incompetent predisposition of the opposite sex.

2. As middle- and upper-class women entered public spheres and illustrated comparable mental capacity to their male components, medical science adapted its diagnostic methodology to include uneducated and lower-class women into the family of hysterics. Hysteria slowly became a malady that afflicted those of unsophisticated mental capacity. It is still commonly presumed by medical practitioners that women (of any class) who cannot articulate their experiences and feelings are more prone to manifestations of hysteria. Later in the twentieth century, as lower-class and uneducated women began to engage in and represent consumerism, medical diagnoses included their behavior within definitions of hysteria. See Roy (1982).

3. The noted sexologists of the time were Kraft-Ebbing and Havelock Ellis.

Charlotte Perkins Gilman and *The Yellow Wallpaper*

He who does not know sick women does not know women. —Mitchell (1972)

The most common treatment for hysteria in the 1890s was the rest cure. It was prescribed, in large part, by neurologists, as hysteria enacted its script through nervous symptoms. One of the most famous American neurologists of the late nineteenth century was Weir Mitchell, and one of his most famous patients was the feminist author Charlotte Perkins Gilman. In 1887, Gilman went to Mitchell suffering nervous symptoms and stress ensuing from an active professional and public career. His advice was to "live as domestic a life as possible," to "have but two hours intellectual life a day," and "never to touch pen, brush or pencil again" (Lane 1980, 20).

Gilman wrote many essays of critical nonfiction addressing women's political and economic conditions on both the domestic and social fronts. But she is best known for *The Yellow Wallpaper*, her semi-autobiographical tale of a woman who goes mad from the treatment prescribed by Mitchell (whose name is used in the story) for her nervous stress, anxiety, fatigue, and intellectual restlessness. The story first came out in the *New England Magazine* in 1891, four years after Gilman was diagnosed with neurasthenia, a symptomatic form of hysteria. After three months of compliance with the terms of the rest cure, Gilman was on the brink of mental breakdown. She cast away Mitchell's advice and returned to work, recovering her health.

In her first-person narrative, the woman (who remains unnamed but is clearly Gilman) is told by Mitchell to abide by the regulations of the rest cure: no excitement, no reading, no writing, no conversation or exercise. The woman's husband, also a doctor, enthusiastically administers the prescribed treatment on the home front; he has long been disgruntled with his wife's career-oriented activities, which seem to make her irritable. In spite of her successes in public and literary spheres, he believes her activities to be unfit for women.

Sequestered in a remote country home, the woman lies for hours in her bed staring at the yellow wallpaper of the bedroom. At first she despises the paper:

> I never saw a worse paper in my life. One of those sprawling, flamboyant patterns committing every artistic sin. . . . When you follow the lame uncertain curves for a little distance they suddenly commit suicide—plunge off at outrageous angles, destroy themselves

in unheard-of contradictions. . . . The color is repellent, almost re-volting: a smoldering unclean yellow. . . . (Gilman 1980, 5).

As time goes by, suffering from lack of any other stimulation, she begins to engage the visions she finds in the paper's mysterious pat-terns. She reaches the apex of her insanity when she becomes over-whelmed by distortions, demons, and cannibalistic creatures that emerge from the walls to consume her. In a final effort to salvage any trace of self-identity and balance, she wages a war against the characters of authority—her doctor, her husband, her professional community—who revealed themselves in the intricate designs of the wallpaper. She fights her own mask of belle indifférence that she wore only to hide the rage that drained the life out of her.[4] She fights her husband's paradoxical constructs of femininity that echo the widespread cultural *male* hysteria: the notion that women are deli-cate, dependent creatures who are dangerous and need to be con-trolled. She comes to understand how her illness is not a personal psychological flaw but something suffered by all women:

> Through watching so much at night, when it changes so, I have finally found out.
>
> The front pattern *does* move—and no wonder! The woman be-hind shakes it!
>
> Sometimes I think there are a great many women behind, and sometimes only one, and she crawls around fast, and her crawling shakes it all over . . .
>
> And she is all the time trying to climb through. But nobody could climb through the pattern—it strangles so; I think that is why it has so many heads.
>
> They get through, and then the pattern strangles them off and turns them upside down, and makes their eyes white! . . .
>
> I think that woman gets out in the daytime!
>
> And I'll tell you why—privately—I've seen her!
>
> I can see her out of every one of my windows! (Gilman 1980, 15)

Charlotte Perkins Gilman sent her completed story to her former doctor, Weir Mitchell. Although he never responded to her directly,

4. Belle indifférence is a symptom of hysteria characterized by a mien of apathy and nonchalance. It was considered by medical practitioners to be a transparent pretense of control and disinterest to counter the intense emo-tional mutability that constituted the hysteric's nervous distress.

FIGURE 1.1 *Charles Dana Gibson,* Design for Wallpaper *(1902).*

Mitchell abandoned the rest cure within a couple years. A colleague of Mitchell's credited this change in clinical practice to Gilman's story.

Charles Dana Gibson

Charles Dana Gibson was a renowned maker of fashion plates and designer of the ideal American woman—the Gibson Girl—from 1890 until World War I. In 1886, while working for *Scribner's* and *Harper's,* Gibson sold his first drawing to *Life* magazine. In 1904 he contracted with *Collier's* and in 1907 with *Cosmopolitan,* where he headed the syndicate that in 1920 bought *Life,* becoming its editor until 1932. During his time as fashion king, Gibson portrayed femininity in the image of the out-of-doors, seeking to metaphorize women's entrance into public life as a liberatory exit from domesticity. The essence of the Gibson Girl was health; she was the consummate sportswoman dressed in tailored shirtwaists or bathing dresses. She was the model of attainable style with an air of serenity and independence. She starred as Daisy Miller in the novel of the same title by Henry James. Meanwhile, Henry's literary sister Alice James was bedridden, along with Charlotte Perkins Gilman, suffering symptoms of hysteria.[5]

5. See Yeazell (1981).

Beneath the Gibson Girl's popular declaration of women's emancipation, a contrary notion of women's status was conveyed. Despite her independent pose, the Gibson Girl was positioned frequently on china, cutlery, pillows, postcards, and wallpaper (FIGURE 1.1)—her excursions into freedom never extending far beyond conventional boundaries. She verified, rather than challenged, status quo Victorian beliefs that marriage and family were primary and that "contentment does not come from careers" (exhibit 1990, Museum of the City of New York).

Darwin meets Philip Morris

The appropriation of power from oppositional bodies or forces is a means of reinstating convention. When cultural resistance is fermenting, those with something to lose take cover and operate from underground. Desperate to ensure their endangered power, they stage a kind of magic show, representing themselves as loosening, rather than asserting, their controlling reins while celebrating the virtues of difference and change.[6] They remake their "face" behind a new scientific theory, or another glossy advertisement, in the name or image of those they exploit; those being erased appear to be doing it to themselves. By appropriating the perceived enemy through a form of mimesis, the adversary is robbed of oppositional power.

Darwinism is an example of late nineteenth-century innovation that represented revolutionary insights in scientific research and simultaneously reinforced hierarchical thinking in relation to gender. Darwin formulated his theory of sexual differentiation at a time of radical change in the social landscape. In ever-increasing numbers, women appeared on the streets, shared jobs with men in the workplace, and engaged in social reform movements and social organizations. It was evident that women, particularly upper-middle-class women, were capable of performing outside of the home and within the public realm. Darwin's theory adapted to transforming reality and the changing cultural manifestations of gender; in acknowledging these indisputable shifts, his theory of sexual differentiation was a radical intervention into the controversial field of scientific genealogy.[7]

6. This dynamic is discussed at length in Faludi (1991).

7. See Shapere (1980) and Ruse (1979) for a more complex sociohistorical understanding of scientific genealogy and Darwin.

Darwin's philosophy supplanted the prevailing Lamarckian view of evolution and sexual identity. Lamarck believed in a model of eternal difference. In this bourgeois worldview, all *men* are equal; for Lamarck, evolutionary theory did not include women at all. Darwin's theory of sexual differentiation liberated women from the Lamarckian designation of absolute inferiority. Unfortunately, he replaced it with a designation of evolutionary inferiority.

Darwin was perhaps the first poststructuralist in his rejection of essentialism and placement of variation at the core of scientific theories of evolution. But in replacing sexual unity with the differentiation of sexes, Darwin did not differentiate symmetrically. Men were further along on the evolutionary scale—and thus "naturally selected"—due to their supposedly advanced diversification. They had advanced further from the primeval soup than women who were akin to children, animals, and savages. In Darwin's evolutionary frame, woman's sex no longer determined her capacity to compete in the public realm but rather the likelihood of her succeeding. Men and women are equal in terms of potential, but women are inferior in terms of realization of that potential.

The tenacity of this scientifically gendered ideology is evidenced in the popularity of Freud's (1965) "little man" characterization of women (118). Rather than female sexuality having autonomous and equal significance to male sexuality, it is perceived as a diminutive sign. Women manifest a mere fragment of advanced male characteristics, while men have no trace of women. While men have full-grown and differentiated sexual organs (penises), women have undeveloped male organs (clitorides). It is no far cry to recognize the stirrings of a theory of penis envy. Penis envy is a cultural conceit endorsed by science as a female perversion so as to void women's power. Female penis envy helps the phallus sustain its erection.

The Virginia Slims cigarette campaign of the early 1990s illustrates the pseudo-emancipatory message of the Darwinian gesture of gender recuperation. In light of undeniable changes in women's participation in cultural politics and professions, Virginia Slims bestows upon women the look of arrogance and self-possession usually assigned their male counterparts. Their ads juxtapose such a modern "liberated" woman against a small insert of a not-so-liberated woman of the past, suggesting a radical change in sexual politics. In one advertisement, the diminutive insert features a woman plowing a field behind an ox; the parodic copy reads, "Virginia Slims remembers when

women were given free reign [*sic*] to advance in their chosen fields."
Foregrounded, is a contemporary woman donned in business suit,
briefcase, and cigarette. We are led to believe that she, unlike her
counterpart from yesteryear, *is* given free rein to advance in her chosen field. The ad performs a dubious tribute to women's progress.

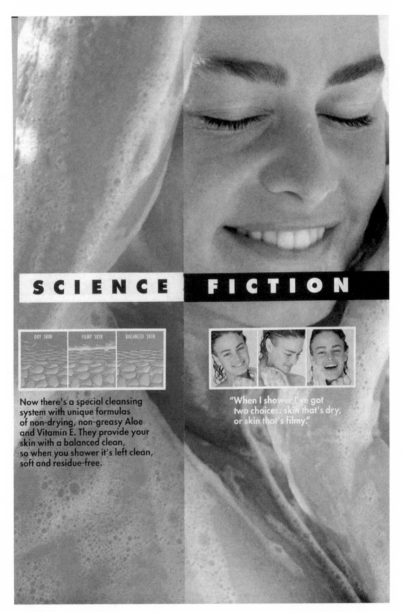

FIGURE 1.2 *Advertisement, "Science fiction," Jergens skin conditioning bars (1992). Reprinted by permission of The Andrew Jergens Company.*

First is the glaring omission of conflicts, failures, and power struggles that characterize women's actual experience today and clearly deny her free rein. Second, the progress being lauded is undermined by the ad's referring to her as a child: "You've come a long way, baby." Clearly, a vestigial marking of women's immaturity and dependence.[8]

Both Darwinism and Virginia Slims ads appear to laud the equality and liberation of women as cultural truths. They do so, however, by simultaneously disguising a reliance upon biologically determined views that advance the inequity of gender. The tension between biologically and socially constructed concepts of femininity is central to hysteria. Hysteria bestows rigidity on a mutable aspect of identity—gender—manufactured by sociopolitical forces. In this blurring of biology and culture, hysteria becomes a "science fiction" through which gender is perceived as a function of sex, representation as a function of truth, and culture as a function of nature (FIGURE 1.2).[9]

Feminization of mass culture

One of the monolithic concepts of femininity that has persisted over the last one hundred years is that women are reproductive, as compared to productive. By being biological reproducers, women have been marked as cultural reproducers—mimics or copies. This reductive and ill-fated correspondence burgeoned at the turn of the century in North America when the rise of industrial capitalism launched an era of mass reproductive technology. The female body was appropriated and represented within expanding circuits of commodity culture. Soon, it/she came to signify the explosive social body itself; female reproduction became a metaphor for mass cultural reproduction.

Huyssen (1986) tells us that the burgeoning mass culture was accused of inauthenticity and viewed as a poisonous adversary to civil-

8. None of the Virginia Slims ads are reprinted here due to the inability to acquire copyright permission from Philip Morris. The tobacco industry is at present under tremendous attack during President Clinton's second term, and Philip Morris's legal counsel claimed they could not risk publishing their advertisement in a book that would be marketed to young adults.

9. It is interesting to note that in this Jergens ad, the woman's body, subtitled "science," is printed in color while the woman's face, subtitled "fiction," is printed in black and white.

ization, whereby the copy, the cheap and banal reproductions of the "culture industry," would create a world of intoxicated, brutish consumers. To ease the threat it was necessary to apply a dichotomy of logic: "the gendering as feminine of that which is devalued" (53). What was devalued, and subsequently feminized, were those aspects of the shifting social and economic landscape that threatened rational bourgeois order. These included the indiscriminating crowd, consumer madness, the reproductive burden of modernization, primitive nature, sexuality, the unconscious, theatricality, and spectacle. With the ideological support of scientific and medical discourses, image-makers of the late nineteenth century merged the excitable nature of the crowd and the nervous nature of women and granted them both a common pejorative status.

In a provocative 1992 advertisement for Dep Shampoo, we see the same woman in profile twice: in the first image her hair is disarrayed in the process of being shampooed and the copy below states boldly, OUT OF CONTROL; in the second profile, the woman's hair is beautifully and neatly coiffed and the copy reads, UNDER CONTROL. Upon closer scrutiny, what we see in the first profile is not merely hair in sudsy disarray, but, in fact, a perceptible crowd of hysterical women, screaming and gesturing "out of control."[10] The image echoes both the labyrinths of Gibson's wallpaper and the internalized demons that possessed Charlotte Perkins Gilman both in her life and in her literary "fiction."

The department store and the stage

One public location where women were welcome at the turn of the century was the fairy-tale department store where upper-class women consumed the products of booming industry. What women wore as they paraded the new marketplaces demonstrated male success in the competitive public arena. Wives and children performed as commodities: personal exhibitions of the wealth, status, and property of

10. Permission to reproduce this advertisement was declined because, according to the president of DEP Corporation, "response to the campaign was poor and we view these ads as negative for both the products and the consumer. We understand your objective is to have the book used as a learning tool and we prefer that you not use this example of poor communication with the consumer" (Robert Berglass, March 1997, correspondence).

the husband and father. The more conspicuously consumptive they appeared, the more respected the man who owned them.

In this era, reproduction and consumption were deemed "uterine things" and dreamlike department stores were the palatial bodies that generated these procreative tendencies. While these places signified women's apparent liberation from domesticity, history suggests that restless homemakers were merely transported to equally isolated *public* rest homes. Designating appropriate public sites for women was to acknowledge socioeconomic change while rendering that change ineffectual.

AUTOBIOGRAPHICAL FICTION

I'm walking through the Galleria Mall, through stalls of neon, Disneyland-ing me into a beguiling nightmare of expenditure. The ad industry has this uncanny ability to sell their commodities in the name of the politically disaffected. Calvin Klein's contemptuous preppies wearing torn jeans. Revolutionary pantyhose and soft drinks donned by post-hip, rock-'n'-roll baby boomers. I hypnotically climb the circular stairwell that delivers me to the balcony level. I'm a bit weary but Philip Morris reminds me that "we've come a long way, baby," mitigating the feminist sensibility that tells me otherwise.

I've always known that obsessive consumption would get me nowhere. But I'm compelled now, some primitive rage guiding me. I walk faster like an amnesiac tracking a memory that will restore my identity, my feet racing through the aisles of some Abraham and Strauss outlet as if to an ageless beat. I'm moving in spite of immense discomfort, my formidable doubt fading, resistance fading, overpowered now in the magnificent convergence of history, childhood dreams, and clearance sales. I am seduced through the gleaming corridors into Neiman-Marcus to the glass counter of the cosmetic section to purchase with my magical money that special perfume. "Krizia, please," my voice emerging clearly though estranged, not mine. It appears, for the time being anyway, that I have suspended all disbelief, and pretend, as if by nature, to be Woman (FIGURE 1.3).

According to the Krizia ad, to secure praise as a woman is to appear as a child. As women pressed for independence, the expectation that women perform a kind of puerilism was cast upon them. To act mature—independent—signified undesirability both to potential husbands and to employers who preferred to maintain authority. Many women chose to act as children: dependent, naive, vulnerable,

FIGURE 1.3 *Advertisement, Krizia Ava Gardner (1990).*
Reprinted by permission of Emanuele Pirella. Concept and copywriter:
Emanuele Pirella. Art director: Enrico Maria Radaelli.

playful, deferring, testing, exaggerating, physicalizing their needs,
even throwing tantrums. But women's faculty for self-preservation
through acting was disregarded in lieu of evaluating the particular
act per se; while appearing childlike was an assignment of desirable
womanhood, when women acted accordingly they were pathologized for that very assignment. Women were judged by *what* they
performed and, ironically, as if they could perform in no other way.
Women, children, and hysterics were viewed as a family of dependent, demanding, and insincere creatures suffering a fixation, rather
than cultivated gift, for dramatic play.

SOME DEFINITIONS OF HYSTERIA

"Dependency is key to [hysterics'] psychopathology." (Chodoff
1982, 280)
"Compensating for basic feelings of inferiority and powerlessness
by stratagems that are essentially demeaning and dishonest,

[hysterics] display a kind of slave mentality." (Chodoff 1982, 279)

Hysterics display an "undercurrent of desperation as they flail about trying to extract total gratification from male figures in one unsatisfactory relationship after another." (Chodoff 1982, 279)

"The hysteric wants what she wants right now! She is trapped in the present." (Chodoff 1982, 280)

"Hysterical puerilism comprises a disturbance in the [hysteric's] sense of reality." (Abse 1982, 175)

"The hysterical personality features egocentricity, immaturity, histrionic theatricality, shallowness of feeling and lack of social responsibility." (Eysenck 1982, 71)

"The hysterical personality is typically described as an overly-dramatic, self-indulgent woman." (Klerman 1982, 219)

"In the hysteric, emotions are labile and exaggerated, yet shallow and unconvincing, rather like poor acting." (Kendell 1982, 28)

It was only fitting that besides department stores, the other public arena in which women were welcome at the turn of the century—as both performers and spectators—was the theater. "Theater in bourgeois society was one of the few spaces which allowed women a prime place in the arts . . . precisely because acting was seen as imitative and reproductive, rather than original and productive" (Huyssen 1986, 51). As long as a woman's role in the public sphere reflected the adage "anatomy is destiny"—as it did in the theater—then her visibility would not be so threatening. Occasional infusions of theatrical stimulation were thought by medical practitioners even to do her some good, perhaps because such stimulation was allied with, and compromised by, the harmless qualities of make-believe, mimicry, and reproduction.

As women gained visibility on the stage, their personas continued to be diagnosed as in-valid, as masquerade.[11] Being "real"—to be a producer, to create reality—remained the domain of men. Theatrical presence was a form of absence, confirming women's role as a mere vessel through which reality passes. Her body was, in effect, an empty

11. Feminist scholars writing on gender and masquerade include Riviere (1929), Modleski (1986a), Russo (1986), Butler (1990a), Doane (1991b), and Griggors (1997).

stage upon which the gender relations of the expanding technological revolution were being performed.

"Above all . . . hysterics are histrionic. They are always on stage and in performance, sometimes to such a degree that they have difficulty distinguishing fantasy from reality." (Chodoff 1982, 278) Hysteria is an ailment that exists but " 'sine materia'—those disturbances which present to the doctor as 'unreal.' " (Ey 1982, 3)

The famous actress Sarah Bernhardt used to visit the Salpêtrière, a hospital of late nineteenth-century France, to study the dramatic poses of the hysterical patients of neurologist Jean-Martin Charcot—Freud's mentor from 1886 to 1888. Many famous men of letters would go to the theater to observe her extraordinary talents. George Bernard Shaw writes his reactions to her performance:

the childishly egotistical character of her acting, which is not the art of making you think more highly or feel more deeply, but the art of making you admire her, pity her, champion her, weep with her, laugh at her jokes, follow her fortunes breathlessly, and applaud her wildly when the curtain falls. It is the art of finding out all your weakness and practicing on them—cajoling you, harrowing you, exciting you— on the whole fooling you. (Gold and Kizdale 1991, 3)

And D. H. Lawrence had this to say:

There she is, the incarnation of wild emotion which we share with all live things, but which is gathered in us in all complexity and inscrutable fury. She represents the primeval passions of woman, and she is fascinating to an extraordinary degree. I could love such a woman myself, love her to madness; all for the pure wild passion of it. Take care about going to see Bernhardt. Unless you are very sound, do not go. When I think of her now I can still feel the weight hanging in my chest as it hung there for days after I saw her. Her winsome, sweet playful ways; her sad, plaintive little murmurs; her terrible panther cries; and then the awful, inarticulate sounds, the little sobs that fairly sear one, and the despair and death; it is too much in one evening. (Gold and Kizdale 1991, 3–4)

Sigmund Freud saw Bernhardt perform in *Theodora*, a melodramatic spectacle of lust and sadism, while studying hypnotism with Charcot.

> I can't say anything good about the piece itself. . . . But how that Sarah plays! . . . Nothing she could have said would have surprised me; I believed at once everything she said. . . . It is incredible what postures she can assume and how every limb and joint acts with her. A curious being: I can imagine that she needn't be any different in life than on the stage. (Gold and Kizdale 1991, 4)

So impressed was Freud with her performance that a photograph of Bernhardt greeted his patients as they entered his office. Perhaps Freud shared Charcot's notion that the arrested imagination of hysterics would be liberated through images themselves—in this case, the dramatic images of Bernhardt.

In spite of the philosophical canon that regarded theatricality as the decline of civilization (Huyssen 1986), the power of tragediennes such as Bernhardt revealed a craving in the audiences to whom she played. Perhaps this deprecating canon was reaction to the seduction, the "plaintive murmurs" and "panther cries" emerging from women's "primeval passions" that instigated fear along with the desire. Through the histrionics of Bernhardt's stage persona came an immediacy, a "truth," that aroused fantasy, dislodging viewers from reality and intriguing them with shameless, near orgasmic, delight.[12]

Of course, not only men attended Bernhardt's performances. Women also hungered to consume hysterical imagery, albeit for different reasons. Bernhardt's images counseled women in the look of "true womanhood" that they had to presume if they were to be seen

12. A *New York Times* (June 1993) front-page headline reads: "So Weak, So Powerful: An 'impossible fantasy'—the child-woman—is back. She's adoring, infantile and, most important of all, unthreatening" (1). The nearly full-page image (in this 1993 Year of the Woman) is a head-shot of Kate Moss on a lace pillow, unfocused eyes staring into space, thumb in mouth. In the accompanying article, Elizabeth Kaye (1993) states that "the public has become accustomed to the child-woman (aka the waif, a near ubiquitous form seen in fashion magazines for almost a year) as the mascot of backlash, the leading signifier that strong women provoke deep uneasiness among certain people" (1). My only contention with Kaye's argument is that this child-woman who is supposedly "back," has, in fact, never left.

at all. Women emulated the great actress who was emulating institutionalized hysterics, as women today emulate ad images that emulate hysterics. Women consume themselves—or rather the *spectacle* of themselves—as men consume them.[13]

The increased visibility of women in stores, on the stage, and, as we shall see, in advertising, implied newfound sources of control and validity for women. But this potential power was discretely framed: actual power became virtual power. Female visibility became a caricatured performance supplanting women's performances as social and political agents. The caprices of Bernhardt were appreciated only when captured and viewed as part of a theatrical phenomenon. On the streets and in the home, such behavior was decidedly abnormal and hysterical. As long as visibility was properly managed, the myth of progress and egalitarianism between the sexes was ostensibly fostered.[14]

The invented disease of femininity spread like a virus through the mind of the social body, subjecting civilization to the horrors of the "wandering womb," a term used to explain the hysteric's frantic search for reproductive opportunities. The "metasticized uterus" broke into the streets and was swiftly arrested; women were quarantined in delusional department stores, on the chimerical stage, and within the ideological confines of reproducer/consumer.

But there was another public frame into which women were abducted into a nullifying kind of popularity. One of the fastest-growing institutions at the turn of the century was the advertising agency. Through photographic technology, the ad agency materialized and reproduced the theatrics of hysteria in mass reproduced images. Tangible and standardized representations confirmed that hysteria was real.

2. THE CRISIS OF THE REAL

The rise of the advertising agency

The first advertising agency was established in 1840 in Philadelphia for selling advertising space in the daily publications. It was not

---

13. See Rubin (1975) and Schneider (1997) for important discussions regarding women's consumption of themselves as mediated and commercial bodies.

14. See Phelan (1993) for an invaluable discussion of the politics of visibility and its bearing on the subjective readings of the female body.

until the 1880s, however, that the advertising agencies expanded their services; rather than merely selling space, they sold copywriting and design skills. These agencies supplanted advertisers themselves in controlling the visual images that appeared in the publications. Authority shifted to an intermediary source negotiating between advertiser and publisher.

At the same time, the photograph replaced the woodcut; the rotary press was invented, allowing for faster printing of larger publications; and publishers recognized that advertising should be more aggressively solicited as an aid to financing newspapers. Advances in transportation technology, particularly the laying of rail, allowed for national distribution of products. Many commodities that previously had only local, geographical appeal, suddenly found national markets. Consequently, the images representing these commodities had national markets. The advertising agency boomed. In offices across America visual texts embraced a more heterogeneous consumer population. With this came the new aesthetic and ethical standards that would ensure the authority of the commercial image (Buzzi 1968).

The advent of photographic technology underlies the tremendous power that these advertising agencies wielded in terms of creating a standardized national aesthetic. Process reproduction, or the use of plates, is independent of any original, as photographic lenses bring out aspects of the original unattainable to a naked eye. Moreover, technical reproduction puts the copy of the original into situations otherwise out of reach for the original itself; it grants a special power to the original as it can now meet the beholder halfway. Commodified women are given a public voice and power that actual women, the "originals," do not have. Photography, as a tool of the advertising agent, profoundly prefigured issues of gender politics.

In the late nineteenth century, objectified images of real people now accompanied the commodities sold to those same real people across thousands of miles. But a certain schism between the representation of the real and the real observer of the representation was created. Advertising images replaced, or at least complicated, individual self-image with the "average" image. Photographic portraits in newspaper ads and magazines determined how women were to pass effectively into the public arena.

Difference was exploding across North America through the influx of immigrants in the late nineteenth century. Exalted and idealized ad images were visual decrees of sameness, purging the import of diverse people, values, and cultures infiltrating American borders. As women's bodies became the site of the ideal, they simultaneously became a site of contradiction and ambivalence; the female body became a sign of homogeneity to diffuse the threat of cultural diversity, of unruly others, of which they themselves were part.

Amid the disarming effects of advertising's culture of falsity was a countereffect: photographic technology had the particular power of granting illusion the look of the real, of truth. Commodities—labeled by cultural critic Orvell (1989) as "monuments of sham"—were marketed as sacred souvenirs of the real world in decay. It was not until this time that advertising came to have the specifically commercial connotation that typifies contemporary advertising. Whether in the form of razor blades that promise a *real* shave, or soft drinks that promise a *real* taste, advertised commodities provide the illusion of authenticity and stability in a postmodern era that produces and glorifies artifice and flux. With women as agents of simulation captured in photography that authenticates, the paradox of hysteria is reinforced; women are configured as *truly fake*.

The ventriloquist and his "real"

Femininity sits like a dummy on the lap of the ventriloquist—the advertiser—who speaks through her. It is often a woman's body that the commodity "wears" to convey its messages; we could say that the commodity is cross-dressed as a woman (FIGURE 1.4). While in the ad for Nic Janik we see the ventriloquy, in innumerable other ads there appears to be no ventriloquist at all. We cannot discern the theatrical means by which female subjectivity is refigured into a dummy to allow for free passage of the ventriloquist's message. Woman is propped up as if speaking for herself, proudly owning the words put in her mouth. The concept of cultural ventriloquism points to the apparatus through which the hysteric embodies the very language that pathologizes her.

The commercial shoot is the aesthetic arena in which ordinary things are made marketable. Advertising agencies spend billions of dollars annually injecting their client's products with animation—referred to in advertising jargon as the "brands' emotional elements"

FIGURE 1.4 *Advertisement, Nic Janik (1994). Reprinted by permission of Escada Elements. Photographer: Walter Chin. Creative director: Marc Balet. Designer: Nic Janik.*

(Russell and Lane 1990, 677). Objects undergo an anthropomorphizing process; humans undergo a dehumanizing process. While the commodity is referred to as the "hero," human actors are referred to as "atmosphere" (John Burger 1991, personal communication). Commodities are repeatedly face-lifted, refurbished, and theatrically lit to endow them with the attributes of celebrities. Like their human counterparts, they must project charisma, grace, determination, and originality if they are to succeed. All this fabricated vitality must appear to be a genuine quality of the inanimate commodity that leaps directly into the deficient place within the consumer. In an exemplary ad for Matsuda, the heroic commodity outlives the (dead) human "atmosphere" that sells it, beaming into the needy eyes of readers (FIGURE 1.5).

Heroic attributes are magically excavated from human luminaries and delivered to consumers in bottles, especially bottles of aromatic

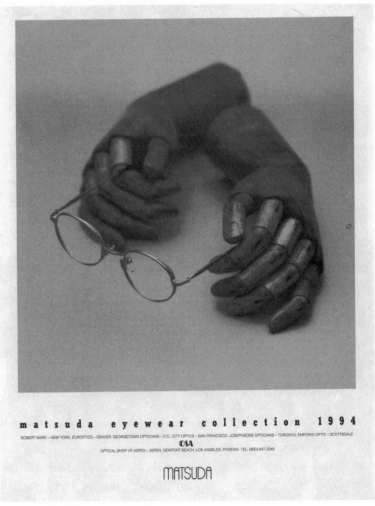

FIGURE 1.5 *Advertisement, Matsuda eyewear (1994). Reprinted by permission of Matsuda, Inc.*

perfume. Parfums Stern Inc. taps the spirit of Cher for their product "Uninhibited"; Elizabeth Arden seizes the essence of Elizabeth
Taylor to sell their perfume "Passion." When we purchase and wear
the product we participate in a chain of alchemical reformulations:
select human qualities are extracted from their ordinary status and
are then exalted by being ascribed to particular celebrity super-
women who loan these qualities to commodities that women must
buy so they can possess the very qualities divested from them,
which having been glorified will make them feel distinguished and
whole. This transference of potency is often illustrated by female

bodies floating, like metaphysical essences, in the bottles of merchandise being sold. It is as if women are preserved or "cured" in the process of sharing their vitality with the commodity (FIGURES 1.6 and 1.7).

Through the eye of the advertising camera, commodity and female body share an identity: reciprocal impersonation (FIGURE 1.8). In a Swatch ad, reprinted here, the woman's dress and the watchband

IT
"
NT
D

FIGURE 1.6 *Trade card, die-cut of barrel (c. 1885).*
Reprinted by permission of General Mills, Inc.

The Rainbath Shower:

WONDERFUL FEELING, WONDERFUL DAY!

Rainbath® Shower Gel
cleanses your skin,
gets it deliciously fresh—
touchably soft!

Neutrogena

rainbath®
refreshing
shower
and
bath gel

FIGURE 1.7 *Advertisement, Neutrogena Rainbath (1993).*
Reprinted by permission of Neutrogena Corp.

are both red, reinforcing the fusion of model and purchasable time-piece. In an ad for Chanel No. 5, a woman places her left hand on the "head" of the perfume bottle and her right hand, curiously, on her own head. Again, both the woman's dress and the tint of the glass perfume vial are red.

An ad for Passion Perfume makes explicit the implicit logic in these ads and so many others like them. A mysterious "man and his passion," as the copy reads, share the top frame of a perfume ad. Elizabeth Taylor stands beside the veiled man in an enchanting swirl of fog and fragrance. In the lower frame, we again read the text, "a man and his passion," but the image has changed: substituting for Taylor is the bottle of perfume. The man in the shadows remains a fixed and predictable quantity, inconsumable; Taylor and the bottle are interchangeable items for the man who can have both.

A look that is pure
draws attention for sure.
By keeping it plain
you show off your brain.
Fancy's a bore.
It's true less is more.
So show off your new
Innocence.

nordstrom

SPRING·SUMMER '90 COLLECTION

POP
swatch®

FIGURE 1.8 *Advertisement, Swatch (1990).*
Reprinted by permission of Swatch AG, SMH (US), Inc.

The obscured subjectivity of the ventriloquists—the capitalist prerogative the man in the ad represents—remains unchecked.

There is more going on here than the visual glorification of women's objective status and the seizure of her subjectivity. Her commodification teaches her *how* to be a consumer. Over the last century, women have earned increased spending power and today exert far greater influence than their spouses over household expenditure. But to become a good consumer, a woman must undergo a form of "market preparation," in which she is "as carefully primed as the materials used in the manufacturing process" (Hebdige 1988, 93). This priming teaches her to know a good commodity by *feeling* what it means to be one. Thus, to "feel like a dummy" is a sign of a "good buy" and, accordingly, of a "good woman," just as to feel hysterical, in the late nineteenth century, was a sign of being a woman.

Maskara

On one level, ventriloquism is a game of vocal sorcery that evacuates power from what is threatening. For it to work it requires a visible figure that can transmit subjectivity. This mask must hold our vision; it must visually distract us from the staging of an auditory trick. Masquerade and ventriloquism go hand in hand.

Etymologically, the term *maskara* is a man in masquerade, a buffoon (Weekley 1921). In common English, mascara refers to a type of makeup worn by women to thicken and lengthen their lashes for self-beautification. These mascaras—whether disguised fools or disguising cosmetics—overtake women with a vision of their own. While the ventriloquist steals her voice, mascara steals her visibility. Even if makeup absolves her of any real responsibility, it also conceals the realness she hopes to embody. Her eyes *become* the eyes of Christian Dior (FIGURE 1.9); her vision *becomes* the objectified vision

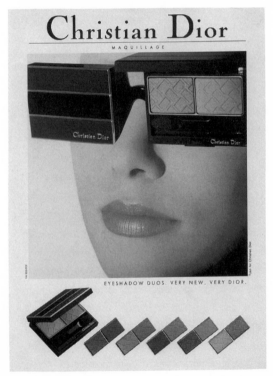

FIGURE 1.9 *Advertisement, Christian Dior eyeshadow duos (1988). Reprinted by permission of Christian Dior Perfumes, Inc. Photographer: Tyen for Christian Dior.*

of the cosmetic. Through consumption of material facades, we serve them, and in so doing we risk the bargain becoming irreversible. We try to take off the facade, to throw it away, but it reappears from within like a bad habit. It spills from our mouths like the unfurling scroll of the master ventriloquist, like Libaio (FIGURE 1.10).

For the female consumers who embody these masquerades, the advertising strategy that masks the apparatus destabilizes self-identity. Women tend to live in their bodies (even those of us who "know better") as if they were real, or unmediated. This deems us all, to a certain extent, hysterical.

SOME SYMPTOMS OF HYSTERIA

Amblyopia—a loss of sharpness of vision.
Diplopia—double vision.
Triplopia—triple vision.

FIGURE 1.10 *Advertisement, Ruffino Libaio (1988). Courtesy of Schieffelin and Somerset Co.*

Dysphoria—a generalized feeling of ill-being; especially an
abnormal feeling of anxiety, discontent, physical discomfort.
Allo-aesthesia—abnormality in the ability to feel sensations.

I feel like Barbie, therefore I am

One of the most pervasive and full-bodied "maskaras" destabilizing self-identity is Barbie—cosmeticized and buffoonish dummy par
excellence. To the delight of multibillion-dollar corporations and
their creative advertisers, the seemingly Faustian deal whereby
women dangle their bodies under the manipulations of corporate
fingers is extremely lucrative. Barbie earned its parent company,
Mattel, $700 million in 1990. To date, approximately six hundred
million dolls (including Barbie's family members, pets, and pal Ken)
have been sold world over (Fleming 1991, 129). Architectural para-
phernalia, such as Barbie's plastic mansions, motor homes, and gyms
are also available at $400, $60, and $22 respectively. Every year Mat-
tel comes up with about fifty new theme Barbies like "Western Fun
Barbie" or "Wet'n Wild Barbie" or "Wedding Fantasy Barbie," average price $15 (130). Recently, Barbie has become available in ethnic
shades and features—all, however, maintain the same body and
vapid expression of the classic blond, blue-eyed, "material girl." As
for wardrobe, Barbie gets about one hundred new outfits a year, and
over the four decades of her existence has had more than 250 million outfits, 1.2 million pairs of shoes, and 35,000 handbags. If Barbie is going to be hobnobbing with the rich and famous, you can buy
her a $120 dress by designer Bob Mackie, the same one who de-
signed some of Cher's revealing body-clingers (131).

    This schizoid-superwoman has survived several incarnations. She
began her rise to fame in 1959 as an adolescent in black-and-white
striped swimsuit and stiletto heels, passed through numerous size
changes, emerged as a precocious astronaut in the 1960s and a surgeon in 1973 (in spite of Barbie's nonfeminist stance). The Barbie we
know today was born in 1977 after serious plastic surgery. From that
date on, her insipid face launched her into celebrity status as it took
on the hard-core working world, then moved through the 1980s and
into the 1990s into her aerobic and executive phases (Fleming 1991,
131). Her mutability secured her fame as an icon, and innumerable
celebrities built careers as Barbie clones. In spite of the human com-
petition, this "dashboard princess" was selected to portray singer/

anorexic Karen Carpenter in Todd Haynes's cynical film *Superstar: The Life of Karen Carpenter*. Barbie, the doll, plays Karen Carpenter (and Ken plays her brother Richard), concert scenes and all.[15]

Barbie's plastic female body is void of explicit sexual assets: she's "all T&A and nonstop legs, everything pert and round and smooth, no belly button, no nipples, certainly no indicated pubic area (similarly, Ken has no penis)" (Fleming 1991, 132). However desexualized in detail, she is nonetheless a hypereroticized icon in general for her targeted audience (ostensibly three- to eleven-year-old girls) and for consumers of Hollywood ideals.[16] Her sexual duplicity cautions against the full-bodied, female sexuality of the celebrities who mimic her. As a plastic doll void of mature sexual signifiers, this sacred prototype is an eroticized child and a celebration of female impotency—notwithstanding Mattel's alterations for the 40-year-old Barbie, which include reduced bust and expanded waist, thus a less violently proportioned female figure.

Teknology

According to Jardine (1987), "machines and women have come alive and to identity at approximately the same time" (152)—the turn of the [twentieth] century. The etymology of *tek*, the root of technology, has to do not only with fabricating but also with begetting form, related to the maternal and an imagined primal feminine allure.[17] "Technology has always been about the maternal body and it

15. The film, in production in the 1980s, was never completed or released as the Carpenter estate is suing Haynes and Mattel for defamation of character.

16. While this may be the targeted audience, Barbie's actual efficacy as a symbolic model extends far beyond this age group. A 1993 adult guest on the Jenny Jones talk show confessed to undergoing eighteen operations for plastic surgery in order to look like Barbie. Her veneration far surpassed a mere desire to mimic her appearance. The twenty-six-year-old woman was beholden to the values, morals, character dispositions, and worldviews that Mattel imputed to its superhero. See Willis (1987) for discussion of Barbie and He-Man marketing and the gendered socialization of children as consumers.

17. See Traweek (1995) for a discussion of the sex appeal of machines and software. "I have been told by old men and young men in the lab that crawling around inside a detector (a room-sized piece of research equipment) and rearranging the detector according to the latest change in theory is 'a very powerful sexual experience'" (211–12).

does seem to be about some kind of male phantasm—but, more, it perceives that the machine *is* a woman in that phantasm" (Jardine 1987, 156).

Automobiles are machines that have been classically construed as feminized extensions of the male ego. The exquisite lines, at once streamlined and curvy, convey speed and efficiency, delectably seductive and smooth. In a 1989 Toyota ad, the image of a car is overshadowed by a larger-than-life woman. She appears to have begotten the car. The ad copy poses, "How many cars that look this good can you rely on?" The tacit question seems to be, "How many good-looking women can you purchase, enter, control, and still rely upon?" Jardine considers the phantasmic correlation of woman and machine an aspect of male hysteria: a male paranoia about real women disguised as female disorder. The Toyota ad disguises this male hysteria by first relating woman and car as intimates, and then reassuring the male consumer of the product's "solid feel," "responsive . . . engine," "substantial package," and "legendary . . . reliability." The hysterical message is: car is woman, car (Toyota) masters woman. Technology is simultaneously feminized and employed to control femininity.

The feminization of technology makes for particularly hysterical logic when related to reproductive technologies. Rosi Braidotti states: "Science and technology were invented to liberate men from real women and . . . reproductive technologies, for example, are simply the last desperate attempt . . . to drain the female human body of 'the feminine' " (Braidotti, quoted in Jardine 1987, 156). Perhaps the vast field of reproductive and medical technologies—artificial insemination, artificial wombs, cloning experiments, and genetic patching—intends to hook us up internally to the technology and commodities we have already begun to look and act like externally. The impossible inscription resurfaces: on the one hand, the disease itself is a reproductive profusion that must be controlled, if not entirely eradicated; on the other hand, reproductive technologies intended to provide the control are likewise feminized.

Barbie would be a perfect spokesthing for Donna Haraway's cyborgs—hypothetical human beings altered for life in an alien environment (much like our late capitalist metropoles) through implantation of artificial organs and other body parts. Haraway knows that "our machines are disturbingly lively and we ourselves frighteningly inert" (quoted in Jardine 1987, 151). Perhaps the hope is that artificial parts

FIGURE 1.11 *Charles Dana Gibson,*
Serious Business *(1905).*

FIGURE 1.12 *Advertisement, Jordache basics (1992). Reprinted by*
permission of Jordache Enterprises. Director of advertising: Shaul Nakash.

will infuse us with animated outlooks and capabilities. Video games, answering machines, nonumbilical telephones, telephone sex, and TV, are technologies that constitute, in part, the external nervous system to which our own nervous systems are sympathetically connected.

Advertising imagery is plugged directly into the masterbody of big business. And the female body, as in the case of Barbie, is molded to s(t)imulate capital, the central nerve of the advertising economy. Consequently, female consumers, symbiotically attached to ad imagery, live the nervous diseases of the social body. Jardine might be suggesting a form of institutional ventriloquism as a cure when she claims that we "can plug the body directly into the machine so as to 'fix it,' plug it directly into capital" (Jardine 1987, 155). I imagine that human nervous disorders will soon be diagnosed and treated as we treat mechanical breakdowns, market crashes, inflations, and recessions. The medical establishment will borrow from the lexicon of capitalism and entrepreneurial economics to understand and control human health and the next "female disorder." Infusions of advertising will be prescribed to keep one in neurological balance with the external world; advertising is, after all, hysterical, and for that very reason it may be just the homeopathic medicine that the doctor ordered.

Who are today's designers of femininity, creating the visual templates for women to plug into? Calvin Klein, creating Woman in the piercing, sultry, have-it-all, envy-me image of untouchable superiority? Thierry Mugler, fabricating Woman as wigged out, buffoonish queens of pretension? Or Irving Penn, who eliminates the female body altogether and fashions femininity in the still-life likeness of sexy Clinique products? They say Charles Dana Gibson is dead, but the resemblance between a 1905 Gibson plate and a Jordache image of 1991 makes me wonder (FIGURES 1.11 and 1.12). I browse through the pages of *Self* and find a woman attired in a conventional bride ensemble advertising Estée Lauder perfume. She looks identical to the award-winning Gibson Girl Bride Doll—hand-painted porcelain, gowned in satin, lace, tulle, lustrous faux pearls and 24-karat-gold accents—advertised the same year, 1991, in *Vogue* as Direct Purchase Doll of the Year.

2

I look therefore I have
photography as consumption

In the mid- to late nineteenth century, female bodies were layered in the ideologies of medical science and industrial evolution. They performed as silent mannequins, displaying and supporting cultural values in flux. They visually broadcasted the messages of a social body undergoing tumultuous change and served as the canvas upon which these changes were appropriately fashioned for consumption.

Interestingly, it became the mission of the male scientific community of the mid- to late nineteenth century to *unlayer* woman and reveal her true nature. Medical researchers were determined to capture the essence of femininity—the *female thing*—by literally cutting and seeing into her. The phantasmic veils they had layered upon her constituted the very magic they were determined to demystify.[1] Through a variety of invasive procedures, medical science exhumed her most private parts. These implicit parts, once revealed, would

1. The medical community that fabricated the fictions of femininity were as absorbed in their "reality effect" as were the consumers to whom they were marketed. There is an interesting parallel here to the advertising community. I am frequently asked whether those who create ads deliberately design a spurious and injurious representation of women. While I believe that a certain degree of conscious prevarication can be accounted for, the politics of gender that informs so many ads mystifies those who reproduce them.

prove the true identity of woman and the origins of her explicit role on the social stage. On a more abstract level, science would unveil and overcome nature. This material intervention toward discovery of an immaterial truth epitomizes the scientific approach to the "confusion of womanhood."

Of special interest were the corpses. Medical practitioners of the era were enthralled with research in human tissue and used almost exclusively female corpses for dissections (Jordanova 1989). According to Jordanova, surgery and dissections of female corpses were sexual acts. Cutting through layers of female flesh consecrated a seemingly ecstatic communion between surgical technology and what we have come to refer to, colloquially, as the "male gaze."[2]

Contemporaneously, there was the advent of gynecological procedures—the opening of women's genitals to evaluation through the use of the speculum, starting in the 1840s. While there was controversy surrounding the use of the speculum, it ultimately came to receive great praise for "employing *simultaneously* both visual inspection and tactile examination" (Smith 1845, 210). According to Shuttleworth (1990), "Technology here offers the fulfillment of the male erotic dream: the male gaze could follow the fingers and penetrate into the most hidden recesses of the female anatomy" (63) (FIGURE 2.1). These probing operations served not only to satisfy medical curiosity but to provide sexual pleasure, as male doctors performed a kind of orgasmic and spiritual "surgery," captured in the satirical verse of a contemporary poet:

> What's more horny than a heart
> heaving with the surgeon's art?
> and the clicking of the clips
> is a series of short trips,
> you're turned on, lit up, elationed—
> quite as knocked out as the patient!
> . . . while the pink peritoneum,
> lovely as an Art Museum,
> strikes you with desire and dumb
> till you very nearly come . . .

2. See Mulvey (1975) for a groundbreaking article on the male gaze, and Kaplan (1983a) for a reformulation of Mulvey by positing the possibility of a female gaze.

FIGURE 2.1 *Advertisement, Natori (1991). Reprinted by permission of Natori Company, Inc.*

> God made this delightful chasm
> for your own intense orgasm!
> (Ewart 1985, 136).[3]

3. This poem was dedicated to Richard Selzer, an American surgeon turned essayist, after Ewart read a review of Selzer (1976) in the *Guardian*. Ewart was satirizing expressed fantasies of the doctor/writer performing surgery on his female patients.

uring the Victorian era, sexual deprivation, mandated for women, is considered the cause of approximately 50 to 75 percent of all ses of hysteria. Physicians treated the resultant anxiety, irritability, ...straction, and sexual fantasies by manually massaging women's vulvas until they experienced relief through orgasm. Pressurized water jets were also used, as were steam-powered vibrators.

Just about the same time that the medical profession instituted gynecology, an extraordinary new invention—photography—metaphorized the invasive practices and pursuits of medical science. The technology of photography was devoted to a form of unlayering, looking into, and capturing; it was, in effect, intimate consumption. Susan Sontag (1977), in her discussion of photography's magical ability to rob one's identity, cites Balzac on his fear of photography: "each Daguerreian operation was . . . going to lay hold of, detach, and use up one of the layers of the body on which it focused" (158).

Photography thus alleged a negative territory that existed beneath the positive surface. Like medical technologies that could diagnose hitherto invisible disease and suggest treatment, photography too, privy to an incisive vision, could diagnose the unsightly, and "treat" it through aesthetic techniques of revisioning. The surgeon's scientific gaze—rendered by knife or through the speculum's cylindrical steel—was now accompanied by a far more socially portentous aesthetic gaze; femaleness could be disclosed by technological as well as human eyes. Under the rubric of "looking," cultural and biological modes of attending to the "female question" were politically united. As these two visions—medical and photographic—joined in a sort of erotic bliss, hysteria blossomed into epidemic proportions.

Along with medicine's explorations in dissection, surgery, and gynecology, came the wax anatomical female models, or Venuses, originally made in Italy at the end of the eighteenth century. There is a strong connection between these Venuses and the photographic realism that was transforming the world of representation. These inert forms were endowed in sexual detail, equipped with removable parts, and contoured to lay seductively flat or in semireclining positions. The male models, on the other hand, all stood upright, muscular, and fleshless (Jordanova 1989). The wax reproduced the texture of the real thing: the coloring was naturalistic and the positions were often imitations from well-known works of art. The move toward realism in medical imagery was a move toward accuracy, toward the notion of an *unmediated* eye; this notion was ushered in with great ferocity with the advent and use of the camera. The Venus models and photo-graphic imagery created a verisimilitude of femininity that became so relentless as to create hyper-realism: a dream space that is also a death space within which consumers become inextricably emersed.

The hyper-realism of photography, unlike that of the Venus models, radically transformed representational politics. Whereas Venuses were discrete objects, photographs—mass-reproduced and nationally dispersed—had an inordinate influence as cultural cur-rency. In "Rhetoric of the Image," Barthes (1977b) explains how the photographic image "innocents" (45), or oversimplifies, the ad-vertisements' dense symbolic messages and semantic connotations; the photograph grants the fabricated ad image an autonomous power that denotes only itself. Barthes calls this "messages without a code" (45). It is the seeming naturalness of the photograph—one cannot deny that "the thing [photographed] has been there" (Barthes 1981, 76)—that particularly lends itself to the rhetoric of the image.

Barthes also addresses the illogical conjunction between the real-ity and unreality factors of photography. The reality factor lies in the there-then of photography: an actual event is captured mechanically. Its unreality lies in its deferred presence into the here-now: the photograph is not experienced as illusion, as art. Through the photograph's stupefying evidence of "this is how it was," it gives us, by a "precious miracle," a relentless reality that conceals something "other," something from which we can remain sheltered (1977b, 44). Sontag (1977) characterizes the photographic process as a way in which slices of the world are presented as "clouds of fantasy and pellets of information" (69). This merger of information and fan-tasy constitutes the "magic of the real" (69). She also notes that "photography has the unappealing reputation of being the most re-alistic, therefore facile, of the mimetic arts" (51).

As the female body was posed, as Venus, photographic model, or surgical patient, she was simultaneously frozen, in wax, on chemically treated paper, and by anaesthesia. In this voiding of life she was endowed with a quality of seamless perfection. In her captured pas-sivity, the signatures of science and art were jointly inscribed into her flesh. Meanwhile, the female body broadcasted a prognosis in the form of a trademark. But it was not necessarily a prognosis regarding *her* identity. The illusion of an originary there-then power was mirac-ulously absorbed into her flesh as a resolute and concrete here-now.

Meanwhile, what was deadened was sexualized, making erotic not only female submission but the very meaning of ownership and possession (Jordanova 1989, 97).

Layers on and off: hysteria and photography

The male surgeons looked and cut in search of the meaning of femininity; alas, they found nothing there at all. Hysterical symptoms, and thus symptoms of womanhood itself, did not reveal themselves in the human tissue or organs anymore than in the waxen anatomical parts. Nearly a century later in 1963, the psychologist Jaspers reminds us that hysteria reflects layers of external impositions and an absence of an organic derivation within the female body:

> In the absence or weakness of a "central core" the hysterical personality seems to consist . . . of different exteriors—to mix a metaphor, a combination of chameleon and onion where the uncovering of each layer serves only to reveal another layer with a different emotional colouration in compliance with the perceived requirements of the interpersonal environment. (Chodoff 1982, 278)

The different exteriors that constitute the hysteric can be understood in contemporary consumer culture as fashion itself. Female identity becomes the layers of commercial signatures that she wears. Fashion designers often inscribe these signatures upon the naked female flesh. An ad reads, "Cindy in her Halston": Cindy Crawford bares all in order to exhibit, to become, Halston. A woman's naked skin, dappled with the logo of René Guinot, "speaks for itself"; Guinot lends her body an identity. "The perfect tan"—produced by the illusion of masterly contrived studio lights—is testimony to a commercial deity, Tanqueray, whose imported and intoxicating rays bestow her, literally engrave her, with "special dry" beauty (FIGURE 2.2).

Photographic commercial brand naming of the female body performs a double feat, one that resembles the contradictory veiling and unveiling processes of medical science. On one hand, brand naming strips layers of identity off; it consumes as it labels. On the other hand, the female body, when imprinted with a trademark, is layered with meaning. And this meaning comes to serve as protection, an identity that redresses the concurrent rape of subjectivity. The vo-

The perfect tan.

Tanqueray.® A singular experience.™
For a 20" x 28" poster of ad, send $5 check or money order (no cash)
payable to: Perfect Tan Print/PO. Box 4314 / Syosset, NY 11791-4314.
Imported English Gin, 47.3% Alc/Vol (94.6°), 100% Grain Neutral Spirits © 1990 Schieffelin & Somerset Co., NY, NY

FIGURE 2.2 *Advertisement, Tanqueray gin (1990). Courtesy of Schieffelin and Somerset Co.*

racious consumption of products—cosmetics, perfumes, lotions, designer clothing—may be women's enactment of this protective layering: women's way of putting back what has been stripped away, to fortify the body against further attack. The irony, of course, is that these layers are impermanent; they wear out or become obsolete, like fashion. And, second, they relay the very femininity that attracts further consumptive gazes.

Photographic images of femininity terminally accompany women's images of themselves (Berger 1972). The observer lives within her psyche as judge, as the ideal that she must fulfill. Simultaneously, she experiences herself as the observer, under scrutiny, and in fear of being unveiled. This visceral, even neurological, terror of being violently seen (through), of being exposed as the very sight that the surveyor is most afraid to see, becomes part of her body and of her performance of self. She is aware of the camera—the public eye, the thief of her likeness—equipped with a consumptive technovision, ready to ambush her at any moment. This everyday story is a lived fiction, as real as the hysterical symptoms that bear witness.

AUTOBIOGRAPHICAL FICTION

I sense a presence lurking just beyond the surface of my body. I am aware of myself as a target, the beholden prey of a disembodied stare. It is imperceptible but so invasive that my flesh and breath chill.

Shortness of breath.

In anticipation of being photographically taken, I succumb to his aim. In a blur of blinding light I hear a round of clicks echo in the chamber and feel the cold draft of the shutter pass in waves across my exposed skin. In the afterflash, I open my eyes and with my remaining senses discern that I have been seized, preserved, and transmuted to print.

A depleted sense of self.

I scan myself as the object scanned. I consume myself as if I was a tourist of femininity. Even when absorbed in a passionate caress, I am alert to the invasive sightseer—especially then, when the lure of pleasure brings vulnerability. Pleasure signifies danger.

Paranoia, oversensitivity, and the tendency to overinterpret situations.

I try to overcome my fear but know that if I surrender to my own desire, I shall be dangerously prone. I chose to stultify my sexuality and remain vigilant.

Sexual frigidity.

I muster a defiant counterglance to the omnipresent stare, unsure exactly from where it issues forth. I face the vast indiscernible eye of the camera, to my left, then suddenly behind me, every sensation a glare that threatens to devour. I am wounded, terrified, staring everywhere and nowhere in space.

In Woodruff, Goodwin, and Guze (1982), the following frequency of symptoms in hysterical patients (by percent) was deduced: nervousness 92, back pain 88, joint pain 84, weakness 84, dizziness 84, fatigue 84, abdominal pain 80, nausea 80, headache 80, dyspnea (shortness of breath) 72, chest pain 72, trouble doing anything because it felt bad 72, constipation 64, depression 64, anxiety attacks 64, visual blurring 64, anorexia 60, palpitation 60, excessive crying 60, fainting 56, dyspareunia (pain during sex) 52, thoughts of dying 48, phobias 48, food intolerances 48, menstrual irregularity 48, sexual indifference 44.

Getting used

Consumption—to use up, eat; to buy; to destroy or do away with; to spend wastefully, squander; to devour; to engross or obsess; to waste away or perish. (Webster's New World Dictionary, Third College Edition, 1988)

The definition of consumption suggests a paradox, not unlike the veiling and unveiling phenomenon described earlier. To consume is to absorb something, to take it into oneself; to consume suggests depletion or eradication. As consumers we purchase products and photographic images and make them part of ourselves. In this sense, photography consumes; it uses up reality, it makes it obsolete, and then, technologically, gives birth to it again.

The concept of waste and refuse is fundamental to the operations of consumption. Commodities not only get used, they also get used up. When images of commodities are compounded with sexual images of the female body, notions of waste become commentaries on gender and power. In an ad for Get Used jeans, a woman stands against a cement wall in a provocative pose; she seems to share the commodity's raison d'être—to get used (up)—by offering her body. In another Get Used ad, two women, scantily dressed, playfully wash a storefront window. Through the soapy glass they scrawl the message, "Keep the World Clean." The innuendo of sexual exploitation is now aligned with positive implications: women must get used—sexually, economically, and symbolically—in order to clean up the social order.

As these representations encode the concepts of exchange and usage, the desires of actual women become representationally passé: they fall into disuse. Differences between women and commodities, between women and photographic images, narrow until there is no distinguishing between them. "We consume images at an ever faster rate and, as Balzac suspected cameras used up layers of the body, images consume reality" (Sontag 1977, 179). In the case of gender, images of women consume the realities of women.

One further reading of the Get Used ads regards the "used look" and the promotion of used commodities: things prewashed, pre-worn, already consumed and discarded. With woman and commodity fused, what is intimated is a woman's impermanence, her kinship to excess and waste, and her ability to be recycled. Woman represents both acquisition and loss, what is taken in and what is thrown away. As recyclable merchandise, she signifies something that lives on and on but as forever alterable.

Photographs are the consummate agents of recycling. According to Sontag (1977), "Nothing is more acceptable today than the photographic recycling of reality" (115). Once in possession of a photographic negative there is the opportunity to make countless reproductions; the notion of waste is factored into production. It is this aspect of photographic technology that, when employed by advertising, fosters the illusion of an inexhaustible supply of commodities, and thus the possibility of more and more buying.[4]

The "get used" concept is at the core of vampirism—the ravaging of another body so exhaustively that all that remains is the passive semblance of a former life. It is interesting to note that the theme of vampirism burgeoned as a cultural myth in the late nineteenth century, just when hysteria was epidemic.[5] *Dracula*, the novel by Bram Stoker, was first published in London in 1897 and has never been out of print. Critics have called it, among other things, a parable of cultural xenophobia, an occult text, a thinly veiled Darwinian or even Marxist tract (Skal 1990). Most agree it taps archetypal motifs that are embedded in our psyche and take diverse cultural forms.[6]

4. Etymologically, consume has been traced to *em*, meaning to take. When Indo-European nomads settled in towns and commerce began, the root -*em* took on the meaning "take by purchase, buy" (Shipley 1984, 96). A warning regarding the dangers of voraciousness—"let the buyer beware" (96)—accompanied the new meaning, thus the words ex*em*ption, red*em*ption. Over time, consumer needs have expanded into a pathological yearning captured in an obsolescent word, "emacity: itch to be buying" (96).

5. See Dresser (1989) for an analysis of vampirism as an enduring American value manifested in legend, marketing, and sexuality.

6. Cinematic renditions of the classical Dracula myth have flourished in the last twenty years. The first cinematic version of the Dracula myth was F. W. Murnau's *Nosferatu* (1922). The classic American release was Tod Brown-

The vampiric transference of power has taken form in the consumptive bite of the camera. But while photographic technology is the culpable "vampire," it is the women being photographed who are represented as the blood-sucking and castrating shrews. While the camera absorbs her lifeblood, she is culturally marked as the wild animal. In the light of such craving for female blood, technological vampirism seems to contest the twentieth-century popularization of penis envy as the predominant dynamic of sexual difference. Perhaps the enduring and gendered images of vampirism evidence a kind of menses envy—envy of precisely that which marks women hysterical.

Vampiric images flourish in popular contemporary magazines.[7] Elongated and exposed necks are one of the most repeated photographic postures of women in advertising imagery (FIGURE 2.3). Whether standing, sitting, crouching, or lying, the backward thrust of her head accentuates, even invites, a state of defenselessness and susceptibility. Several ads feature the typical Bela Lugosi bite: men, gripped with desire, lurching forward aggressively into the radiant, timeless, uncovered expanse of a woman's pulsating neck. Anthony (1982) and Klerman (1982) include vulnerability and helplessness on their lists of hysterical symptoms.

Many contemporary ads, however, feature a kind of "displaced bite." An advertisement for Martell cognac exemplifies this evolved, sort of *photographic bite*, springing from the eyes and carried resolutely in the protracted gaze. A man delicately touches a woman's neck, his fingers perhaps nostalgic for the toothy bite of yesteryear. Her head pulls gently away from his touch and rests against the mirror behind her; there in the mirror's reflection we see the man's penetrating stare. The ad copy declares, "The Art of Eye Contact." Vampiristic contact has become an optical transaction, with the looker in command. Women today suffer from a pervasive need to appear attractive and

---

ing's *Dracula* (1931) starring Bela Lugosi. Several other productions, mostly American and British, appeared in every decade of the twentieth century. There were comedic and parodic renditions including *Dracula's Dog*, *Dracula's Widow*, and *Dracula and Son*. One of the most compelling versions is Werner Herzog's *Nosferatu* (1979), and one of the more recent is Francis Ford Coppola's *Bram Stoker's Dracula* (1992). The list is extensive since 1992.

7. Interestingly, more and more vampiristic images in magazines of the 1990s feature only women, cloaked in black, hovering over each other, or glaring at consumers like packs of ravenous beasts. See Fuss (1992) and Copjec (1991).

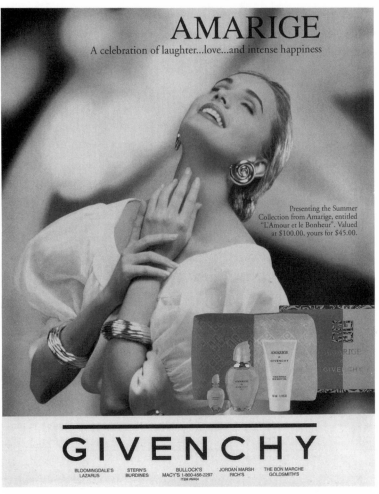

FIGURE 2.3 *Advertisement, Amarige perfume by Givenchy (1994). Reprinted by permission of Parfums Givenchy, Inc. Photographer: Claus Wickrath. Model: Berry Snither.*

usable in the eyes of a disembodied camera; they have a need to become erotic still lifes.

Desire and tactility:
the Grecian bend and fashion babies

With women and technology forced into orgasmic intimacy, commercial ad photography becomes a form of commodity pornography. Dreams of ownership and power are not only eroticized but made tactile; economic control is an affair in which sexuality and materiality are intertwined.

An essential component of women's liberation at the turn of the twentieth century was clothing reform. Previously, corsets and excessive layers greatly inhibited movement, restricted women's breathing, pressured internal organs, cramped the stomach and nullified the appetite (thus conforming to standards of feminine frailty and self-denial), and caused physiological disorders. Together, these afflictions were known as corsetitis.

Corsets worn with bustles thrust the woman's bosom and bottom into exaggerated positions known as the "Grecian bend." The posture accentuated sexual and carnal readiness precisely at the time when wearers were expected to sublimate or transcend such physical preoccupations (FIGURE 2.4). These restrictive conventions of Victorian dress needed to be refashioned to address women's increasing entry into the urban marketplace. In their place, fashion designers in the early 1900s conceived of women's clothing with flexibility and movement in mind.

The appreciation for texture and detail that depicted earlier Victorian clothing remained an element in new fashion plates. The minutiae of a garment's composition were made manifest in the designs themselves, reflecting the primacy of substance valued in engravings and lithographs of the time. Along with mobility, the aesthetic of the times emphasized touchability and indissolvable materiality. This materiality was evidenced in "fashion babies," pasteboard dolls created in France at the turn of the century, dressed in miniature versions of the latest haute couture. These cardboard "babies" were a tribute not only to fashion itself but to an era marked by an increasing regard for that which could be handled and possessed.

While dress that physically forces the emblematic arch is unpopular today, the assumption of the look that it produced remains a mainstay within commercial photography—another means of materializing a representation of desire. Whether waxen, cardboard, or photographic, Grecianesque models embody the everlasting possibility of entry. In a 1992 advertisement for Everlast, Cybil Shepherd poses in a standard Grecian, while ESPRIT features the posture on all fours (FIGURE 2.5). Material clones of the female body, thrust into speculative curvatures and inviting protrusions, abound in ad imagery and help amass a very sexy profit. Her muted and overdetermined body is a symbolic passageway to conquest; in materialized form it performs as a "trophy," a monument to victory.

FIGURE 2.4 *Advertisement, Yes clothing (1991). Reprinted by permission of Yes Clothing Co.*

Photographs can be conceived as two-dimensional trophies. They have the power to concretize a virtual likeness into an object that both erases and exalts the power of the imaged. They can transform culture into couture, spirit into ESPRIT. Sontag (1977) captures the hysteria of facsimiles when she states: "Photography is a kind of overstatement, a heroic copulation with the material world" (30). While it denies presence, it simultaneously bestows hyperpresence.

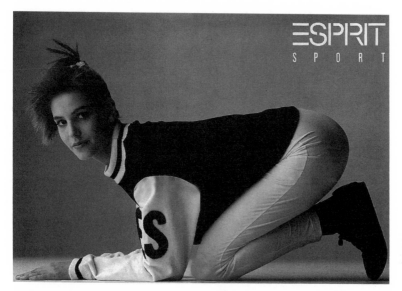

FIGURE 2.5 *Advertisement, Esprit sport (1988). Reprinted by permission of ™©Esprit de Corp., San Francisco, California (1981).*

Hysterical symptoms are such ambivalent overstatements as well. They are emphatic attempts to rupture the expected looks of femininity while embodying that femininity at the same time.

Photo as symptom

Barthes (1981) says that the photographic image "flows back from presentation to retention" (90). It possesses us in its still life and it holds us there in its evidential nature. At the same time, a framed segment comes to epitomize a larger (out-of-frame) space. "In all photographs we have this . . . act of cutting off a piece of space and time, of keeping it unchanged while the world around continues to change" (Metz 1990, 159). Metz argues that in the definitive photographic click of the shutter there is a kind of castration that marks the place from which the look has been averted forever. The photograph itself—the in-frame, the place of presence inside of absence—is haunted by its borderlines and by all beyond them that is lost.

This photographic transposition of an object displaced into another register is comparable to hysterical construction. The hysteric's body is a site for displacement; hysteria, like photography, produces a snippet of "truth" in the form of a symptom. This symptom, like the photograph, is a visible fragment of the larger unseen story. It is a trace, or physicalized memory, that exhibits itself so dramatically and absorbingly that what is absent—what is beyond the frame of the somatic manifestation—is forgotten. Both the metonymical photograph and symptom assume an autonomous, fetishistic identity with a fixed metaphorical meaning.

Walter Benjamin (quoted in Buci-Glucksmann 1987) compares image and symptom: "The woman's body . . . stands as a metaphor for extremes: desire/death, animating/agitating, life/corruption . . . and serves to materially convert that 'petrified anxiety,' the image 'that knows no development'" (228). For Benjamin, the hysterical symptom is displaced evidence. It is a material recording of a living death and, like the photograph and fetish, it gathers a kind of consummate and luminous power.[8]

The structure of displacement and its lustrous fallout has critical potential, evidenced through a parallel: there is a connection between photography as a visual fragment of experience and the symptom as a fragment of the body. The sequencing of photographs and symptoms forms a montage that challenges conventional narrative and historicism (Benjamin 1969). Sontag (1977) has pointed out that a book of photographs is very much like a book of quotations, thus granting a body of images a similarly critical advantage. A hysterical attack is a story of physical quotations: incongruous corporeal gestures that together question conventional narratives of health.

Photograph and hysterical symptom speak a similar language; they impart images, they *show* reality in lieu of verbally narrating it. An ad for Liz Claiborne, featuring a model who is "all legs," sells hosiery with ad copy that declares proudly, "Legs have a language of

8. Regarding the symptom, Freud conceived of this "death" as a psychosexual inability [of women] to successfully master the Oedipal—a kind of frozen impotence leading to a suspended state of castration. I prefer to think of it as a cultural and gendered debauchery—a kind of deliberate ensnaring of one's substance leading to a suspended state of desire. The shift heeds important issues of culpability and victimization; in Freud, the little deaths that accompany hysteria (as well as their remedies), remain the responsibility of women. My modified explanation redirects attention to the cultural strategies, ideologies, institutions, symbols, and people, that rig the "killing" and yet remain safely concealed behind that rigging.

their own." While the ventriloquist's master narrative divests both hysteric and commodified woman of social value, her graphic corporeality speaks nonetheless, albeit in a different register; she talks in gestures, poses, and movements. Innumerable advertisements sell their product through the language of body parts, through seemingly "unreadable" signs (FIGURE 2.6). In this way, they sell the mysterious facades that secure capitalist structures of power. But they also gesture accusingly toward them, just as symptoms gesture accusingly toward an underlying disease. Photographs are similarly muted and incomplete; they too suggest that a bigger picture is not merely cut off and hidden but, in fact, is challenged by what remains in the photograph itself.

The verbal language of the hysteric is often afflicted. One of many hysterical symptoms that relates to language aberrations is known as

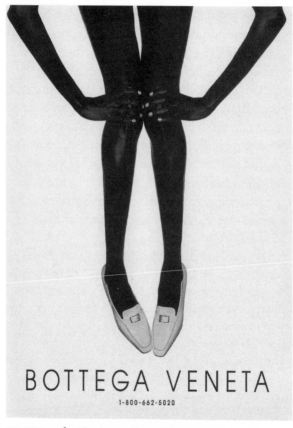

FIGURE 2.6 *Advertisement, Bottega Veneta (1991). Reprinted by permission of Bottega Veneta. Photographer: Marc Hom.*

the "hysterical twilight state," or the Ganser syndrome. Sufferers offer approximate or nonsensical answers to questions, or provide peculiar elaborations and circumlocutions referred to as "talking past the point" (Whitlock 1982, 201). "We cannot fail to recognize how in their choice of answers the patient appears to deliberately *pass over (vorbeigehen)* the indicated correct answer, and to select a false one, which any child would easily recognize as such" (186). For instance, when asked, "How many noses do you have?" the patient responds with a reply such as, "I do not know if I have a nose" (186). According to Critchley (quoted in Whitlock 1982) these are early stages of sensory, or jargon, aphasia.

The Ganser syndrome alludes to a kind of savvy that the hysteric, at least in this instance, developed within the constraints of her circumscribed social status. Ganser's hysterical patients were all incarcerated prisoners on remand. Given these circumstances, they might have found the rather obvious questions suspicious, some sort of trick, and, not knowing what the catch was, deliberately gave approximate answers (Whitlock 1982, 202). The language they spoke was impudent and ironic and suggests hysteria's potential as a political stratagem.

The hysterical symptom, like the photograph, is a material by-product of mass-reproduced culture that connotes something other than material reality. The hysteric's body—a female body—is a snapshot and a condemnation of the cultural politics of gender; *it is a living paradox.* Its oscillation between convulsive freezing and fluid recycling, between inclusion and exclusion, links woman to photography: she *lives* the symbolic dying and rebirthing that distinguishes the photographic message.[9]

9. Several scholars have written about the photograph in ways relevant to the paradigm of hysteria. See Sontag (1977) on the hyper-real and surreal aspects of photography, the photo image as a primitive trace and a material token of absence, the relation between photography and voyeurism/tourism, and the photographic rendering of reality as an item for exhibition. See Graham's (1982) discussion on "manufactured memory," in which the will functions as if it were the semi-somnolent, isolated, hypnotized unconscious of the spectator lost in a dream. See Benjamin (1969b, in English translation) and Buck-Morss (1989). See Buci-Glucksmann (1987) on the "mimesis of death" (225) and the visible "massification" of feminine bodies (223). Finally, see Metz (1990) and Barthes (1981) on the relation between photography, death, and the fetish.

The surrealists

The age of mechanical reproduction demanded reconsideration of authority, subjectivity, and authenticity. It was by virtue of photographic methodology, in large part, that symbols became objects and objects symbols, deeming signifiers and signifieds indistinguishable. This photo-induced quality of a hypertactile "really-real" was, indeed, surreal; photography and surrealism shared a kind of teleological "posture of alienation" (Sontag 1977, 80). The surrealist photographers were particularly interested in deliberately employing photographic potentials to blur what they saw as false boundaries between reality and illusion.[10]

The hysteric, considered incapable of distinguishing real from unreal, served as a perfect paradigm for this ambiguity. In fact, according to the surrealists, hysteria was a paradigm for modern life itself; we all had a touch of the "disorder." As far back as 1888, Möbius, who influenced Freud's work on hysteria, discerned the hysterical constitution of industrial capitalism (Roy 1982, 146). He declared that hysteria was ubiquitous, and to varying degrees we all suffer it. But it was not until the surrealists' aesthetic exaltation of hysteria that it became a glorified pathology.

The surrealist community, under the direction of André Breton, adopted hysteria as their aesthetic emblem.[11] Dalí's *Phenomena of Ec-*

---

10. Related to this alienation of photography and surrealism, Krauss (1990) discusses the "true copy" and the "false copy." The true copy is a valid imitation, truly resembling an original, a copy of the inner idea of a form and not just its empty shell. The false copy puts into question the very question of differentiation:

> The false copy is a paradox that opens a terrible rift within the very possibility of being able to tell true from not-true. . . . The false copy takes the idea of difference or nonresemblance and internalizes it, setting it up within the given object as its very condition of being. . . . Photography, in its precarious position as false copy—the image that is resemblant only by mechanical circumstance and not by internal, essential connection to the model—served to deconstruct the whole system of model and copy, original and fake, first- and second-degree replication. (23–24)

It was this paradox that the surrealists celebrated.

11. This community, growing out of dada influences, included a large number of writers, painters, sculptors, and photographers, and thrived in the

stasy seems to be literally derived from Jean-Martin Charcot's elaborate late nineteenth-century iconography of hysteria, which is discussed in depth in Chapter 3. In honor of the fiftieth anniversary of Charcot's studies of hysteria, the surrealist collection includes photographs of Charcot's patient Augustine: "the most beautiful hysteric" (Weiss 1989, 93). The surrealists were also celebrating the "aesthetic" of hysteria, which they defined "as a supreme form of expression" and the "greatest poetic discovery of the nineteenth century" (93).

Breton was strongly influenced by Freud and psychoanalysis. Breton's fascination with *l'écriture automatique*, with dreams, the unconscious, and repetition, all derive from his understanding of Freud. The surrealists were offering a language, so to speak, to their exalted but muted hysteric. But this language would ultimately imprison her as did the supposedly curative language of Charcot's hypnotism and iconography, and aspects of Freud's psychoanalytic discourse.

The surrealists manifested their fascination with the unconscious in actual photographic technology. Just as psychoanalysis introduced to surrealists and dadaists the world of unconscious impulses (Benjamin 1969b), the camera introduced the optical unconscious (Krauss 1993). The implications of "unconscious optics" are sensorially profound. Dark elusive hallways extending back into the vanishing points of visual memory seek knowledge that no conscious light could ever reveal. The surrealists developed such photographic techniques as collage, montage, rayography, solarization, doubling, and negative printing in an attempt to sever the questionable seamlessness that photography often rendered. Through the phenomena of overlaying and repetition, the paradox of reality was constituted as a sign: presence was positioned alongside absence, altered by representation, made spatial, and transformed into movement (Krauss and Livingston 1985b). The surrealist aesthetic was thus constituted as hysterical; it displayed the unceasing stutter of information across the modern, increasingly visual landscape. Photography enhanced the surrealist aesthetic because of its power to reference coincidentally illusion and the real.

1920s and 1930s. The writers included Breton, Tzara, Eluard, Apollinaire; the artists included Duchamp, Dalí, Ernst, Tanguy, Picabia, Chirico, Miró, Magritte; the photographers included Man Ray, Bellmer (also painter and writer), and Brassai.

The female body itself undergoes a technological transformation in the hands of the surrealists. For instance, whether we conceive of the technique of doubling as the essence of meaning (as surrealists Breton and Man Ray did), or as a deformation of meaning (as surrealists Bataille and Hans Bellmer did), the female body is codified by doubling and all that doubling means; she is more than herself, not herself, two-faced, reproducible, a copy, replaceable, extra, excessive, and ornamental.[12]

Unfortunately, regarding the female image, the surrealists reproduced the stigmatic elements of the hysterical iconography. Their photographic representations revered hysteria as an abstraction but failed to understand or celebrate the rebelliousness of hysterical women per se. Perhaps, as feminist Xavière Gauthier suggests, in embracing hysteria the male surrealists were using woman to work out their own rebellion against the Father.[13] Perhaps blind to the

12. Breton valorized the primary process of the unconscious with the intent of creating the "marvelous," whereby opposites are reconciled and desire is given free rein. He advocated dialectic idealism. Bataille accused the surrealists of "pretentious idealist aberrations" and nauseating utopian sentimentality, and proposed a heterology, something more parodic (Weiss 1989, 90). He was interested in transgression by means of a pure, wasteful expenditure, or nondialectical materialism, the goal being individual sovereignty rather than collective social revolution. Differences between Breton and Bataille resulted in Bataille's being exiled from the surrealist camp.

Man Ray's work was a valorization of the female body that represented classical Bretonian surrealism and the languor of the fashionable woman of the times. He made his living, in large part, doing fashion photography for *Harper's Bazaar, Vogue, Vanity Fair,* and *Charm.* Hans Bellmer's work (as an advertising designer in Berlin in the 1930s) spoke more to Bataille's nondialectical theory of transgression. Bellmer's work foregrounds the sadistic component of scopophilia, where the sculptural and photographic effects disarticulate the female body into a sign of violence, possession, and masochistic pleasure (Weiss 1989, 93). Of particular interest, however, is Bellmer's photographs of his constructed *Doll* (wood, metal, plaster and papier-mâché, produced in 1934) that appear to be deformed and parodic versions of the Venuses. See Grundberg (1990) for discussion of Bellmer's preoccupation with sexual ambiguity, fetishism, and substitution. See also Cindy Sherman's dummies deployed in sex acts. They resemble Bellmer's Poupées and suggest a more Bataillesque interpretation of doubling.

13. See Suleiman (1990) for a discussion of feminist interpretations of surrealism.

misogyny and sexism that the technology of photography inscribed culturally, they fell victim to the very paradox they tried to illuminate. It seems that under the influence of their own artistic obsessions they failed to recognize the male hysteria to which they contributed. Weiss (1989) claims that "the iconography of hysteria, much like the photographic iconography of Surrealism, is not merely a scenario of women possessed by demons but also (and perhaps above all) of men possessed by the phantasms and images of the women they love, desire or imagine" (94).

Fashion and art photography: still life and beyond

Art and high fashion became intimate allies in the 1930s, with surrealist manipulation as their common trope. Photography was particularly predisposed to surrealist visions. And fashion, with its pervasive addiction to an un-real, to glamour, was somewhat surrealist from the start.

Fashion photography is "based on the fact that something can be more beautiful in a photograph than in real life" (Sontag 1977, 104). It is accomplished by the conjoining of two different promises of the photographic image: (1) it will provide real information about the world, and (2) it will thrust that realness into a distortion that is quintessentially surrealist. The aesthetics of hysteria informed the developing industries of fashion and art photography.[14]

By the 1950s, photography popularized a merger of fantasy and reality, and of past and present in a forever here-now relatively unburdened by historical references. It also began to bridge modernism's contested categories of high and low art. Photographic artists began designing the mise-en-scène of advertisements, the seemingly basest form of popular culture. But the advertising industry, bent on the sales of affordable wish-objects manufactured to fall short of the promises their jingles offered, was fertile territory for artists and designers. Advertising was ardently engaged in artistic explorations intended to rend human beings from the constraints of reality and cloak them in the phantasms of the imagination. Artists prided

14. While practices of art photography are, of course, employed by fashion photographers (such as Man Ray), art photography is a much more expansive field and cannot be reduced to fashion photography. I thus consider them separate, albeit nondiscrete, categories.

themselves on uplifting the debauchery of mass-reproduced "art." They projected their abstract sensibilities upon the ever-malleable female form of popular currency. Newsstand images were made superlative by art photographers' dramatic lines, mysterious shadows, and exquisite facades. Sadly, their increasingly chimerical aspects did not discourage dissatisfied women from ripping the images out of magazines and bringing them to beauty parlors and boutiques as illustration of the visual dreams they wanted desperately to embody.[15]

This magical power is manifest in surrealism, and profound in Man Ray's rayographs, created primarily for his fashion images in *Harper's Bazaar* and *Vogue*. In one rayograph, a human hand is permeated with a delirious kind of emptiness that grants it an uncanny presence—one that can never be possessed. Ray had a particularly widespread influence on post–World War I advertising aesthetics. While the rayographs were not created for his advertising commissions, imitations of them abound in contemporary advertising design.

The still life particularly resonates with Ray's surrealist tradition and frequents the pages of popular magazines, both in ads and fashion spreads. Still-life photographers, such as Wright Morris, have the extraordinary ability to evoke the lives of people who are absent from the pictures they take. One of photography's gifts is that it lets us see more than it shows. "Morris can make a newspaper-lined drawer of cheap flatware tell a poignant tale of the lives and times of all who ate with those knives and forks night after night, year after year" (Edwards 1990, 67). Jan Groover, featured in *American Photographer*, photographs only those special objects that, in her perception, possess animate powers. She claims: "Objects have attitudes. Apples sit around and don't do much, but bottles become little characters" (quoted in Squiers 1989, 43). The still life, like the symptom, arrests attention and extracts a piece out of something larger; it transmutes ideas and lives into substances. It simultaneously endows the substance with another life, one infused with fancy, implausibility, even danger by haunting it with all that remains invisible. By changing the way things look, the very nature of reality is altered.

15. Berger (1972) traces the development of visual culture from oil painting to publicity images, covering issues of tactility, glamour, envy, the culture of social relations told through pictures, and the importance of wealth, buying power, and capitalism, in transforming our concept of seeing.

Of relevance here is the work of commercial photographer Irving Penn. Penn is well known for his renderings of Clinique products. The following description of Penn's 1972 still life, *Cigarette 34*, exemplifies the magical transmutation:

> Penn had not resorted to abstraction to disguise his odd subjects, nor had he glamorized them in any obvious way. Though dramatically enlarged, meticulously studied, and presented in luminous platinum prints, the discarded cigarettes were clearly what they were—yet a transformation had occurred that turned the grimy, stamped-out butts into objects unlike anything anyone had seen before. Brooding and irresistible, they became strangely moving monuments to time and loss. With each "portrait," Penn's alchemy had taken something despised and made it worthy of attention; but he had not changed it at all, only the way we perceived it. (In a testimony to the power of such alchemy, I never see a cigarette butt lying on the sidewalk without a sense of recognition, as if I know it now for all that it is). (Edwards 1990, 67)

It is when photography (art, fashion, or commercial) uses the female body as its object that "gender reality" itself is technically altered and abstracted. The female body is translated into inertia representing something larger than the female body, but the extraordinary presence she exudes does not fill the emptiness made to allow for it. The recognition that Edwards speaks of—man to still-lifed/ennobled cigarette butt—is not the sense of recognition of woman to still-lifed/ennobled female body. For her, a vacancy remains through the spectacular rebirth. Photography, in spite of its alchemical talents, can serve as a weapon that "spirit[s] away "politics". . . to the advantage of a socio-moral status" (Barthes 1987, 91), of a gender status.

In the photographic iconography of hysteria produced by French neurologist Jean-Martin Charcot, the hysteric's photographic image functioned to "spirit away" the very gender politics that invented her. The hysteric's ambivalence and ruptured reality was swallowed up and recomposed as an abstracted series of visual types that did not transport her out of hysteria, nor alter the political nature of her reality. The visual types that medical photography pathologized a century ago are today mass-marketed through advertising. Photography in the service of late nineteenth-century medicine fashioned the hysteric per se; photography in the service of late twentieth-century advertising fashions the generic condition, hysteria. As ad imagery breeds more and more hysteria, it also, paradoxically, "spirits *back*" politics. Or rather, as we become more literate in reading the politics of hysteria that infuses mass image-making, the more advertising itself becomes a pedagogical site of critical parody.[16]

16. This thought foreshadows Chapter 6, "Representation is dead, long live representation," in which I pose the critical potential of the radical femme and of advertising imagery itself.

Arrested

3

I. INVENTING TYPOLOGIES

Psychiatric photography and Hugh Diamond

More than a hundred years ago, the camera was employed in the service of medical science toward diagnosis and treatment of pathologies. It was in application to psychiatry that the first systematic practice of clinical photography was undertaken (Gilman 1976, 5). Through what was termed photographic physiognomy, the invisible conditions of psychological health were coded in new classifications of gestures, expressions, musculatures, facial characteristics, and proportions. Visible types were discerned to correspond to maladies, such as religious melancholy, melancholy passing into mania, mania, suicidal monomania, nymphomania, catalepsy, depression, incurable insanity, insanity accompanied by epilepsy, and, eventually, hysteria (FIGURE 3.1).

Hugh Welch Diamond was a trained medical doctor and resident superintendent of the Female Department of the Surrey County Lunatic Asylum in England from 1848 to 1858. Fascinated by new developments in photography (particularly the calotype process, which made duplication cheaper and simpler) and devoted to the spirit of scientific inquiry, Diamond popularized the use of the camera in detecting types of insanity, earning himself the title "father of psychiatric photography" (Gilman 1976, 5). He saw photography as having

FIGURE 3.1 *Hugh W. Diamond,* Suicidal Melancholy *(1852). Reprinted by permission of The Royal Society of Medicine, London.*

three important functions in the treatment of the mentally ill: (1) it can record the appearance of the mentally ill for study, which can be subsequently typologized and used for future diagnosis; (2) it can be used in the treatment of the mentally ill through "the presentation of an accurate self-image. . . . By freezing the features of the inmates, the camera was able to present an indelible image of the patient for the patient's own study" (8–9); (3) it provides a visual record of patients to facilitate identification for future readmission and treatment. The portrait was becoming accepted as empirical proof of psychiatric symptomatology and, simultaneously, as a representational form through which the "mentally ill" were to imagine and interpret themselves.

Women at asylums were now accompanied by images of themselves that exposed and named them within a spectrum of insanity. The parallel to how women consume themselves through advertising imagery is stated clearly by Berger (1972):

A woman must continually watch herself. She is almost continually accompanied by her own image of herself. . . . From earliest childhood she has been taught and persuaded to survey herself continually. And so she comes to consider the *surveyor* and the *surveyed* within her as the two constituent yet always distinct elements of her identity as a woman. . . . The surveyor of woman in herself is male: the surveyed female. Thus she turns herself into an object—and most particularly an object of vision: a sight. (46–47)

Williamson (1986b) provides an ideological link between the diagnostic, medical still lifes and the still lifes that typify capitalist realism—a link between notions of female aberrance and notions of exclusion and property. Referring here to contemporary advertising images of women, Williamson's comment is relevant to female inpatients of the mid- to late nineteenth century: "What is taken away in reality . . . is re-presented in image and ideology so that it stands for itself after it has actually ceased to exist. . . . All these images of 'otherness' have as their referent an actual Otherness which was and is still being systematically destroyed, first by European then by American capital" (116–17).

The othering of women as insane is, in part, a function of being invalidated and isolated within the political and economic life of capital. As pathological tokens, women are "killed into art" (Gilbert and Gubar 1979, 14–17); as advertising currency, these still lifes generate profit for those who create them. One visual format of this aesthetic invalidation is to highlight a part, a detail, of the body—such as the nose of the Jew, the lips of the African-American, the jaw of the criminal—toward a characterization of the whole. A single physical feature is employed as a clue into one's larger nature; representational art becomes science.

Sander Gilman has contributed extensively to the study of stereotypes and categorical images, explaining their geneses and psychological functions.[1] In his examination of Diamond's work, Gilman offers evidence of the surveyors' pleasure in their readings of these photographs. Ernest Lacan, for instance, does not mince his romantic rapture in his reaction to Diamond's work (FIGURE 3.2):

1. See Gilman (1985a, 1985b). See Lombroso (1920) for visual codification of the criminal.

FIGURE 3.2 *Hugh W. Diamond, asylum patient suffering depression (1852). Reprinted by permission of The Royal Society of Medicine, London.*

One's eyes are captured by the portrait of a woman tormented by suicidal monomania. This woman, of a mature age, must have been quite attractive when in the bloom of youth. Misfortune came, and then illness, but they did not succeed in depriving her features of their beautiful composure. And yet, what sadness, how many complaints, how many disappointments are to be found in those eyes! What anxieties, morbid thoughts and ominous schemes are written on this wrinkled forehead. How many tears, scarcely dried, are on these shrivelled cheeks. How much bitterness, and restrained grief, how many swallowed sobs, are in this mouth, whose smile must have been so graceful in the past! Should not the expression of despair stamped upon this pallid face show a profound revulsion against life and the omnipresence of morbid thoughts, the wide scar this unfortunate person bears on her throat would reveal all. This photograph is a moving drama. (Ernest Lacan, quoted in Gilman 1976, 22)[2]

2. This passage recalls previous reference to the orgasmic poetics of the medical surgeons describing the process of cutting through the flesh of a fe-

Diamond's photographic plates of patients were the bases for determining their internal state. Of course, the women were not consulted as to whether the appraisal was meaningful to them; knowledge was a function of an abstracted and depersonalized diagnostic process. Many of the looks captured by Diamond—such as the fierce and maligned look, the demure and lamentable look—are

male corpse, the sexual excitement of performing a gynecological examination, and the amorous adulations of writers and doctors overwhelmed by the presence of Sarah Bernhardt.

FIGURE 3.3 *Hugh W. Diamond, diagnosis unknown (1852). Reprinted by permission of The Royal Society of Medicine, London.*

FIGURE 3.4 *Advertisement, Request jeans (1994). Reprinted by permission of Stephanie Pfriender, photographer. Model: Berta Elite. Hair/make-up artist: Patrick Swan. Client: Request Jeans Advertising.*

recognizable in innumerable commercial ads (FIGURES 3.3 and 3.4). But perhaps more profound, contemporary ads create their own visual iconography. Capri gives us a choice of a dozen types of women—dramatic, bold, outrageous, outspoken, flashy, surprising, elegant, original, modern, sensational, contemporary, and spontaneous—and displays how each looks. Vitabath ministers to its own visual spectrum of personality "fanatics"—"psychological fanatic," "sensual fanatic," and "intellectual fanatic"—two of which are reprinted here (FIGURES 3.5 and 3.6).

In 1858, Diamond's earlier photographs inspired a major series of essays by John Conolly, *The Physiognomy of Insanity*. In his description of each kind of insanity, Conolly refers to photographs, taken by Diamond, of patients in various stages of their treatment. This process of correlating an appearance with a psychopathology grew rapidly within medical science, reaching a peak after 1885 with the work of Jean-Martin Charcot at the Salpêtrière, a hospital for the mentally impaired in Paris.

FIGURE 3.5 *Advertisement, "Sensual fanatic," Vitabath (1990). VITABATH advertisement reproduced with permission of Tsumura International Inc., owner of VITABATH copyrights and registered trademarks.*

FIGURE 3.6 *Advertisement, "Intellectual fanatic," Vitabath (1990). VITABATH advertisement reproduced with permission of Tsumura International Inc., owner of VITABATH copyrights and registered trademarks.*

The Salpêtrière and Jean-Martin Charcot[3]

Charcot, with whom Freud worked at the Salpêtrière during 1885–86, engaged in a photographic iconography of hysteric female patients.[4] He was seeking clinical types and, particularly, a way to differ-

3. I owe much of my thinking in this section to Copjec (1981).

4. Charcot's early and most extensive work was almost exclusively with female hysterics. After 1886 he did work more extensively with male hysterics,

entiate hysteria from epilepsy. His iconography charts the various stages of hysteria captured by medical photographers pioneering the field of electrophysiology (electrical excitation of muscles).[5] Charcot articulated the hysteric crisis into four phases: the epileptoid phase of convulsions; the phase of large movements of salutation; the hallucinatory phase of passionate attitudes (such as terror, repugnance, irony, supplication, eroticism, ecstasy, crucifixion) (FIGURE 3.7)[6]; and the phase of terminal delirium.

Resident hysterics were posed and photographed in each of these phases, producing a kind of "double-representation": the images were representations of staged reenactments of their somatizations (Russo 1986, 223). These graphic freezes were mounted visibly in an amphitheater designed by Charcot, in which crowds could gather and view the images, charts, drawings, graphic diagrams, statuettes, plaster casts, and portraits that served as visual auxiliaries to his lectures. These, however, were mere accessories to the primary illustration, the hysterical patient herself, whom he brought from the wards to the classroom or gallery to replay the hysterical fit or illustrate a particular expression. Frequently, they were hypnotized into automatons to simulate an attack for the audiences, encouraging a kind of unconscious habituation of their dysfunctional nervous systems. Charcot had, in essence, created the "living pathological museum" (Charcot's term) starring the "leading ladies" of hysteria (Copjec 1981, 183). Their responsiveness to hypnotic suggestion earned them special status as medical commodities, exchanged from one French hospital to another for scientific viewing and experimentation.[7]

---

but did not continue his photographic documentation and treatment with the men as he had with the women. This is not to say that there was no visual pathologizing, or hystericizing, of men during this period in time. There was a developing discourse of male hysteria in the late nineteenth and early twentieth centuries, and the diagnosis fell on some male bodies more than others. See Gilman (1991).

5. Charcot received the professional assistance of Duchenne de Boulogne and Albert Londe. De Boulogne was a medical photographer and pioneer researcher in the field of electrophysiology, experimenting with the electrical excitation of muscles and the subsequent production of expressions. Albert Londe, the photographic director of Charcot's laboratory, developed a visual system to diagnose mental conditions based on these facial expressions (Copjec 1981).

6. See the similarity in attitude in figure 5.9.

7. These experiments paralleled those of other enterprises expanding in

FIGURE 3.7 *P. Regnard (photographer),* Repugnance, *from Jean-Martin Charcot's* Iconographie photographique de la Salpêtrière *(1878). Reprinted by permission of New York Academy of Medicine.*

PORTRAIT OF A SALPÊTRIÈRE HYSTERIC

Blanche Wittmann, the prima donna of Dr. Charcot's public séances at the Salpêtrière, later moved to the Hôtel-Dieu hospital, where she was investigated by Dr. Jules Janet. After achieving the "first stage of hypnosis," that is, lethargy, Jules Janet modified the usual technique and discovered that Blanche had a second personality, much more balanced than the other. Blanche II, supposedly unconscious, was always aware of everything that occurred during the many demonstrations when Blanche I acted out the "three stages of hypnosis." For many years the silently raging Blanche II assisted at experiments to which Blanche I submitted with complacency. Jules Janet kept Blanche Wittmann in her second state for several months and found her remarkably improved by his treatments. She returned to the

---

the last quarter of the nineteenth century, such as ethnographic studies amid remote primitive tribes in exotic locations. A kind of "intellectual tourism" took hold in medicine as well as in the marketplaces of mass culture and fields of academic research.

Salpêtrière to take a job in the photograph laboratory and in 1900, when a laboratory of radiology was opened, she was employed there. Since the dangers of radiology were not yet known, she became a victim of radiologist's cancer. Her last years were a calvary that she crossed without showing any hysterical symptoms. She suffered one amputation after another and died a martyr to science. During her last days, Blanche was interviewed by Doctor André Baudouin, who asked her whether the hysterical episodes of her youth had been simulated and thereby had made fun of the doctors. Wittmann replied, "There is no truth at all in such rumors. Those are lies. We had these spells and were in these lethargic states because we could not do otherwise. Besides, it wasn't a bit of fun." She added, "Simulation! Do you think it would have been easy to fool Dr. Charcot? Oh yes, lots of fakes tried; he gave them one look and said, 'Be still.' "[8]

In spite of Charcot's seeming preoccupation with objective standardization, his methodology and personality deeply afflicted his clinical practice. Charcot was known for his piercing gaze and as an intimidating and domineering character who sought to duplicate his own will in the brains of his subjects. At the same time, Charcot was a participant in the hysterical masquerade that was being displayed and studied. On the wards, he would mimic the painful contortions of his patients, supposedly as a way to sympathize with, and thus understand, the hysterical experience. Whether this "taking-in" of the hysterics' bodies into his own enhanced his compassion and/or diagnostic acumen is difficult to determine. Did it constitute a kind of erotic voyeurism? Was it a way of transforming his fears of abandon into something he could possess and control? Might it not signify the attractiveness of women positioned on the boundary between the social order and the mysterious beyond—a way to merge with the mysterious wisdom of women, configured as both the dangerous, exciting seductress of the otherworld and, if tamed, the protector who keeps evil away?

Whatever the intentions behind his methodology, under the tyrannical Charcovian microscope, the female personalities he studied dissipated. Charcot concluded that hysterics lacked the crucial

8. This historical portrait, along with those that follow, are cited from the program notes of the theater production *Dr. Charcot's Hysteria Show*, performed in New York City in June 1989. See Schutzman's (1990) review/article on this ensemble production.

inhibitory mechanism necessary to subordinate emotional excess and suggestibility, thus exhibiting a kind of psycho-physiological mercuriality. In his attempt to provide portraits of physiological stigmata that would hold up in the medical community, what he finally contributed was an overdetermined and self-reflecting portrayal of female psychology: one that demanded constant attention, spoke foul language, displayed deceit, coquettishness, lying, exaltation, and despondency.

PORTRAIT OF A SALPÊTRIÈRE HYSTERIC

Desirée was the only child of a minor government official who was an adherent of positivist philosophy and a close friend of Dr. Charcot. Desirée's mother was well educated and the family frequented the theater, the ballet, the opera, and art museums. Desirée was planning a career as a ballet teacher when she was subjected to a series of frightful incidents. She was admitted to the Salpêtrière at the age of twenty because she said that whenever she tried to move in her dancing classes, her body was permeated by vibrations from horrible sights. Desirée claimed to be possessed by a demonic force that took over her body whenever she started to move. She became a permanent resident at the Salpêtrière where she was proud of her role as an exhibit in Charcot's public lectures. She died in the hospital at the age of thirty-eight, in 1893, a few months after the death of Charcot.

One of Charcot's standardized visual attitudes, labeled *Extase* in approximately 1878, featured Augustine, one of the most facile hysterics of the Salpêtrière (FIGURE 3.8). Similar models of such "ecstatic" women in various stages of rapture or sensual bliss, hands and face uplifted to the heavens, fill the pages of magazines in the 1990s (FIGURE 3.9). Another of Charcot's attitudes was labeled *Erotisme* (FIGURE 3.10); a woman, still rapt in ecstasy, lies prostrate, wrapped in her own arms. In many of the images of Charcot's iconography, as well as in those of Hugh Diamond and Man Ray, the backgrounds are scratched out or indistinct, and the face or body fills the entire frame. It is "as though the image could reveal immediately what it was, *as though existence and meaning were identical*" (Copjec 1981, 25); the picture itself showed everything there was to know. This aesthetic element in Charcot's three-volume *Iconographie Photographique de la Salpêtrière* (Bourneville and Regnard 1877–80) was due, in part, to Charcot's unique appreciation for both the classical look of beauty—defined by precise composition from drapery to lighting—and, in part, to the

FIGURE 3.8 *P. Regnard (photographer)*, Extase, *from Jean-Martin Charcot's* Iconographie photographique de la Salpêtrière *(1878). Reprinted by permission of New York Academy of Medicine.*

sensibility of photographer Paul Richter with whom he worked. This appreciation distinguished the photographs of the *Iconographie* from other medical photographs of the period in auguring the "art" that would link medical and advertising disciplines.

FIGURE 3.9 *Advertisement, Savvy (1992). Reprinted by permission of SWAROVSKI JEWELRY U.S. LIMITED.*

The aesthetic fusion of existence and meaning in the photogaphs was an embodiment of Charcot's very definition of hysteria. For Charcot, as well as the mainstream medical community of the turn of the twentieth century, hysterical symptoms were, on the one hand, not real; there was no organic lesion of any kind that would explain the recurring symptoms. On the other hand, Charcot believed that hysterics were neither malingerers nor simulators; they were not fully conscious of their motives and thus could not be accused of feigning illness for secondary gain. Thus, the paradox: for Charcot, hysteria was a real but unfounded disease.

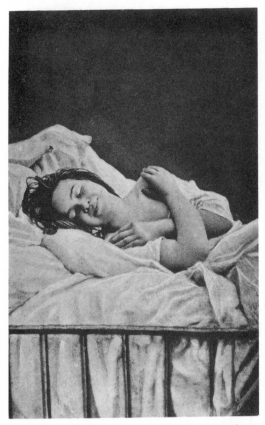

FIGURE 3.10 *P. Regnard (photographer),* Erotisme, *from Jean-Martin Charcot's* Iconographie photographique de la Salpêtrière *(1878). Reprinted by permission of New York Academy of Medicine.*

Charcot's definition of hysteria typifies the contemporary commercial fusion of "not real" and "real" that predicts our crisis of representation, wherein the representation of the real thing *is* the real thing. His definition also foretells the diagnostic method of hysteria, which relies upon a subjective reading of a performance or surface. Hysteria, and representation itself, cannot be *about* the real because the real is hysterical.

Charcot recognized hysterical psychosis as a sudden and dramatic onset with transient and volatile symptoms. From his experiential data, he concluded that shiftiness, trickiness, slipperiness, and lewdness were characteristic of hysteria. Copjec confers that, statistically speaking, hysteria is an incomplete kind of disorder, unpredictable and always receptive to new forms of expression. Hysterics at the Salpêtrière exhibited convulsive, fitlike behavior only after being housed in the same ward with the epileptics, and then only when some medical practitioner was around to view their behavior. Unlike epileptic fits, hysterical seizures did not occur when the patient was alone or out of reach of an audience. Astasia-abasia (the "hysterical gait") also requires an audience. The patient walks normally, never falls, when unobserved. When observed, however, she appears to be *trying* to fall. The presence of a witness is still considered a criterion for a hysterical attack (Pincus 1982). Furthermore, one-third of Charcot's hysterical patients never exhibited attacks at all, and of the other two-thirds, not all exhibited the full attack: the formal display of all four phases, in proper sequence, which distinguished hysteria from epilepsy. In fact, what was presented in the medical gallery were repetitions of each phase in several different patients. It usually took numerous patients and/or photographs together to illustrate the whole picture that corresponded to the codified definition of a hysterical attack (Copjec 1981, 27).

In spite of Charcot's theoretical affinity for medical indeterminacy, his iconography and hypnotic stagings gave the lability of hysteria an appearance of rigidity and completeness. Charcot secured the indefiniteness of hysterical reactions into a formulaic progression. Meanwhile, within the prevailing school of medical associationism, mental pain was perceived as a patient's lack of mental capacity—a deficiency of her brain. Images, or products of the imagination, were viewed as inferior things or copies of real things. Associationists also traced mental dysfunctions to certain areas in the brain. With the brain as the original site of images, disorders of imagination and thought were diagnosed as disorders in specific locales within the brain. The hysteric, relying upon bodily imagery, was perceived as inferior due to improper brain functioning. Medical photography and Charcot helped pave the way to neurological surgery.[9]

The catalog

While medicine was busy cataloging female qualities to piece together a scientifically accurate and typical woman, advertising was busy cataloging commodities (FIGURES 3.11 and 3.12). Montgomery

9. Copjec (1981) offers an excellent explication of associationism and hysteria.

FIGURE 3.11 *Gold rings advertised in* Montgomery Ward & Co. Catalogue and Buyer's Guide, *No. 57, Spring and Summer (1895): 165.*

Ward and Sears, America's thriving mail-order marketplaces, offered page upon page of commodities in detailed and subtle array. Products and women seemed to be undergoing a similar ritual of assimilation into consumer consciousness. Both assumed a magical versatility, their identities embodying the emerging ethics of interchangeability, disjunction, and artifice. But this versatility was fixed and codified into recognizable samples, models, and types. The commodity was lauded and marketed for its adaptability and its

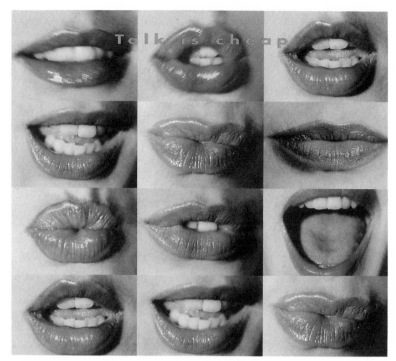

FIGURE 3.12 *Advertisement, Rampage (1993). Reprinted by permission of Arnell Group. Photographer: Peter Arnell.*

classifiability at once. The paradox harks back to Charcot's formulation of hysteria wherein the hysteric's lability was exalted and studied within a visual system that arrested that lability.

Entrepreneurs Montgomery Ward and Richard Sears (known as the "Barnum of merchandising") were the giants of the cataloging industry (Ewen and Ewen 1982, 65). Looking to circumvent the general store and offer another retailing possibility, they built an empire on picture books: dreamy catalogs from which potential customers could order whatever they wanted and more. Ward's folksy style and benevolent "personal friend" appeal, resulted in his catalog, the *Great Wish Book*. From a one-page sheet in 1873 it grew to a 24-page booklet in 1874 and a 544-page catalog by 1893. "People eagerly awaited the coming of the catalog; through this window on a world of apparently unlimited possibility, people caught a glimpse of things to come and received advice on how to get these things in the here-and-now" (64). Appealing to immigrants and urging them to order in their native tongues, the catalog was a vehicle for Americanization: "the pictorial images spoke an easily understood, universal language, demonstrating what an American appearance was all about" (65).[10] In 1946, the Grolier Club Book Society selected the *Great Wish Book* as one of the hundred most influential books on American life, a catechism of "the standard of American middle-class living," and apostle of "creature comforts" (65).[11]

In similar fashion, Sears developed his catalog, first called *The Farmers Friend*, and later referred to as the *American Dream Book*. Through wishes, dreams, and American nationalism transformed into objects, ordinary people could encounter prosperity, something grand. A new way of life appeared, one that masked the realities of wage labor, factory production, and corporate goods. It was a life of mass imagery that heightened the ambivalence and contradictions of the rise of consumer culture. The commodity body hides the very process of its production, just as the commercialized female body hides the process of its production as hysterical. The social disorder contaminated the female body; accordingly, hysteria exploded across the face of American society. A century later, hysteria is second-nature to women's psychic life as are the societal efforts to deny its invention and meaning.

Pressing and stamping

The cataloging concept of changeable fragments took on another form in the notoriously homogenizing 1950s. Hysterics—almost

10. An article entitled "American Beauties" in *Lears* (November–December 1988) includes studio photographs of six women, each accompanied by a short stereotypical synopsis including nationality, profession, and the fragrance they represent. For instance: "NATIVE AMERICAN Imo Brockett, 50, farmer, wife, mother, grandmother. The fragrance for the country woman, Lauren by Ralph Lauren; FRENCH AMERICAN Lorna de Wangen, 41, art consultant. The fragrance for the original woman, Red by Giorgio; CARIBBEAN-AMERICAN Elaine O'Neill, 44, social worker. The fragrance for the romantic woman, Halston Couture by Prestige Fragrance."

11. See Bernays (1928) for discussions on the alliance of advertising and nationalism, the growth of the propaganda specialists, and the workings of invisible government. See Graham (1982) on post-Hitler capitalist advertising whereby modern corporations expressed technological might and heaven-sent power through a neutral style of rigid formalism and high-tech Hollywood spectacles of space-age gleaming luminescence.

exclusively women except for the victims of post-traumatic stress syndrome following World War II—were often found to be suffering multiple personalities (Abse 1982).[12] Different identities and unstable personas constituted a loosely bound whole, one whose frayed edges needed to be concealed. In order to present an image of emergent American pride and domestic perfection, the seams of her multiple selves were skillfully blurred. Fortunately, on the industrial front, the 1950s ushered in the aesthetics of streamlining—a look first piloted in the late 1930s, derived ideologically from science-fiction utopian-future genres (in numerous fields) and executed through the technological processes of pressing and stamping.[13] Streamlining established itself as the embodiment of the American dream with Cadillac's El Camino reaching luminary status as the "Dream Car." It also established itself as a method for weaving multiple personalities into seeming a coherent whole.

The engineering innovations of pressing and stamping were intended to package within a sheath the dirty, mechanical, functioning aspects of modern labor, to create an image of sleekness, cleanliness, convenience, and ease. Economically, these techniques fostered the ethics of mass reproduction and accessibility on large scale industrial terms: a million streamlined Chevrolets, a billion streamlined radios, streamlined trains, refrigerators, bathing beauties. Streamlining also worked as a cultural blueprint that defined consumer identity and its relation to the market. The emphasis was on style, superficiality, decorative function over use function, and comprehensive design. The era of management science was launched, and American dreams and fantasies were engineered as deliberately as material objects (Hebdige 1988).

Simultaneously, advertisers, aware of the trend toward the super-

12. Multiple personality is one of the dissociative forms of hysterical reactions.

13. Through stamping and pressing techniques parts of a product were mechanically stamped out whole and subsequently welded together. Geometric or "rectilinear" forms were stamped and pressed into "curvilinear" forms in the streamlining process. Streamlining was a concept in physics whereby "a material may meet with least resistance" (Ewen 1976, 107). It became a cultural allegory whereby a product was designed to pass through the greatest amount of popular resistance and enable a consolidation of capital. See also Hebdige (1988).

fluous and of the alienating effects of a culture uprooted from tradition through mechanical reproduction, marketed products as "real" things: the real cleanser, the real Coke, the real shave. It was a way to combat the empty, the pretentious, and the narcissistic—all signs of hysteria—that characterized prevailing Americanization (Orvell 1989). Women, along with consumer objects, signified this double identity of vacancy inside and glossy perfection outside. A contemporary advertisement for silk clothing offers its merchandise as the vehicle for reconciling this breach: "Seem a Dream, Prove Real." Another exemplary ad is a four-page spread for the Liz Claiborne perfume "Realities." The first three pages display different versions of "reality": a man and woman embracing on the street, a family scene, and two men kissing opposite cheeks of the same woman. The last page displays only the bottle of Realities Perfume with copy that declares, "Reality is the Best Fantasy of All." The brilliant transformation of reality into fantasy helps sell fantasy products as solutions to real problems.

Women, simultaneously primary consumers and objects of consumption, were pressed and stamped along with commercial products. Representing a stage of Americanization, in which form did not follow function as in classic design, women expressed a streamlined passage of signifiers across a wide range of unrelated products from TVs to tupperware. A woman's body was the malleable stand-in for lingerie, cars, cosmetics, island vacations, home appliances, and jewelry. Sanctioned femininity represented something so versatile that she could reincarnate as the essence of any new fashionable ideal; in each manifestation she was advertised as hypertight, extra-complete, unbroken.

The composite commercial woman of advertising was much like the composite hysteric of Charcot's gallery and stage. Both illustrated a femininity that could hold graciously all its contradictions. But it was an unlivable femininity; in real life she broke apart. Hysteria—in its 1950s manifestation of multiple personalities—was perhaps a symptomatic breaking up of this prevailing look of streamlined femininity, a reflection of the shards of her self-image that commodity impersonation had instilled in her. Survival for many women consisted of wearing this "packaged" personality as cover while privately entertaining a repertoire of antagonistic internal selves. What surfaced was another symptom that reflected her "made-to-order" identity (FIGURE 3.13). It was la belle indifférence.

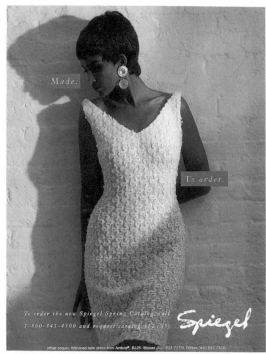

FIGURE 3.13 *Advertisement, Spiegel (1991). Reprinted by permission of Spiegel, Inc. Agency: McConnaughy Stein Schmidt Brown. Creative director: Jim Schmidt. Art director: Steve Juliusson. Photographer: Erie Michaelsen.*

Pierre Janet was a renowned French psychiatrist at a time when many of his colleagues believed that hysterical symptoms were "put on." Janet (1920), however, believed such symptoms were not under voluntary control. As an associationist, he hypothesized that they were the result of some kind of failure in the level of brain functioning. Janet was the first to use the term "la belle indifférence" to describe the seeming nonchalance that hysterics exhibited toward their own pain. But his astute description of the symptom—"facade *covering profound anxiety*" (Lewis 1981, 222)—has been lost and transmuted into a sign that women really do not suffer from the overwhelming depression (or any other psychophysical illness) that la belle indifférence signifies. All that is recognized is the facade itself.[14]

14. See Lewis (1981) and Klerman (1982) on the relation between hysteria and depression.

From reproduction to mutation

What is it that the advertiser repeats that the hysteric repeats or performs in her own body? Soon after the turn of the century, the catalog industry launched a campaign of ritual repetition. With repetition being the modus operandi of hysteric and commodity, the ritualization of repetition in turn normalized both. In a Clairol ad of 1989, advertisers pose the ontological question: "Who Do You Think You Are?" In late capitalism, the answer lies in your mimetic politics; that is, in who, what, and how you repeat. For instance, perhaps we cannot choose whether or not to be hysterical or objectified (we simply *are*), but we can choose the particular face of hysteria/commodity we want to wear. Clairol, of course, suggests that we wear/be Clairol: "Clairol Highlighting Collection is who you really are." It may seem that the choices are no choices at all; that, in fact, all choices succeed in deferring, not satisfying, the desire to answer the question. That we never find our identity, we just keep buying. But *how* we repeat who and what we repeat is critical: repeating does not necessarily enforce habituation and compromise; in repetition there is the potential for change.

There are contradictory interpretations of repetition: (1) Broadly speaking, repetition suggests dumbness, stuttering, and the inability to articulate or originate ideas. (2) Repetition links production with reproduction, humanity with machinery. It is the emblem of machination and arrest. Wherever discipline and precision are primary processes—as in cataloging—repetition is as well. (3) Reproduction is a subset of repetition which identifies the "quintessential copy"—there are no changes whatsoever in the remake. Reproduction is the least performative of the various forms of repetition. (4) Repetition suggests a deliberateness born out of randomness. It places an image (or text), no matter how fragmented or decontextualized, into movement, thus granting it a kind of self-referential power. (5) Repetition imbues an image with a kind of immortality, potentially creating something greater than itself, as photography illustrates. (6) Repetition defies essentialism and fixity. As repeated imagery crosses our exterior landscape and our inner psychic screen, it prompts uncanny dreams, memories, and events. The repeated thing overflows itself and creates a theater of doubles, shadows. (7) Repetition, in the sense of repeated performances, intimates mutations that can appropriate or subvert the power of what was repeated. This is the form of repetition that most challenges the quintessential unchanging copy.

Repetition does not necessarily institute a one-way tyranny by which female consumers internalize prescribed body aesthetics so completely that they are transmuted into the image. The possibility of repetition that transgresses what is repeated always lurks within the realm of popular culture. The space of repetition promises change and mastery as much as it does repression and ignorance.

Freud's theory of repetition compulsion conceived of repetition as a patient's attempt to manipulate actively her own powerlessness. Speaking of the child's fort-da game, Freud (1961) notes, "At the outset he was in *passive* position . . . but by repeating it, unpleasurable though it was, as a game, he took on an *active* part. These efforts might be put down to an instinct for mastery that was acting independently of whether the memory was in itself pleasurable or not" (10). Through a repeat performance comes an opportunity to alter the experience and thus change its effect. Modleski (1982) discusses how female spectators repeat images of villainesses on TV soap operas. But, being uncomfortable with these images, they repeat them in an attempt to reconcile the discrepancy they feel. The repetition both reinforces powerlessness and yet allows for mastery and change.

Being that mimesis is a primary tool of the hysteric, a critical question arises as to the hysteric's potential to manipulate her own powerlessness. Are the hysterics' mimetic inclinations a sign of contest or of submission, of self-healing or affliction?[15] The discrepancy of interpretations of repetition provides a picture of the treacherous psychic territory through which the hysteric, and perhaps most consuming women at large, navigates in attempting to answer the riddle of her identity, Who Do I Think I Am?

What precisely do women mimic? Hysterical stereotypes—histrionics, exhibitionism, and lack of emotional control—are still

15. Similar questions have been raised regarding repetition in ritual, carnival, and parody. Does the replaying of unpleasant memories and behavior constitute transgression on some level? Or is the potential power of taking action canceled within an institutional frame that allows this play? See Bakhtin (1984) and Stallybrass and White (1986).

models for contemporary middle-class working women. But perhaps today's women are more aware of the stigma, that there is no viable secondary gain to be had in playing those particular types. New hysterical styles have emerged. A predominant late twentieth-century enactment of hysteria is superdenial, a numbing refusal to see oneself or project oneself as suffering in any way—la belle indifférence taken to an extreme. While "dying" may have always been a hysterical symptom, in the 1990s we are cultivating a slow, repetitious death of the self.

From vibrancy to vacancy to vibrancy

David-Menard (1989) tells us that what the hysteric repeats is bodily position: image. And she then adds: "a bodily position is indeed not a fact" (37). Nonetheless, certain coordinates of the (moving) female body are halted, paralyzed, as if they were signs of a significant, perhaps primal, scenario that must be held in suspension, then repeated. It was representation of these arrested positions that Charcot conceived of as the treatment for hysterics, particularly the treatment of psychic or physical paralysis.

Charcot's contemporary Pierre Janet believed that the hysteric's paralysis was caused by a failure of the imagination; the hysteric could not form the image of her limb that was necessary for her to move it. Charcot granted the hysteric more imagination and more intelligence. Charcot explained hysterical symptoms as corresponding to the patient's "idea of a symptom." That is, he credited his patients with the ability to manifest a physical sign that corresponded to a thought. Thus, for Charcot, paralysis was caused by a fixed idea, by an *image* of paralysis. He also credited his patients the ability to undo the imagination through imagination. Both the hypnotic performance of the hysterical attack and the photographic image of the hysteric in a hypnotized state were imaginative forms intended to treat the patient's imagination.[16]

16. The relation between images, ideas, and pain is relevant to our discussion but far too vast to address here. Briefly, Freud speaks of an injury to the "idea of the arm" when faced with hysterical paralysis and no organic cause (David-Menard 1989, 11). For him, the idea of the arm denoted a psychical (not physiological) repository from which pain or symptoms might originate. Nearly a century later, Merskey (1982) states that pain can result from ideas.

It is important to remember that these "curative" performances and images are presented in advertising, as well as in medical photography, as real; ventriloquism and photography masterly enhance the illusion of nonillusion. Imagined female body positions are repeatedly broadcast as evidence of female disease; image is taken as fact. They are even mistaken by those who invent them. It is no surprise that these positions, when repeated by consumers, are read medically as pathology. The very "imaginative" treatments produced by Charcot to liberate her arrested imagination were created simultaneously as proof of her arrested psychic development; the "cure" she repeats is as arresting as the thoughts and body positions it intends to let loose.

Let us turn to the arrested poses themselves. Generally speaking, each arrested body posture reduces an array of movements, experiences, and contexts into a singular look. David-Menard (1989) calls the hysteric's display of a repeated posture, "presentification" (111). Through presentification, an excessive presence compensates for a predominating absence. In a Charles Jourdan advertisement reprinted here, legs "presentify" her whole body (FIGURE 3.14). Speaking of the hysterical attack, she states that what is projected is "the tail wagging the dog, the prosthetic hysterogenic body rending the physical body of which it has literally lost sight" (xvii). If we agree with David-Menard that the origin of hysteria lies in the relationship of a subject to her own body, then consequently, the female consumer knows herself in relation to the body that is "presentified" commercially; for instance, she knows herself as a pair of sleek and sexy legs. She perhaps knows this other body better than her own, for it is imaged in such abundance, consumed daily, and exudes more presence than her own. This process of presentification also renders history nonoperative by appropriating past and future into a perpetual present, bearing no signs of context, genealogy, or means of production. Detached from these forces, the hysteric who presentifies shows and shows but does not communicate; she indicates and marks the hegemonic memory but only as a token, an arrested memento of what society does not want to remember.

Merskey is referring primarily to Couvade's syndrome, a hysterical symptom whereby a person experiences pain in his or her own body through sympathetic thoughts about pain that someone else is suffering. See David-Menard (1989) for detailed discussion of the relation between pain and thought in hysteria.

FIGURE 3.14 *Advertisement, Charles Jourdan (1994). Reprinted by permission of Charles Jourdan USA, Inc. Agency: In-House. Photographer: Christopher Weil.*

One of these enduring visual mementos is the look of death. Its recurrence in contemporary imagery evidences the process of depletion that mass technology incites. One of the characteristic features of the death aesthetic is the embalmed look, visible in ads for Yves Saint Laurent, Krizia, and Serge Lutens, to name only a few. The whitewashed face of death not only obliterates depth and difference but represents female gender as an evacuated shell, an empty place where time as well as movement has stopped (FIGURE 3.15). Another common representation of death is the nearly full-bodied corpse,

FIGURE 3.15 *Advertisement, EXP jeans (1993). EXP jeans advertisement with the permission of Express, Inc.* ™ *Express. All rights reserved.*

lying motionless, staring blankly into space. (Unlike the image in the Charles Jourdan ad, the presentified body is often a full body.) Sometimes her body seems strewn randomly, as if she were victim of a crime, half-naked and abandoned while an unapprehended perpetrator disappears out of frame. In fashion photography, the mien of death is designed figuratively. Issey Miyake, for instance, invokes the arty specter of death through a dusky charcoal overcoat, hanging in midair, limp and disembodied like a flimsy and shriveled skin.[17]

How do women relate to their own deadened bodies? The mirror held up by Yves Saint Laurent or Miyake swallows what it sees and returns it in a vapid echo of a former self. How do women relate to representations of women made socially valid by voiding them of contour, expression, subtlety, and vitality? To reenact these extraordinary images of devitalization has always had dire social meaning for women: the public display of melancholy or depression—of grief—carries a negative stigma. Freud claimed that to publicly express grief would carry a sorrowful subject from melancholia into a curative mourning. But for women, it was, and perhaps still is, confirmation of her "disability" rather than of psychic healing.

17. For fascinating historical examples of sham-deaths see Strouse (1980) and Gold and Fizdale (1991) (providing images of Sarah Bernhardt playing dead at home in her coffin).

Privatization of these emotions has equally damaging repercussions. Emotions, like memories, tend to distort when they go unrecognized. Should opportunity for contact with another present itself, the repressed emotions become flushed with energy. Often they appear overdetermined, even caricatured. This response is also stigmatized by medical professionals as hysterical in the sense of being histrionic.[18]

Popular imagery reflects the oscillation between devitalization and hyperexcitement. Alongside innumerable images of death and dying, are innumerable images of women masquerading as the opposite. From the cast of death she is exuberantly reborn. She performs "sheer energy," unencumbered by grief, literally lifted off her feet and cast into outlandish flailings and contortions that portray freedom and carefreeness (FIGURE 3.16). A woman so delighted by her hose jubilantly plays hopscotch in the streets. Another, perched on one leg,

18. Very few doctors recognize that these histrionic displays are a function of a *relationship* in which a female patient reacts to the demeaning insensitivity of those who abuse, consciously or not, their privileged gender role. See Eliot Slater (1982).

FIGURE 3.16 *Advertisement, Sheer Energy (1988). Reprinted by permission of L'eggs® Products, a division of Sara Lee Corporation.*

blows her tuba in the park in tribute to her newfound soft drink. The vacillation between the two extremes of pretension in advertising—vacant facade and inchoate energy—are comparable to the extreme conditions that characterize the arrested body of the hysteric.

No-body or all-body? The hysterical choice

Hysterical behavior swings between two prototypical conditions: artifice and essence. Artifice is a "state of pure face," all surface and *no body* or substance. This condition refers to the hysteric's being disgusted by the sexualization of her body, thus choosing to have no body at all (David-Menard 1989, 65–74). Something in the history of her body could not be formulated; there was, supposedly, a failure of symbolization. Visual signs or physical forms take the place of utterance. While this no-bodyness can be taken as a psychopathological denial that must be overcome, it can also be seen as a refusal to accept the female body as it has been forged by societal authorities.

The other prototypical condition is essence, a "state of pure potency." In this instance, we have energy without channel or vehicle, thought without language. The hysteric's body "thinks" prosthetically; it claims its will to pleasure through symptoms, through extensions or parts, although it lacks the means, socially, through which to experience that pleasure. This can be understood as a state of *all-body*. Hysterical thought remains primal, unexpressed except in convulsive gestures and corporeal displacements. Her arrested pleasure becomes a metaphor for inchoate femaleness that must be infused with spirit, speech, and symbolization if it is to possess exchange value in the "civilized" world of culture.[19]

19. Nervous disorders, of which hysteria was one, only came into existence after "civilization" emerged; that is, nervous disorders reflected an inability to resist ideological/cultural influences on the body. The female body was configured in the eighteenth century as the inscribable body. Scientific theory imaged the feminine as easily written upon by outward signs, her nature being much more fragile, porous, and insubstantial than that of men. It was on a basis of such scientific theory that women were considered capable of spontaneous combustion. Nervous ailments reached epidemic proportions by the end of the eighteenth century: two-thirds of all diseases at this time were considered nervous disorders. Nerves were referred to as a "disease of civilization" as early as 1733 by George Cheyne, author of *The English Malady*, cited in Logan (1993, 3–4).

The hysteric's condition is one in which both of these bodily conditions—no-body and all-body, artifice and essence—coexist without mediation in the form of a vacillating body. In the hysteric's desire to have and exercise a healthy erotogenic body, that which she is denied, she speaks out with an hysterogenic body that knows no negotiation or subtlety (FIGURE 3.17). She is heard, by default, through a language of "all or nothing" (David-Menard 1989, 135).

FIGURE 3.17 *Advertisement, "Subtlety," Clairol highlighting collection (1989). Reprinted by permission of Clairol, Inc.*

If advertisers tried deliberately to represent the hysterical mode of communication they could not have done better than a 1992 Coty ad for their product, !ex'cla.ma'tion. A woman sits seductively on a circular bottle of perfume the size of a beach ball surrounded by enormous exclamation marks. Her body is an exclamation as well, though there is no "sentence," no content, that precedes her. The ad copy states succinctly: "Make a statement without saying a word!"

Clownism

When Charcot hypnotized his hysterics for the crowd of curiosity seekers, they exhibited behavior similar to the creatures in ads who are thrown into depression by an unsuccessfully bleached shirt or, conversely, into ecstasy by a successfully waxed floor. Within the psychosocial amphitheater of both medical physiognomy and advertising, doctors and advertisers alike script similar sagas of psychic killing and rebirth (FIGURES 3.18 and 3.19). Hysterics were hypnotized, as are the mediated women of ads, to better absorb the hysteria of their respective hynotizers. Describing hypnotized hysterics, Showalter conjures a scene of female puppets exhibiting the projected terror of medical puppeteers:

FIGURE 3.18 *Advertisement, Banana Republic (1993).*
Reprinted by permission of Banana Republic.

New York, 836 Madison Avenue, Tel. 212/517.9339, Fax 212/439.6032

FIGURE 3.19 *Advertisement, Missoni (1995). Reprinted by permission of Missoni. Photographer: Tiziano Magni.*

Some of them smelt with delight a bottle of ammonia when told it was rose water, others would eat a piece of charcoal when presented to them as chocolate. Another would crawl on all fours on the floor, barking furiously when told she was a dog, flap her arms as if trying to fly when turned into a pigeon, lift her skirts with a shriek of terror when a glove was thrown at her feet with a suggestion of being a snake. Another would walk with a top hat in her arms rocking it to and fro and kissing it tenderly when she was told it was her baby. (Showalter 1985a, 148)

Charcot's second phase of hysteria is known as the "phase of clownism," and his female patients were praised for being excellent comediennes. Copjec (1981) reminds us that women were aligned to comedy through an essentialist reading of female vapeurs, or humours; they were seen as possessing an inherently amusing dispo-sition. This alignment conformed with the prevailing notion of woman as naturally sick.[20] Today, Charcot's phase of clownism is re-ferred to as fasen psychosis, or the buffoonery syndrome, in which the patient "makes disconnected, caricatured grimaces and gestures and indulges in a number of contrived, stupid, and silly acts" (Whit-lock 1982, 203).

Numerous contemporary images of women are pure spectacles of amusement and buffoonery: women in striped clown ensembles spin through the air (Weekend Exercise), sprawl across furniture in impossible positions (XOXO), and ride cows backward on the beach (Perry Ellis); Lagerfeld women wear their hair as volcanic eruptions or record high beehives; Arnell/Bickford dresses a woman in a pre-posterous breast plate and matching hat made out of a plastic Mountain Dew bottle; in an ad for Barneys, a woman kisses a chim-panzee while balancing a shoe on her head (FIGURES 3.20 and 3.21).

An exceptional number of these ads include images of animals. Women and beasts are represented as intimate cohabitants of sym-bolic space, co-trainees in a laboratory of obedience and tricks. Both are posed as reminders and cautioners of a wilder, more ribald uni-verse. On the one hand, they exhibit surges of disobedience, bad taste, and indiscretion. On the other hand, they are clearly domesticated: resigned captives in a world of foolishness, subservience, and insult, in which their undertakings are chancey and their identities ambiva-lent. Both oscillate between life and death, inclusion and exclusion.

Many of the comedic images exalt instability and ambivalence. The commodified she-creature/hysteric masks her own social dying with images of overexaggerated exhilaration and health; she obscures with her own body the power politics that her body econ-omy suffers. Part of the humoral quality of the hysteric derives from this precariousness issuing from a female body oscillating between incongruous positions. One advertising agency captures brilliantly the precarious condition of the female consumer: the copy reads, "Ann Taylor is your lifestyle," alongside a visual of a woman in Ann Taylor shoes walking on eggs. The implication is of a lifestyle with a grounding that will shatter if you dare to put your foot down, to assert your presence. "Walking on eggs" is perhaps a

20. Copjec (1981) calls for a theory of hysteria that theorizes women out-side the vapeurs, as well as outside the "poverty of the image" (40).

FIGURE 3.20 *Advertisment, Barneys New York (1991).*
Reprinted courtesy of Barneys New York.

cultural metaphor for "walking in women's shoes." Women's place is visualized here as a serious gamble: if she applies her weight, she does so at the risk of obliterating her fragile and fertile, reproductive essence. Unisa expresses the precariousness and lack of grounding by posing a woman on the spikes of a white picket fence; for her to stand, or to walk, is allied with pain if not futility (FIGURE 3.22).

When women rehearse the various lifestyles that advertisements visualize, they embody tentative positions. They repeatedly try on and act out the contrivances of each fiction they are sold. With enough practice, the illusion passes as an archetype, the sham as prototype, the hysteric as model woman.

PORTRAIT OF A SALPÊTRIÈRE HYSTERIC
Augustine's father, according to her mother, died right after Augustine was born. Augustine's mother showed anger and bitterness whenever she was

FIGURE 3.21 *Advertisement, "The Dreamtime by Serge Lutens," Fall (1992) makeup collection. Reprinted by permission of Shiseido Cosmetics America Ltd.*

asked about him, growing impatient with Augustine's many questions. At the age of thirteen, Augustine took a job in the store owned by her mother's lover, who told Augustine her eyes would someday get her into trouble. Kept late one night to work in the storeroom, Augustine was raped and then left on a cold floor drenched with pails of water her mother's lover threw over her in an attempt to wash blood away from her stomach, thighs, hands, and hair. She was sent to the Salpêtrière in 1875 because she said she saw blood everywhere and did not know who she was when she looked into a mirror. She complained that love and sex were not what she thought they would be.

The subject of a famous series of photographs published in 1878, Augustine became an icon personifying religious fervor combined with female sexuality. Intelligent, coquettish, and eager to please, Augustine's poses suggested the exaggerated gestures of French classical acting style. She

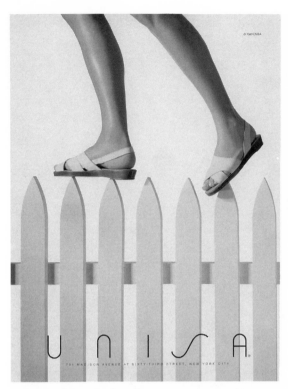

FIGURE 3.22 *Advertisement, Unisa (1993). Reprinted by permission of Unisa. Photographer: Dennis Blachut. Art director: Josiane Ohana.*

divided her hysterical attacks into scenes, acts, tableaux, and intermissions, and she was able to perform on cue and synchronize with photo sessions. Though at first she was cheerfully willing to assume whatever pose her audience desired, in 1880 she rebelled against hospital rules, having periods of violence during which she broke windows and tore her clothes. She was able to use the histrionic talent that had made her a star of the asylum when, with the help of a sympathetic doctor, she managed to escape from the hospital disguised as a man. She is rumored to have spent her adult life as a cabaret performer and impresario in Chile.

The return of the carnivalesque

Stallybrass and White (1986) speak of hysteria as the return of the carnivalesque: a version of rebellious disenfranchisement and socio-political buffoonery made manifest in the area of gender. What has been repressed and excluded from social identity, and all that is associated with the lower body stratum, return as negative representation in the hysteric "wh[o] become[s] phobic precisely through the law of her exclusion. . . . (You must not be *that*.)" (183). What is emphasized in carnival is an uncensored and yet deeply ambivalent indulgence in inappropriate behavior. Inappropriateness in every form is heralded; languages marked as vulgar—particularly those of the "obscene" body—are shamelessly expressed.

Carnival is an enactment of internalized disgust for one's own body, and the simultaneous opportunity to embrace that disgust—to revel in the body parts and functions that since childhood were disowned as filthy. Cardinal (1984) speaks of a hysterical patient who "heals" herself by making associations between her illness, clownery, and the masquerade of bourgeois innocence, thus accepting those parts of her body she previously refused:

> I was an invalid and it was while I was laughing that I made the discovery. I was made to think of circus clowns who slap their great shoes in the sawdust, seemingly unaware of a little red bulb which lights up their rear ends as they say with exaggerated and pretentious mimicry: "I'm sooooo smart," making the children laugh. They are grotesque because they appear to ignore what is happening at the base of their spines. (174–75)

She turns, like many hysterical patients, to unsterilized and unmediated ordeals of the carnivalesque, through which she may recognize herself *without* disgust. For once, what she sees represents accurately how she feels, and through this alignment comes a semblance of sanity and gratification.[21] Freud (1962, 17–18) speaks of agencies of disgust to describe the forces that jeopardize the cure of hysterics if such forces remain repressed and unexpressed. Only when these "repulsive" forces are unleashed and analyzed can the hysteric recognize her own pain and conflict and overcome them. These are the

21. One might ask why carnivalesque images provide a healing that advertising images do not if both relay a merger of woman and the beastly, woman and the grotesque, and images of disgust. One response is that carnivalesque imagery is not sterilized and packaged as are advertising images. For instance, a 1993 Nike campaign represents the look of different emotions: "disgust" is presented as a well-dressed, upper-class woman with a broken golf club. More important, it is worth considering that ad images *are* potentially healing; see Schutzman (1998) for an investigation of the radical potential of hysterical buffoonery.

same forces that, when publicly displayed at carnival, mobilized authorities to *outlaw* carnival.

The hysteric is a designated outcast, one of "the contained outsiders-who-make-the-insiders-insiders (the mad, the criminal, the sick, the unruly, the sexually transgressive)" (Stallybrass and White 1986, 22). These outsiders, however, are central in that they secure privilege to those who debase them. They embody the struggle between sanity and madness, law and disobedience, health and sickness. Ironically, they are represented as stereotypes. As Owens (1983) puts it, it is in the stereotype that "the body is apprehended by language, taken into joint custody by politics and ideology" (7). An ad for Bijan stereotypes and takes into custody the femme fatale (FIGURE 3.23).

PORTRAIT OF A STEREOTYPE

She is "the right woman," everything he wants her to be, the prototype of authorized femininity. But "sometimes you meet the right woman on the wrong night." Unfortunately, her fateful femaleness erupted and surfaced the night he was on duty. He arrested it. She was mug-shot and finger-

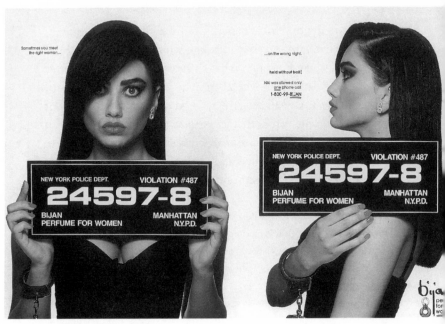

FIGURE 3.23 *Advertisement, "Violation #487," Bijan (1991). Reprinted by permission of Bijan Fragrance.*

printed, her violating *insides* confiscated like contraband. As official civic property, she is neutralized and society is made safe. She is beautiful but dangerous, desirable but evil, vibrant but vampirish, appetizing but unclean, exotic but, ultimately, criminal.

The Bijan ad suggests, paradoxically, that the stereotypical woman—the requisite woman—needs an official scent to redeem her, to free her by fumigating the horrors of her interior, the stench of her carnivalesque emissions. "Niki was allowed only *one* phone call—1-800-99-*BIJAN*." And yet Bijan represents the police, precisely those who will restrain her. Countless ads targeted to women sell cleansers, perfumes, health, or beauty products. They reinforce women's need to purify themselves of their excess, toxins, fanaticism, and criminality. (It is interesting to note that peddlers at late nineteenth-century fairs—a site of excesses and physical indulgences—sold primarily soap, mirrors, hygienic products and commodities of a cosmetic nature [Stallybrass and White 1986, 39].) The recurring message is that bleeding femaleness—that which is unnegotiable and marked odious—must be transformed. In order to be commercially rehabilitated, she promises not to bleed, she promises to defy her biological body. She betrays herself and hysterical disgust erupts. Of course, she is arrested, again.

Just be yourself

Contemporary advertisers offer counsel to women on how to maneuver through the morass of multiple and contradictory versions of themselves. Should they identify with the illusions of animality or propriety, of vibrancy or death, of clownery or impotence, artifice or essence, exaltation or debasement? Ironically, women are advised to mimic their authentic selves. "All you have to be is you" (Liz Claiborne). "Be what you want but always be you" (Paul Mitchell). "Try to be like yourself" (Palmettos). "Be who it is you say you are" (Side 1). Mimesis itself—a performative act—is reduced to an exercise of cloning an original, natural self, however implausible that self may be. The tropes of masquerade and deception are championed by the ad industry to convince the female consumer that she is void, that she has no identity at all. Internalization of this image then makes her a prime target for commodities that promise to help her "be herself."

Blanche Wittmann, during her stay at the Salpêtrière, occasionally took on the role of a person she referred to as "Odette" and described as a photographer's model. As "Odette," Blanche enacted scenes in which she would try to take off her clothes with one hand while putting them on with the other. After 1876, when André Brouillet completed his famous painting "A Clinical Lecture at the Salpêtrière," which features Wittmann, "Odette" disappeared from Blanche's repertoire.[22]

Jacques Lacan's (1968) notion of mimesis is particularly helpful in understanding this hysterical predicament of putting oneself on while taking oneself off, of literally robing and disrobing oneself in identity. In the mirror stage of development, the child experiences a critical moment of misrecognition. He or she becomes conscious of a difference from the mother, but this difference is constituted by a representation. Thus, for Lacan, mimesis is a camouflaging gap that separates other (image) from self. In this interpretation, the self is dispossessed and the subject experiences a de-realizing effect.[23] Lacan's theory presupposes a social "I" with the Imaginary as the necessary condition of being-in-the-world, rather than being-in-the-world as a prerequisite to imagine. For all subjects the Imaginary is the precondition (not the replacement) of the unconscious. The subject caught up in the lure of the Imaginary projects itself out of itself. By becoming *unreal*, the subject becomes inserted in the world as *meaning*.[24]

What meaning? What particular unreality? The Lacanian narrative (along with poststructuralist narratives) tells us that we are *all*

22. Wittmann's performance illustrates an ambivalence that typifies hysterical identity. It is particularly fitting that the vehicle through which she communicates the confusion over "who to be," is clothing. The passage also harks back to the issue of photography. In this case, once Odette has become a photographic certainty she is no longer an active personality for Wittmann; Odette has been appropriated and cultivated as a social celebrity and perhaps no longer bears any oppositional value in Wittmann's repertoire of hysterical personalities. This suggests that the therapeutic value of medical physiognomy was entirely adaptive (rather than progressive).

23. This differs from Sartre's version whereby mimesis signifies the self being possessed (not dispossessed) by the positivity of another, and whereby the world (not the subject) experiences the de-realizing effect.

24. See Anthony Wilden (1968).

fictions, that there is nothing but fiction to be. We are led to believe that all fictions carry the same truth valence. But in fact, the same fiction on different bodies conveys very different functions of power. While faking or deceiving is a cultural exercise that everyone engages in, fakery, as an ontological state, is reserved primarily for women. The female body is the form through which deception is marketed. Therefore, when women claim rights to material space, body, or voice, it is interpreted as a contradiction of accepted social codes. A contemporary ad for diamonds states, "Sometimes a woman's best defense is pretense"; an ad for women's clothing pronounces boldly that faking it—and making it appear as the real you—is the way for women to achieve public validity. The real self becomes something women are invited to contrive. We put on who we really are as we put on any other false face. Thus, the Lacanian notion of misrecognition is a psychodevelopmental reality for both men and women, but a demonstration of gender per se in the case of women only.

Puffery

"The pretentious opinion of salesmen and advertisers, exaggerating their wares, magnifying value, quality, and attractiveness to the limits of plausibility and beyond." (Preston 1975, 3)
"Legalized lying." (Preston 1975, 4)
An "advertiser's opinion of a product that is considered a legitimate expression of biased opinion." (Russell and Lane 1990, 689)

Advertising relies on mystique and subterfuge. The tenets of early advertising giants such as Elmer Wheeler are still taken as gospel. His first holy commandment of 1950s salesmanship captured the essence of puffery: "Sell the sizzle," he professed, "not the steak" (Ewen 1976, 62). Meanwhile, ad executives like to believe that their businesses have undergone complete demystification (Metter 1990); while at one time advertisers were hidden persuaders, today, they imagine their devious skills are common knowledge, neutralized by consciousness and public critique. Spin—the body of persuasive marketing including perception shifts, image-molding, and brand personalities—is supposedly "out of the closet." According to Bert Metter (1990) of *Ad Age* magazine: "Manipulation is part of the game. . . . Spin is naked to the world. And the more naked spin is, the more naked advertising is" (36). Metter confesses, however, that "it pays for the naked to be in good shape" (36).

In impersonating ads, women spin themselves. To avoid arrest or, rather, to "escape" the unavoidable state of arrest, they shape-shift.

The fugue: the hysterical escape

Dissociative types of hysteria take various forms. Besides multiple personality, others include hallucinations, hysterical twilight states (cloudy states of consciousness), stupor (assumption of a motionless posture), pseudoseizures (attacks of sudden unconsciousness usually accompanied by dramatic motor manifestations), and fugues, or dream states (Fenton 1982). The fugue is understood as a temporary flight or escape from reality or consciousness. Characterized by aimless wandering, it is a state of psychological amnesia during which the subject seems to behave in a conscious and rational way; however, upon return to normal consciousness, she cannot remember the period of time previous nor what she did during it.

This semiconscious being lost in a fugue state is the ideal advertising target. In fact, it epitomizes the capitalist dream state that advertisers propagate as the ideal state of susceptibility. What is desired are thousands of ephemeralized sleepwalkers only half in control of their lives. Many ads feature women in a petrified state of wonder, appearing lost in an endless daydream. An ad for Gianfranco Ferre clothes portrays a lifeless woman with shoulders rounded and head thrust forward as if being pulled by invisible strings across the room. Consumers are most exploitable when they are not thinking too clearly, when they don't remember their last commercial nightmare, when they are wandering aimlessly through malls. The female consumer in particular needs to be programmed to believe that the only way to expand the constrictive condition of her femaleness is by leaving her body entirely. Möbius, a nineteenth-century neurologist, states:

> The necessary condition for the pathogenic operation of ideas is . . . a special frame of mind. It must resemble a state of hypnosis; it must correspond to some kind of vacancy of consciousness in which an emerging idea meets with no resistance from any other—in which, so to speak, the field is clear for the first-comer. (Möbius, quoted in Roy 1982, 175)

Hebdige (1988) tells us that "advertising provides an endless succession of vacatable positions for the 'desiring machines'" (211). Advertising images are created for the disgruntled to encourage them to spend their money on dreams, to reinvest their capital in the great unknown expanse beyond their limited realities. But first, these textual images must be certain to rouse discontentment, fear, and powerlessness. The desiring machines, usually female consumers, must be made aware of their vacancy before that vacancy can be filled.

> It is our job to make women unhappy with what they have. We must make them so unhappy that their husbands can find no happiness or peace in their excessive savings (chairman of Allied Stores Corporation, quoted in Hebdige 1988, 87)

> Advertising helps to keep the masses dissatisfied with their mode of life, discontented with the ugly things around them. Satisfied customers are not as profitable as discontented ones. (*Printer's Ink*, advertising trade journal, 1930, cited in Hebdige 1988, 93)

Advertising success—the ability to create fugue states of epidemic proportions—relies upon mass regulation of desire. One of advertising's most insidious tactics is "want formation.[25] Before achieving the desirable semiamnesiac fugue state, consumers are first readied vis-à-vis several incisive messages that stir self-doubt. Dep ads, for instance, remind readers that their breasts are "too big, too saggy, too pert, too flat, too far apart, too close together," before rushing in with their heroic hair-styling products: "At least you can have your hair the way you want it. Make the most of what you've got." Michelob evokes all our failed self-improvement campaigns by sending missives about jiggly hips and thighs, body hair aversions, aging problems, weight problems, and sex problems. Then they offer "a more refreshing message": "Crack open a cold, clean, extremely smooth Michelob Light and enjoy yourself. Just the way you are. Relax. You're OK. Improve your beer."

Through ad copy, consumers are reminded of their deep personal failure in fulfilling their own wants and simultaneously invited into a fugue state. Through dissociative means—such as applying Dep shampoo to your hair to treat your imperfect breasts, or drinking

25. The notion of want-formation is fundamental to advertising ideology and practice and is discussed in innumerable sources. See Packard (1961), Ewen (1976), Meyers (1984), Clark (1989), and Williamson (1986a).

Michelob Lite to remedy your flabby arms—consumers are transported into an illusory state of fulfillment. Referring to the hysterical fugue state, writer and psychologist Abse (1982) states: "The dissociated personality in fugue is acting out a wish fantasy, and consciousness is suffused with feelings of well-being; these replace the consciousness of frustration and the feelings of ill-being that preceded the fugue" (175).

Thus consumers are first launched into existential frustration, and then quickly offered a new want, a fashioned material-dream that can be possessed posthaste. The purchasable product, the "hero," whether it be jeans or hand lotion, brings you out of the aimless blur of discontent and back into focus. It retrieves you from the ephemeral haze of dissociation and invisibility. But this commercial brand pseudo-psychoanalysis, whereby repressed stuff is continually reimaged (supposedly liberating the consumer/patient), simultaneously stimulates desire and erases choice. There are several ironies here. First, the possibility of being healed is contingent upon first entering a sickness (the dissociative state). Second, in order to accomplish this healing one must forgo her own subjective desire and copy a type (for instance, the one wearing the jeans or using the hand lotion). In order to feel better about herself, the consumer must dissociate from herself and align with an image; she must imitate the imitation. Only then will her dreams become realities. The product becomes the redemptive force, as long as one can become it. And, of course, one cannot; one can only impersonate it.

We desiring machines roam haphazardly in ad-inspired fugue states, ever shopping, seeking self-improvement and satisfaction. When we fail, as we always do, we try again. Capitalist cheerleaders root us on: "Big girls don't cry, they go shopping" (Virginia Slims). But in our search for happiness, commodities deliver us to the Pearly Gates shortsighted and impotent. Our ephemeral dreams were masterfully packaged in things that leave us only smoke and mirrors, just as the profiteers intended it. Yet as hope is dissolved, it survives, glimmering in those undying things: ever-ready batteries transcending time, Barbie dolls spinning impossible perfection, fashion-makers casting spells upon the latent wannabe within each of us. It is this recurrent and contrived collusion of promise and futility, mysterious auras and industrial merchandise, that reproduces in compliant minds the willingness to search and spree again, to copy the copy over and over, and to sustain an epidemic of dissociative fugues, women in flight.

What does man want?
the fetish and the anorexic

4

Man Ray probably thought he was doing some form of homage to femininity when in 1924 he designed his model/lover Kiki in the image of a classical Ingres odalisque: a female slave or concubine in a harem. The violin f-holes—saluting Ingres's musical avocation—are imprinted in her flesh like the signature of a master artist on his work, endowing her form with his worth. More than sixty years later, Moschino Inc. retains Ingres's classical pose but endorses her body with a far more dubious inscription than did Ray: a large question mark, the supposed signature of femininity itself (FIGURE 4.1).

Enigmatic femininity is packaged in innumerable objects—clothing, perfume, makeup, high heels—that women are told they need. Neediness and deficiency are aroused in women's notion of their femininity as well as in their wardrobe. Moschino implements the question mark to intimate both the female "lack" that characterizes some psychoanalytic discourse (What do women want?), and the answer to that lack that characterizes consumer capitalism (They want merchandise, in this case, Moschino). There are several popular advertisements that explicate this Freudian/capitalist complicity. An ad for Saks Fifth Avenue inscribes the question mark across a woman's face. Another displays a lavish boudoir strewn with women's lingerie. We see a half-naked man and a much smaller image of a woman (face only) reflected in a mirror. Ad copy reads: "What do women really want? That's VICTORIA'S SECRET." The

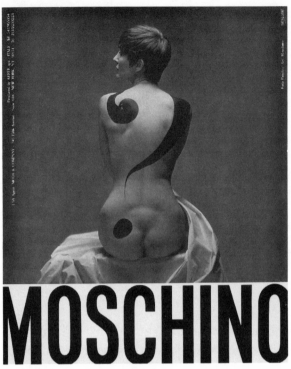

FIGURE 4.1 *Advertisement, Moschino (1990). Reprinted by permission of A.E.F.F.E. Art design: Moschino. Photographer: Stefano Pandini.*

commodity, once again, is the answer afforded to the oft-posed question regarding female desire.

The question of language

Freud's discovery of the unconscious was a revolutionary achievement: beside the conscious mind was another mind that, if tapped, would not only subvert the impervious mask of consciousness (the notion that consciousness is all), but heal it as well.[1] When the hys-

1. The advent of psychoanalysis challenged the false consciousness of psychic reality in much the same way that Althusser's Marxism challenged the false consciousness of the working class. Both Freud and Althusser (by virtue of his alliance with Marxism) were part of the "hermeneutics of suspicion" (Ricoeur 1970, 28). Freud deemed the unconscious organized as a language, Althusser believed ideology operated through language, and for both, language is fundamentally mythic (not based on laws of nature). In rejecting Hegelianism, both were criticizing the prevailing concepts of a rational, analytically neutral identity.

terics in Freud's care were given verbal access to their "thoughts without language"—to free associative talk, termed the "cathartic method" by Dr. Josef Breur, and the "talking cure" by his patient Bertha Pappenheim—the symptoms of hysteria would dissolve. It was as if the hysteric's body was suddenly endowed with mind, her mind invested with lost memory, and her memory graced by language.

PORTRAIT OF A FAMOUS HYSTERIC

Bertha Pappenheim (1859–1936), known in psychiatric history as Josef Breuer's patient Anna O., suffered a hysterical collapse in 1880 at the age of twenty-one, during a period when she was responsible for the prolonged day-and-night nursing of her father Siegmund, who was dying of tuberculosis. Dr. Breuer arrived to treat Bertha as an old-fashioned physician with black bag in hand, but she quickly changed their relationship by falling into autohypnosis and commencing to mutter in an apparently absentminded state. She was intrigued by the good-looking and highly cultivated, successful Dr. Breuer from whom she received massages on her head and legs—standard treatments for paralysis. Breuer and Pappenheim spent many hours in hypnosis, while she told him sad and fanciful stories, "talking herself out" until she was "clear in mind, calm, and cheerful." Breuer described her case as "the germ cell of the whole of psychoanalysis," and attributed her cheerfulness to the talking, not to his presence on the scene. Bertha fantasized a love affair with Breuer; the infatuation seems to have been mutual, though unconscious on Breuer's part. After many months of hearing reports of his fascinating patient, Mrs. Breuer grew jealous and angry. Surprised, and probably feeling guilty as well, Breuer suddenly determined to end the treatment. He announced his intention to Pappenheim and prepared to depart on a trip to Venice with his wife. Pappenheim responded with a hysterical childbirth to summon Breuer back for another session. He was shocked to find her in bed with abdominal cramps, which she explained with the words, "Dr Breuer's child is coming." He calmed her with hypnosis and abandoned her to a colleague.[2] But Anna O., under

---

2. This is Freud's version of the case according to Jones (1953). It has been contested by other sources; Hirschmuller (1978), for instance, suggests that Bertha and Breuer together decided to terminate her treatment upon reenacting the hallucination and traumatic events precipitated by her father's death two years prior. Hirschmuller does, however, acknowledge several conflicting reports and documents regarding the case, suggesting the impossibility of accurately reconstructing the historical events.

hypnosis, of her own accord, began to describe the details surrounding the first appearance of her particular symptoms; she contextualized historically and psychically her paralyses, contractures, inhibitions, and states of mental confusion. Having given birth to psychoanalysis, Pappenheim went on to become an important figure in the history of the German Jewish women's movement and in the history of modern institutionalized social work. In the same year that Freud and Breuer published *Studies on Hysteria* (1895), Pappenheim, at the age of thirty-six, became headmistress of an orphanage she founded in Isenburg, Germany, near the birthplace of her mother, Recha Goldschmidt. This orphanage became the headquarters for Pappenheim's forty-year philanthropic career. She spent her life rescuing and sheltering abandoned and abused women and children. In 1954, Pappenheim was honored by the Republic of West Germany as a "Helper of Humanity." (Program notes from *Dr. Charcot's Hysteria Shows* (1989), New York City)

Even though Anna O. "gave birth to psychoanalysis" (that is, psychoanalysis "lent" her a language whereby she could translate her symptoms into a genesis myth and thus undo them) the process of extricating contemporary women from their culturally muzzled status is still ongoing. Within advertising, women continue to be the site of public (and profitable) acts of strangulation and silencing. The visual metaphors of Apriori clothing ads appear to be informed by psychoanalytic precepts. One ad declares, "The creators of Apriori clothing are always surprised by where their designs wind up." One page of the ad features a huge spool of thick unwoven hemp; on the next page, it seems no surprise (to me) that the hemp has wound up across the mouth of a woman in the form of a fashionable cowl. Such images repeat a pre-psychoanalyzed Anna O. The somatic body still awaits narrative enlightenment. Within the psychology of advertising, the psyche itself is gendered: ego is male, libido is female; Egoiste perfume is targeted for men, Passion perfume is targeted for women.

It seems imperative to pose several questions here. Did the hysteric's story ever get told, or ever get translated? Did it ever leave the doctors' offices and enter the social body? While Anna O. talked herself into the realm of the symbolic, thus securing her cure, in whose language did she speak and in answer to what questions? Were the social origins of the hysteric's conflict brought into analysis and/or did her "successful" analysis in any way shift accountability for female disorders to the male hysteria that inscribes social power dynamics?[3] These questions are perhaps related to a more encompassing one: Whose story is told when the hysteric speaks? It is critical to understand psychoanalytic case histories and "cures" as an interactive process across gender and across sites of power.

PORTRAIT OF TWO HYSTERICS

Sigmund Freud was born in 1856 in Moravia and died in London in 1939. In 1884, he was introduced to the "cathartic method" by Josef Breuer. *Studies in Hysteria* (1895) was the result of Freud's and Breuer's collaboration on the treatment of hysteria, which was for Freud the starting point of what later became psychoanalysis. Ida Bauer, known in the history of psychoanalysis as Freud's Dora, was born in Vienna on 1 November 1882 and died in New York City in 1945. In her young life, Dora's father, Philip, a wealthy textile manufacturer having an affair with Frau K., hands Dora over to Herr K. in exchange. When Dora finally objects, Mr. Bauer brings her to Freud (who had cured him of syphilis six years earlier).

Dora's case of hysteria can be understood as a continuation of Freud's ongoing self-analysis—a fragment of his own case of hysteria. First, Freud's own dreams revealed the existence of a "wandering male organ" rather than the "wandering womb" that typifies discourse on hysteria. Second, in his analysis with Dora, he acknowledged that this transference was occurring. Third, through his own ambivalence about the literary aspect of relating his patients' stories, and the relation he saw between such writing and hysterical fantasies (Freud 1953, 256), Freud suggests an uneasy awareness of his own hysterical potential. Lastly, unable to let Dora go, he reproduced in his own consciousness the certainty of Dora's illness and of her need for him. In his desperation to cure himself, he insists that his own text of her story is fragmentary, full of detours, gaps, and omissions but that its logic differs from Dora's hysterical disjunctions and incoherent narrative.

3. Very likely they did not. Psychoanalysis has undergone tremendous theoretical and methodological changes over the last sixty years. But during Freud's early days of research and practice, psychoanalysis was not renowned for its inclusion of historical and cultural inequities. "Freud's apolitical theorizing discards the hypothesis that clinical hysteria and mass hysteria might be the same" (Schulz-Keil 1988, 73). The particular bias toward individual responsibility for one's mental health—and a seeming lack of focus on social constructions of illness and thus self-victimization—plagues some contemporary psychotherapies.

The linear narrative that he as analyst was supposedly to help her create was not possible for him to do within the context of their relationship.

Symptoms, like language, can be overdetermined. To Freud's credit, Freud's career was, in part, a negotiation with his own hysteria. The text entitled, "Case of Dora," was one of Freud's overdetermined symptoms. Dora, who suffered from recurrent aphonia (loss of voice), depression, fits of coughing, globus (lump in the throat, or inability to swallow) and catarrh (inflammation of the mucous membrane of the throat), terminated their analysis before completion.

Freud attempts to cure the hysteric by lending her symbolic language. The question of whether the language of her cure does, in fact, cure her (rather than reinscribe her into a symbolic order that repeatedly heals *itself*) can be investigated vis-à-vis the rhetoric of narrative. If the story of how "progress" is effected—how primal passions are made socially viable—resides in the female body, then her body can, metaphorically speaking, be equated with narrative (Logan 1993). She tells the story of civilization's production, just as the commercial object, or "hero," tells the story of a commodity's production. But this is also a self-canceling narrative, twisted into symptoms. Having found something to say, she is not allowed to say it from her marginalized perspective within the narrative. Part of the ceaseless treatment of womanhood involves censoring her story to remove any threats to the *reproduction* of male power. She is encouraged either to concur with the story of the master narrator or remain silent. Thus, the story of *production* that she is literally aching to tell—a complex one of ambiguities, contradictions, and waste—is both inscribed upon her and buried within her, as its full disclosure would subvert the prevailing order of public life. It is through this process of physicalized a(voidance) that women become the catchall for what cannot be explained. Her hysterical body performs the contradictions between "evidence" (or "truth") and all that challenges it, producing symptoms and pains that cannot be pathogenically justified.

The riddle of hysteria

Hysteria is a riddle that has plagued generations of medical science:

The task of accounting for hysteria resembles the work of Sisyphus. In fact, with hysteria always presenting the same riddle, the authors have sought explanations rather than a true answer. . . . Theories arose one after the other, one against the other, different from one another, and yet there seems to be no progress in sight. . . . When the hysteric presents her riddled body to the physician, even though mute, she poses her question. . . . The questioning one is the hysteric. (Wajeman 1988, 2–3)

Hysteria, an illness with no medical evidence, is the mark of inquiry itself, hovering suspect over the physician's wisdom, over the wisdom of Western medicine itself. The hysteric's role regarding patriarchal knowledge is ambiguous. She identifies with the structure of speech expressed as a question-answer: she asks, "Tell me who I am," and then she herself responds, "I am who you say [I am]" (Wajeman 1988, 12). But what he says she is, is never quite right. The conundrum unfolds like this: (1) by posing a question and requesting an answer, hysteria generates knowledge itself; (2) responding to the symptom, knowledge states what the hysteric is (a witch, a goddess, a patient, a whore, an odalisque); (3) no answer settles the hysteric's question because all answers fall short of the truth she experiences; no answer masters its object, thus none can silence the hysteric. "Disengaged from the truth, knowledge fails to account for hysteria" (15).

This three-part indeterminant process echoes the advertiser's creation of vacuous positions for the consumer/female to try to fill, to fail to fill, to try to fill again, ad infinitum. GUESS represents the unsolvable mystery of female desire by employing the question mark as both logo and allure. In GUESS ads, woman is the question; GUESS shirts, jeans, men, and perfume, as the case may be, are the answers. All answers are external to her self. Neither absorbing the doctors' knowledge nor the advertisers' ideal products reconcile her conflict. In fact, they generate it. Although the doctor/advertiser provides an answer to her suffering, the next day her illness has not abated but only moved to another part of her body.

It was in studying the hysteric (who, among other things, lacks the subject-object distance that constitutes symbolic knowledge) that Freud discovered a psychic knowledge that does not know itself: the unconscious. According to Kolbowski (1990), hysteria is a collapse into one's own story. Rather than figuring the story, the hysteric becomes the figure *of* it, merged with the subjectivity of the story's fragmented parts. Thus, hysteria signifies a lack of "lacks." In turn, the female body represents both lack and compensation for that lack.

According to the hysterical ordering of gender, when women gain access to patriarchal knowledge, "knowledge" itself is cast into doubt. Her authority to "know" (a function of being intimate with patriarchy) must be qualified by something that marks her as secondary. If she is to represent power or ownership visually, then she must be marked as other than her male counterpart. Early psychoanalysis and advertising sexualized that mark, fusing the signs of inchoate sexual passion and of possessability upon the female body. In a Calvin Klein ad for jeans, two bikers—one male, one female—stand beside their bikes in passionate embrace. But the woman is entirely bare-assed, aligning her more with the sexy, rideable Harley than with the male biker.

Historical interlude: the 1920s, psychology and advertising

While both advertising theory and psychoanalytic theory developed independently, both relied, in large part, upon research with women. In the 1920s, a more prominent affiliation was forged between the two. At the end of World War I, there was an accelerated need to increase consumption, and psychoanalysis, flourishing in Europe, became popular in the United States. Advertisers consciously employed the psychological notions of instinctual/sexual drives and unconscious motivations to institute a scientific study of women as consumers. It was not long before notions about the nature of women, the principal consumers, became embedded in the analyses of how consumers functioned (Ascher 1987).

Advertising theorists took some of Freud's concepts and used them for their own purposes. While Freud postulated only sexuality as an instinct that transcended history, consumer theorists produced lists of other natural instincts. Frederick (1929) listed eighteen "female instincts" including sex-love, mother-love, love of homemaking, vanity, love of mutation or change, love of prestige, and love of reputation. She even ennobled a "love of trading" to instinct status in the attempt to rationalize and justify women's new consumer function (43–53). In the eyes of the admen, however, emotionality and irrationality were enduring base components of all these instincts and the mainstays of consumer/female nature. The psychoanalytic concept of an individual's subjection to unconscious drives was vulgarized and naturalized by advertising theorists. Culturally determined traits were designated as inherent instincts and society was thus absolved of any responsibility for their existence (Ascher 1987, 49).[4]

While contemporary culture has supposedly evolved beyond such outmoded metaphors for gender analysis, the tendency to reinstate them predominates in current advertising. A 1993 ad for Apriori clothing juxtaposes a waffle-iron with a woman, shown from neck down, in a waffle-textured dress. The implication is that women's advancement into new spheres will bear her abiding "instinct for home-making," that she will remain umbilically linked to her "natural" status. Her headlessness seems to be offered as further reassurance that her progress is limited to physicality and dumbness, and will not interfere with prevailing intellectual prowess. Similarly, female domestication is insinuated in a 1991 image that accompanies a fashion editorial entitled "Out of the Kitchen" (*New York Times*, May 1990). The women are photographed out-of-doors, one wearing a tea-towel linen skirt with a border depicting cutlery, another wearing two aprons. Wherever they may be going, they are evidently taking the kitchen with them.

This latter spread becomes particularly interesting viewed in the context of 1920s economic developments. The *Ladies Home Journal* (1920s) intimated that feminism and communism were foes of the home and motherhood, and that any woman who did not chose to stay home and raise children was "aiding the red cause" (Ascher 1987, 46). At the same time, industrial ideals and developments suggested that women get out of the home at least to buy the family's needs. Efficiency kitchenettes were the ultimate progression in the trend of the shrinking kitchen that began in 1900; by the end of World War I, they were a sign of middle-class prestige, indicating that the husband's earning power freed the wife from menial productive labor. Just as upper-class women at the turn of the twentieth century paraded the department stores in glorious fashion, flaunting their husband's economic mobility, women of the 1920s paraded

4. Freud (1963a) described Ida Bauer's (Dora's) mother Kathe Bauer, as afflicted with housewife's psychosis. She was obsessed with cleaning the Bauer apartment and kept certain rooms locked at all times, keeping the sole key in her possession. With the scientific authority that attended Freud's work, the notion of a homemaking instinct (documented in Frederick [1929]) was bestowed both a physiological and pathological status.

their husband's middle-class status simply by consuming packaged foods. The "Out of the Kitchen" images resurrect the seeming mobility of the postwar climate, and simultaneously show that women can never entirely leave their home-bound status at home.

By 1920, the specialization of rooms within the single family home and the segregation of women working within them, were common economic realities. Abraham Myerson, employing popular psychoanalytic notions of human needs while supposedly championing women's rights, claimed in his popular book, *The Nervous Housewife*, that the cure for the epidemic of female neuroses would not be found in the privatization of women. In fact, such privatization, he continued, wreaked tremendous damage on women:

> Man . . . has deliberately isolated his household—on a property basis. . . . This is good for the man . . . but not for the woman. Her work is done all alone, and at the time her husband comes home and wants to stay there, she would like to get out. Work that is in the main lonely, and work that on the whole leaves the mind free, leads almost inevitably to day-dreaming and introspection. These are essentials in the housework—monotony, daydreaming, and introspection. (Myerson 1920, 77–78)

Myerson, nonetheless, maintained an ideological commitment to the single-family home with its specialized quarters and male advantages. He professed, ultimately, that adventure and freedom could be gained through romantic love, and that security and nourishment were available through family life. Women's questions and problems were returned to her once again; they were believed her responsibility, not society's. Thus, the answers that Myerson provided only betrayed her pain and conflict into invalidism.

The fetish

With life choices increasingly reduced to commodity choices, consumers turn more and more to advertising for clues to satisfy their needs. But the clues, embedded within the images, are obscure in terms of sexuality and gender. They are frequently offered within the ambivalent frame of the fetish.

I have already invoked, indirectly, the (sexualized) commodity fetish in numerous ways: (1) through the structure of the advertiser's question mark inscribed on the female body as lack, and the commodity as advertiser's answer to, or compensation for, that lack; (2) in the notion of hysterical knowledge whereby the subject-object distance that characterizes symbolic knowledge is absent, and thus one collapses into her own story; and (3) in fusing signs of sexual desirability and ownership on the site of the female body, thus exalting and discrediting her simultaneously.

Theories of the fetish are invaluable in recognizing hysteria as an ambivalent commemoration to—perhaps a ritual of—consumer capitalism. Within the constructs of hysteria, we discover a codification that both valorizes the female body as a reproductive/sexual icon and maligns it as a pathological vestige of cultural production. The medical profession that defines, if not invents, the hysteric disguises its intentions in her construction; the language, fantasies, and traditions that inform much of medical science are exempted from the perceptible design of female invalidism. In the realm of advertising, a similar construct is manifested whereby insatiable profit-making is both valorized and concealed; an object, a commodity, exudes an aura of seduction so arresting that it masks the materialist underpinnings of its construction. In weaving hysteria and the fetish, I weave a story of consumers who cannot see their desperate, perhaps ailing, reflections in the commodities they buy. Confounded in quixotic spells of purchasing we fail to see ourselves as exploited and pathologized performers in a much larger industrial machine—a social system whose organizing principle, according to Marx, is capital.

As I have invoked hysteria as a cultural analytic, I invoke fetishism as an analytic. Pietz (1993) reminds us that Marx's theory of fetishism is a way to reopen the question of materialist criticism and provide a path out of the hall of mirrors conjured by the representational politics of advertising. While fetishism is employed in the ad industry to help fashion this hall of mirrors and collapse critical consciousness, it also, like hysteria, calls attention to this fashioning and this collapse.

Marx claimed that a commodity is a fetish: a "sensuous supersensuous thing" that stands in for *and also critiques* the capitalist social process as a whole (130). He characterized this whole as an everyday religion, a normative magical language that exploits labor. Marx's use of fetishism was, in part, satirical: he used the term to evoke notions of primitive worship to critique the atheological sacrality with which the commodity was treated; he was attempting to subvert the power of the fetish through a radical, historical, and materialist theory of fetishism. How does this relate to hysteria? As the female body is commodified and fetishized in advertising imagery, it assumes its fantastical misrepresentation, its hysterical address. Her mediated image must be theorized satirically as well. Thus, my "theory of hystericism" intends to subvert the power of hysteria by pointing to the material reality of the historical hysterical body and to acknowledge the misrepresentational nature (the sensuous supersensuous thinglikeness) of representation itself.[5]

As a commodity fetish, the female body stars in the phantasmic staging of its own consumption in the aura of Things. Concurrently, still marked as a threatening possessor of sexual difference, she performs the role of psychic fetish within the male imaginary.[6] The psychic fetish is evoked when objects of purchase are offered as phallic stand-ins for the male authority that is absented from images of the female body in ads. For instance, an ad for pantyhose foregrounds a woman's long stockinged legs and scanty skirt, photographed from the rear. It reads, "Pantyhose for men" (FIGURE 4.2). Of course, this ad is not suggesting that men buy and wear pantyhose, but rather that men will derive pleasure from the women who do. Subtly, the ad suggests that pantyhose stand-in for men, or male attributes. Clothing and fashion itself (things a woman can crawl

5. Because of the emphasis in this book on synthesizing theories of multiple disciplines, I do not engage in more depth the very relevant and insightful theories of capital and commodification that would enhance my argument. I refer readers to Pietz (1993) for his perspective on Marx's conception of economic fetishism in contradistinction to numerous semiological readings of Marx in which "the concept of materiality is always either replaced altogether by a concept of objectified form, of the pure signifier, of else abstracted on a textualist model as sheer heterogeneity and contingency. . . . In this way, all dualities between form and content, sign and referent, exchange value and use value, subject and object, difference and contradiction, are 'overcome,' as is the need for dialectic" (127). The value of Pietz's comments to this study of hysteria is twofold: (1) in keeping vigilant to the ever-present danger of treating hysterical formulation as merely metaphor or ideology, as if there is no concrete experience to be considered, and (2) in escaping the perniciousness that accompanies the necessary engagement with the slipperiness of signification in media culture. See also Marx (1993).

6. For an excellent elaboration of psychic fetishism and commodity fetishism see Emily Apter's introduction to Apter and Pietz (1993).

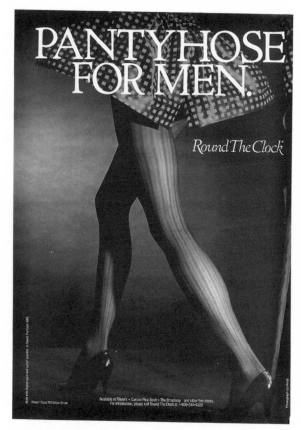

FIGURE 4.2 *Advertisement, "Pantyhose for men," Round the Clock (1989). Reprinted by permission of Romann and Tannenholz.*

into like a new skin) can, supposedly, remake her into him. In many ads, her "lacking" femaleness is bedecked in fringe, beads, and sequins—stylish versions of male genitalia. One ad displays an array of seductive male accoutrements accompanied by the fanciful reflection, "The best things a man ever gave us." In assuming the wardrobe and brand names (such as Hanes and Jockey) traditionally associated with men, she becomes "an extension of his ego," and with no great leap of imagination, his phallus (FIGURE 4.3). These messages imply that women can, and must, acquire what a man already has if she is to have her own power, ego, and desire; she cannot directly access these goods. Within advertising mythology, the female body performs the role of fetish; she borrows his attributes (phallus, clothes, language, knowledge) but plays an ancillary (and thus non-threatening) version of him.

An extension

of the ego.

Ultra Silk.
In 17
couture
colors.

THE LADY PREFERS
Hanes

© 1989, Hanes Hosiery, Inc.

FIGURE 4.3 *Advertisement, "An extension of the ego," Hanes (1989). Reprinted by permission of Sara Lee Hosiery, a division of Sara Lee Corporation.*

When woman herself is fetishized—made to be a surrogate for male power—she becomes Freud's "little man" (Freud 1965, 118). She is "little," for her power is postured slanderously, a copy or extension, primitive, invalid, and unevolved. Fears of her otherness, of difference, are warded off through her power and knowledge's being viewed as imposture. When woman becomes a fetish, her own female body assumes the phallus; this is intended to "cure" her by making her same (as him). But, of course, she cannot actually become the same with equal access to his social power; she must be marked same and less-than-same at once. She must maintain her difference—designated marks of inferiority—to prevent her from being perceived as a real contender. She remains equipped, for instance, with exaggerated breasts, buttocks, or legs, that point to her sexual and/or reproductive purpose. Through the fetish she is at once defeminized (masculinized) and extrafeminized. Hysteria too is marked by such oversignification of sexuality. The hysteric's sexuality is, symbolically and medically, exaggerated but empty, reified but objectified, aestheticized and yet anaesthetized. Subsequently, the actualization of herself as a sexual subject is obstructed.

As women's bodies are sexualized and taken out of context, they become fused with commodities that can be disposed of and replaced, while the power of the capitalist machinery remains mysteriously protected. The commodity-fetish-as-mediated-female-body broadcasts a collective imaginary (the illusion of capital), while holding captive (in image) real laboring bodies, real women's bodies, that if revealed in their material reality would destroy the illusion they service. When the illusion of capital is inscribed on female bodies and consumed as daily (phantom) bread, a gendered practice of mystification is elevated to the status of an unconscious socioeconomic ritual. I posit hysteria as a "disease of capital" in which labor, bodies, desire, meaning itself, become fetish objects alienated from their actual social value; meanwhile these fetish objects, hysterical themselves, are a "mask of the disease of capital," keeping the production of hysteria obscured. It is this ambivalence, this satirical power, that vests the hysteric and the fetish with an uncanny ability to flatter and defy, veil and reveal, the social system that creates them.

The uncanny

Freud's notion of the uncanny provides a metaphor for the magical terrain in which advertising imagery flourishes. It also illuminates the techniques used by advertisers to invest the sexualized fetish with metaphysical powers. Finally, it provides a launching pad from which to evoke real bodies (marked by race and class, as well as by gender) that at once advertising exalts and diminishes.

For Freud, an uncanny event is one that occurs by virtue of assistance from a special, magical power (Freud 1957c). He considers this a kind of doubling phenomenon, not unlike the mechanics of the fetish, whereby reality appears as more than itself, as guided by an inexplicable force. Freud offers many manifestations of the uncanny including animate objects that appear lifeless, and conversely, inanimate objects that appear animate (dolls, wax figures, and automata). Freud extends this category of the uncanny to include the following: epileptic fits and manifestations of insanity that "excite in the spectator the impression of automatic, mechanical processes at work behind the ordinary appearance of mental activity" (226); dismembered limbs (244); the compulsion to repeat (238); something familiar that has been repressed (247), or something repressed that recurs (241); residues of animistic mental activity brought to expression; silence, darkness, and solitude (246–47). Freud repeatedly cites, too, a generic uncanniness that he describes as "something that ought to have remained hidden but has come to light" (241). The hysteric renders this uncanniness. In the form of a fetish she comes to represent not only woman but something more than woman: "something that ought to have remained hidden but has come to light."

> An uncanny effect is often and easily produced when the distinction between imagination and reality is effaced, as when something that we have hitherto regarded as imaginary appears before us in reality, or when a symbol takes over the full functions of the thing it symbolizes, and so on. It is this factor which contributes not a little to the uncanny effect attaching to magical practices. (Freud 1957c, 244)

Advertising creates a virtual reality to substitute for and complement experienced reality. It relies upon animism, an investment in an image or inanimate thing to awaken something repressed, something still alive but starved. Advertisers, with their subtle and strategic deployment of visual signs, are masters at evoking the uncanny through the aura of the fetish. In a Liz Claiborne ad, a woman sits with her upper body hidden behind a newspaper, her legs conspicuously long and surrounded by flowers. Copy reads, "My horoscope: 'Things will blossom for you today.' Uncanny." Legs, horoscope, and flowers signal a hidden sexuality, a cosmic mystery, that will "blossom" and animate her eclipsed body.

Freud investigated the "something that ought to have remained hidden" (241) to uncover aspects of female sexuality and desire that would not necessarily benefit privileged male subjectivity. When Freud (1957b) proclaimed that female desire was a "dark continent" (212) he was not condemning women to an ontological state of primitivity, but acknowledging the research that would need to be done before fully knowing what women want. His use of the term was an admission of his own limitations and a decision to leave the mystery of female sexuality to potentially more insightful women analysts and the future of psychological inquiry.

But within advertising imagery, female desire has been aligned pejoratively to the "dark continent." Sexuality, race, and uncultivated "nature" are managed secrets of the capitalist machine; the ways in which they inform living subjects are controlled through the mechanism of the fetish. They are disparaged and romanticized, held up as objects of danger and yet inured within the landscape of popular culture.

The "dark continent": female sexuality

In the case of the fetish, too, interest is held up at a certain point— what is possibly the last impression received before the uncanny traumatic one is preserved as a fetish. Thus the foot or shoe owes its attraction as a fetish, or part of it, to the circumstance that the inquisitive boy used to peer up the woman's legs towards her genitals. Velvet and fur reproduce—as has long been suspected—the sight of the pubic hair which ought to have revealed the longed-for penis; the underlinen so often adopted as a fetish reproduces the scene of undressing, the last moment in which the woman could still be regarded as phallic. (Freud 1959, 201) (FIGURE 4.4)

If advertised commodities (clothing, shoes, stockings, perfume) can point to that last blissful moment before disenchantment is revealed (she doesn't have the penis after all! she *is* different), then it will likely sell. Such psychoanalytic notions of fetishistic practices converge with the interests of consumerism to impart an uncanny thinglike power to the female body/commodity.

Freud states that female genitalia have a particularly uncanny power because they represent something long established in the mind from which we are alienated: our beginnings in the womb and our passage out through the birth canal. While this passage out of the female body may be construed as desirable "progress" out of the

FIGURE 4.4 *Editorial fashion feature, "Special effects," Vogue (1990). Reprinted by permission of Condé Nast Publications, Inc.*

"dark continent," the female body signifies, nonetheless, a nostalgic domain both feared and desired. The fear ensues from an insecure male interpretation of difference: female genitalia, lacking in men but residing somewhere in primal memory, signify a loss, or castration. Woman is fetishized, loaned the phallus, negating her difference and her threat. The pleasurable domain of female sexuality can then be fearlessly engaged. Freud tells us that the multiplied genital symbol "is perhaps a preservation against [his] extinction" (235).[7]

The female as fetish is hysterical. She is designed to double as lack (the imperfect commodity) and cure (the perfect commodity). She is excessively visible and never quite unmasked. Finally, both psychoanalysis and advertising lend women a symbolic language for the purposes of her "liberation" into social visibility and health, but it is the same language that humiliates and imprisons her, that turns her into the hysteric. Barthes (1987) speaks of the "spectacle of a terror which threatens us all, that of being judged by a power which wants to hear only the language it lends us. We are . . . deprived of language, or worse, rigged out in that of our accusers, humiliated and

7. It is interesting to note that Freud used nearly identical terminology in discussing narcissism, which he claimed was a defense against the death instinct (Freud 1959).

condemned by it. To rob a man of his language in the very name of language: this is the first step in all legal murders" (46).

The issue of language is critical to an understanding of the hysteric. According to David-Menard (1989), Freud was unable to fully understand the language of hysteria *as experienced by the hysteric*. He focused on the causal link between psychical events and physiological symptoms while the hysteric experienced her repeated body positions as a subjective language that goes on in its own register, her symptomatic body being the only reality. For David-Menard, Freud failed to treat body positions as a function of the hysteric's relationship to her own body.[8]

David-Menard (1989) claims that the fact that a subject adopted a certain position in a given scene does not explain *why* that position has become symptomatic or why it is even accompanied by pains. Instead, we must see what is expressed by the *attention* she has conferred on it. The very origin of hysteria lies in this attentive relationship of a subject to her own body (38). Judith Butler (1990b) addresses the importance of this relationship in her discussion of gender performativity: "The body," she states, "is not a self-identical or merely factic materiality. . . . One *does* one's body" (272).

The "dark continent": animality

The female body accommodates the body positions and "brands" of other, less evolved, species. In 1992, prints of untamed animals, predominately cheetahs and leopards, dominated women's fashion, from handbags to body suits, from K-Mart discount items to the fashion wardrobes of Jean Paul Gaultier. A collusion of sexual prowess, female gender, and bestiality unfolds in hundreds of images in popular magazines (FIGURE 4.5). In an *Elle* (October 1992) fashion spread, femininity is erected as the "law of the jungle" where "fashion's new animal magnetism roars," where "animal-patterned fabrics are stampeding out of the hills . . . dressed to kill" (176). On

8. David-Menard (1989) views Freud's treatment of body positions as too literal, as a fact. In Freud's (1895) "Psychotherapy of Hysteria" (in Breuer and Freud 1955) there are several references that indicate that Freud took very little as literal. While I believe that Freud thought in terms of symbolism, David-Menard elaborates an important relationship to those symbolic symptoms that Freud did not emphasize in his case studies.

GIANFRANCO
FERRE

Boutiques

New York
845 Madison Ave at 70th Str

Washington DC
5301 Wisconsin Ave

Beverly Hills CA
270 North Rodeo Drive

FIGURE 4.5 *Advertisement, Gianfranco Ferre (1992).*
Reprinted by permission of Gianfranco Ferre.

one model, the leopard pattern of a donned bathing-suit extends beyond the fabric into the flesh of her legs, across her back and arms,
eradicating any trace of unbranded, human skin. Her wild mane is
shot from behind, concealing her human face. Another model man-
ages a close-up animal impersonation: her face and neck are intri-
cately marked with spots, bright red lips purr with a combination of
ferocity and cublike playfulness. But while fierceness is insinuated,
domesticity reigns: the barks and growls are only whimpers and
groans, the slithery separates and tiger-print bustiers, busting out
with feral passion, blend into leopard bedspreads, curtains, aprons,
pillows, towels, lampshades, dishes, and gift-boxes. The forces of

colonialism interplay with the forces of primitivity within the fetish of the feminized dark continent.

Signifiers of animality are often supplemented with related signs of natural splendor: feathers, beads, twigs, shells, rope, exotic flowers, undeveloped landscapes. These align femaleness with a raw incompleteness ready for processing into usable forms.[9] Black women, as well as white women, immerse their commercial bodies in "savage styles," an oxymoron. But the psychophysical terrain that is being invoked is clearly black: black Africa, the "heart of darkness." Accordingly, the legendary colonizers are white. The factor of race is critical in orchestrating advertising's visual interplay of natural resources, female sexuality, the dark continent, the uncanny, the fetish, and, of course, "progress."

The "dark continent": race

Race, as a physical marking, tends to reappear on women's bodies, thus aligning race (particularly blackness) with gender (particularly female). In one fashion editorial we find "basic black unleashed": a woman lies dressed in that velvety fur look that Freud linked with the last blissful moment before her sex is revealed. "This season," the ad declares, "basic black shows its dangerous side in powerfully graphic ensembles that emphasize the body beneath" (Bensimon 1991, 137).

The suggestion of a dark unknown confers uncanny and fetishistic qualities upon female sexuality. Women (of any color) share their "feminine nature" with this symbolically dangerous and contagious dark space. One rarely finds white male models half-naked or fully adorned in "native" African motifs or shuffling off to Wall Street carrying cheetah-skin briefcases. It is almost exclusively white women (not white men or black men) who double with black women in the racist images of a menacing "Africanness" and black

9. See Bensimon (1993). It features the work of several international designers. "Designers are heading back to nature. . . . In light of the burgeoning interest in all things wholesome, it seems appropriate that designers should find themselves. . . . seized by a desire to work with materials that are the antithesis of synthetic. . . . Belgian designer Ann Demeulemeester takes the theme to its logical conclusion, constructing a primitive-looking necklace of twigs and feathers" (74). The model wearing this "natural" fashion statement is black. She is wearing a crumpled straw hat, scant makeup, and her expression is plain, suggesting a kind of rural naïveté and deprivation.

eroticism. Benetton ads are particularly provocative in maneuvering through the tangled terrain of race, gender, and commercial imagery. While overtly proposing unification, the visual contexts within which this message is relayed are highly contentious. For instance, many Benetton images display stereotypical oppositions of white and black that are self-incriminating and naive. Others present a natural or cultural disaster (such as Haitian refugees dying in sea crossings, or the death of a person with AIDS who looks very much like Christ in his last moments) that powerfully suggest any attempt to work toward the "United Colors of Benetton" could result in catastrophe. One Benetton ad foregrounds a black albino woman within a small and undeveloped African village of fully pigmented black women. On the one hand, she appears a freak, even sickly, in her relative whiteness. On the other hand, the others receive no better racial rendering as they are represented as "black natives," physically robust but culturally "primitive."

Benetton ads employ several traditions that illuminate the race politics of advertising. First, "blackness" is worn differently by white male bodies and white female bodies, making race a subset of gender differentiation. Blackness, as a concept, can be "tried on" by either white men or white women, but because of its symbolic fusion with femininity, it cannot be entirely "removed" by women. Second, black and white are less differentiated on the female body than on the male body. With women's cultural value defined by pretense and what can be transmuted, the risks of racial integration can be played out on her body without fear of serious repercussions. Finally, even when blackness is obviously visible on the female body, it must undergo re-visioning. While African-American cultural heritage is often alluded to with pride (one brand of beauty products is named "African Pride" and one of its ads in *Ebony* magazine lists the forty blacks in the 103rd Congress) ad imagery and copy frequently undermine this pride. A large number of other ads found in *Ebony*, targeted to an African-American readership, sell products that promise to relax and straighten resistant black hair—to sell standards of white beauty under the guise of enhancing black beauty.[10]

10. See Doane (1991a). For analyses of popular culture that focus on the link between gender and race see hooks (1992), Wallace (1990), Willis (1991), Larkin (1988), and Bobo (1988). See also two anthologies: James and Busia (1993) and Morrison (1992).

Woman as adornment

Regarding race, advertising is willing to blur the difference between black and white as long as this obfuscation is performed on the female body. Similarly, regarding gender, the female body is frequently masculinized, while the male body is rarely, if ever, feminized in commercial imagery. Woman serves as an ornament, a titillating hint of contrast, that accentuates prevailing hierarchies of race and gender. While the marketplace would have us believe that "it's what you add that counts"—evidenced in ads for shoes and handbags, cosmetics, perfume, and jewelry—in fact, it is what the addition embellishes that counts.

The female body is codified as adornment to the social body; similarly, the female mind/spirit is codified as adornment to social knowledge. In one Samsonite advertisement, a young woman in a 1950s polka-dot dress prances fancifully through a field of blooming flowers. When she announces metaphorically, "My accessories [my Sammies bag] are an expression of my perky inner spirit," she seems to communicate a delight in her interior state being somewhat supplementary, petty (FIGURE 4.6). In another Sammies ad, copy reads, "You don't go to the beach with just any old bag." The elderly woman walking on the beach is apparently the unnecessary "old bag" you want to replace with a new (Samsonite) bag. Both ads stage woman as fetish in that they first summon, and then trivialize something feared. In the first instance, her vital "inner spirit" is evoked only to be undermined by equating it with expendable objects, accessories. In the second instance, the elderly woman, the "old bag," is presented only in order to get rid of her; her obviously un(re)productive status makes her disposable.

Advertisements conjure another kind of fetish when the female body itself becomes an accessory, dangling like fringe or a handbag from some other body external to her. This is visually established, for instance, in ads for Secret deodorant that pose the entire female body against the backdrop of the male body. Images of muscular and solid men performing "manly" tasks—jackhammering, weight lifting, carrying the world on their shoulders—fill the background in timeless black and white, evoking the eons of labor and mastery by which man supposedly created the very foundation of existence. As the story goes, the secrets of the unknown are his to engineer and uncover. She leans against him as if from another world—a fresh

FIGURE 4.6 *Advertisement, Sammies (1991).*
Reprinted by permission of Samsonite Corporation.

touch of red or yellow splashed randomly across his more seasoned canvas. In other ads, women are spotted on hoods of cars and decks of boats, frozen wisps of good luck gracing some mechanical device and/or its driver. She is tabooed marginalia exalted to form an erotic memento, an adorning and superficial keepsake.

Finally, Donna Karan's (DKNY) female mascot "goes all the way." She sits poised in readiness atop a Porsche, her shirt broadcasting a personal ad for a passionate man. She seems to get an immediate response in the solid thrust and drive of the steel beneath her. With the backing of the mighty DKNY conglomerate, she rides orgasmically into a billion-dollar calendar year; on the following page she is wearing a suit, brandishing a cigar, and luxuriating in the profit with the aplomb of a veteran mobster.

DKNY is not faking its excitement or self-satisfaction, having spawned four new companies in 1992. What is of interest here is the ambiguous gender construction of the DKNY empire. On the one hand, it is firmly masculinized in the lean-back, enjoy-it-all visage of the suited CEO licking his chops after a successful kill. On the other hand, DKNY represents the killing moment itself as an ecstatic female souvenir screwed into a car hood. The fetish is, necessarily, marked as both masculine and feminine.

In the various ads reviewed here, the imposition of maleness on female bodies is trivialized through repeated insinuations that this intrusion, in fact, heals her. Women wear maleness, absorb it, and learn to think of its internalization as essential to their survival. The magic of it all rests on women's believing, perhaps unconsciously, that periodic inoculations of phallocentric imagination into their own self-image is vital to their self-worth, as well as their social worth.

The bisexual fetish

Seemingly astute to expanding roles of women, advertising provides lots of chic women dressed in business suits, girls hanging out at the ballpark, female warriors, military recruits, and revolutionary insurgents. With increasing standardization of such imagery, these social exhibitions of gender-blurring are normalized. But advertisers simultaneously broadcast the female body as the epitome of sexual confusion.

In 1992, for instance, an ad campaign in *Elle* introduces "DUDES." The Wild West is subjected to a postmodern reincarnation as female cowboys parade as city slickers. A pin-striped, skintight bodice keeps the man's dress shirt and silk tie tightly cleft to her unmistakably feminine torso; her bared and supposedly male chest, clothed only in narrow suit suspenders, conspicuously announces female breasts. The style encodes the female form as sexually ambivalent and mysterious. Code West Footwear props a woman suggestively atop a restaurant counter wearing cowboy boots and very short shorts. The caption reads, "It's been proven through history that wimmin's a mystery."

Perhaps most troubling regarding this transference of maleness upon femaleness into a bisexual fetish, is not the cross-dressing so much as the ascribing of sexist habits, proclivities, and attitudes to the female. Magazine images proliferate with "very Charlie" women grabbing a man's butt (Revlon's Charlie perfume), pretentious female "wise guys," and "feminist" babes claiming, "There's nothing wrong with putting a man first as long as you enjoy the view" (Virginia Slims). Finally, women don the uniforms of war, moral righteousness, and national honor, assuming the bearings of their hawkish cohorts. A zealous female spokesperson for the U.S. Navy, dressed in male navy attire, declares, "I wish I were a man." Another woman, selling cosmetics for a new Estée Lauder campaign (called "Neutrality"), is decked out in the raiments of the Queen's army. A Philip Morris cigarette ad asks, "Ever wonder where we'd be if history were herstory?" The copy accompanies an image of a woman fully decorated in military regalia. With women portrayed as mere clones of war-driven men, the visual answer to the rhetorical question is, We would be in the same bloody waters we are in now.

What I find particularly pernicious here is not the act of mimicry itself nor the suggestion that mimicry belongs to the feminine (in fact, I discuss the subversive promise of mimicry at length in Chapter 6). The perniciousness rests in the particular choice of "male qualities" mimicked in ads: sexist and/or assaultive practices (from pinching butts to soldiering) that women have protested publicly for decades. The staging of the female body in gestures of seeming power appropriated from a traditional male repertoire of social misogyny, underscores the politics of the bisexual fetish in its more nocuous form.

In keeping with fetishistic tradition, the female embodiment of the male ensemble is also clearly marked as insubstantial. The navy recruit is ridiculously cute; the "wise guy" looks idiotic with tongue hanging out of mouth and eyes rolled back into her head. Gaultier as well provides a dubious portrait of military valor when situated upon a woman's body. The image of her armor is so extravagant that she looks like a fierce crystal chandelier, a symbol of courage recycled as drooping jewelry. War worn on women becomes an affectation and her combative ardor appears a charade.

Such gender positionings are the insignia of advertising warfare. The objective is to win consumers and conquer maximum market shares. To do so, admen target-market through ground maneuvers of typology and demographics. They neutralize competitors through focus groups that cleverly feedback subliminal messages from the field and recirculate them in the next pioneering offensive. They strategize with snake-framed Barbarellas in combat hats. They insert decoys as cover girls, while master schemes are rehearsed for execution in future layouts.[11]

Bisexual fetishization provides a clue to the quintessential hysterical question. It was a question posed by Ida Bauer, Freud's Dora, during the course of her psychoanalysis: "Am I a man or a woman, and what does that mean?" (David-Menard 1989, 129). We have seen how fabrications of female gender propagate women's (hysterical) uncertainty regarding their own identity. Modern advertising, however, intimates that this question plagues men as well as women. Male models for Jordache and Calvin Klein glance down at his and her private parts, respectively, perhaps seeking conclusive evidence regarding identity. Advertising wields its destabilizing power not only upon those who embody it, but upon those who fabricate it as well. As consumers we are all prey to how the fetish conducts its enchanting orchestration of modern knowledge; we are all subject to the vicissitudes of a hysterical sensibility within the social body.

The hysterical social body

Hysteria is animated irresolution. It lives as both idea and thing, as reified trash and trivialized power, as a sign of terror and desire at once. But how does one live this contradiction? What are the imperatives upon embracing, as women do, this irreconcilable double-bind? We can gain insight into the hysteric's body by way of the "social body" she consumes. This larger social body oscillates between excessive speculation (wasting) and starvation (conserving). Consumer fluctuation is reflected in the binging/purging motif of the lived female-body economy. Eating (consumption) disorders are of epidemic proportions in the late twentieth century, with 90 percent of all sufferers being female (Bordo 1990, 49–50). Women are bing-

11. See Ries and Trout (1986).

ing on false promises, and as they deny their bodies what is necessary for health, they grow desperately out of shape and out of order.[12]

A 1990 editorial fashion spread features images of women in men's sportswear. The accompanying article is entitled "Girls Will Be Boys." Figuratively speaking, if girls will be boys and boys will be boys, what happens to the girls? Virginia Superslims, among others, responds by foretelling the possibility of her immanent disappearance. She grows slimmer and slimmer, nearly vacant, as her hips, buttocks, thighs, abdomen, and chest (the same body parts overexaggerated in other ads as signs of her immoderate womanliness) now fall under siege. Looking in the mirrors that *Elle*, *Vogue*, and *Cosmopolitan* provide, she is a mere ghost of her former self. In an ad for Elle Decor, a woman stands before a mirror, her reflection represented as three flimsy vertical lines, gently curved and entirely devoid of volume. She smiles as she beholds this depthless signature of her diminishing materiality. In an ad for Superslims, a barely perceptible curl of smoke represents a female body struggling to achieve the aesthetic norm. But even this ethereal puff has too many calories: "Kiss that fat smoke goodbye," ad copy states, "and say hello to the first low smoke cigarette for women." In a Maybelline fantasy, a woman is perched precariously on the edge of a huge revitalized fingernail. She unfurls her hopelessly puny wingspread and surrenders herself to the gargantuan expanse of the commodity, the painted false nail. These ads from popular magazines of 1990 serve as metaphors of the continued epidemic of anorexia among teenage girls and young women. They also appear as disconcerting aestheticized renderings of cancer patients. As the models attempt to look like a cigarette—thin, elegant, sleek—they manage to romanticize the disease nicotine induces. The deathly withering away of the cancerous body, of the anorexic body, is engraved in these images as a mark of glamour, creating something of a contemporary analogue to the romantic, tubercular death of the nineteenth century.

The frail, pale consumptive female we associate with today's anorexic has much in common, at least visually, with the late nineteenth-century hysteric who characterized the "cult of invalidism" (Ehren-

12. Regarding the female body economy specifically as an ambivalent and contentious sign of the ideological social body, see Bordo (1993), Butler (1993), Crawford (1984), Chernin (1985), Evans (1989a), Gallagher (1987), and Jacobus, Keller, and Shuttleworth (1990).

reich and English 1973). But the roots of hysterical invalidism lay in a broader scientific and theoretical cult. In the late nineteenth century, Darwinian ideology tempered economic theories as well as medical beliefs. For example, the English philosopher Herbert Spencer (1820–1903) argued for a correspondence between the bodily organism and the social body, between the circulation of blood and the circulation of money. He claimed there are two organizing categories for the social, as there are for the body: those of waste and those of repair, or nutrition. For Spencer, profit in the commercial sphere was analogous to nutrition exceeding waste; the unimpeded flow of both blood and consumer goods constituted health, and any blockage or interference overthrew the system as a whole. Spencer paralleled the obstruction of menstrual flow, and thus the retention of blood, to the poisonous attributes of waste (speculation) overcoming dependable nutrition (reliable and profitable exchange).

> Just as blockage in the female economy would lead to hysteria and insanity, so in the wider social system it led to its equivalent economic form: uncontrolled speculation. Spencer's physiological theories of the social economy place on a material base the traditional associations between the fickle, uncontrollable operations of credit and the female sex. (Shuttleworth 1990, 58)[13]

A 1935 image from the theatrical production of *A Little Girl with Big Ideas* illustrates the widespread belief that a healthy woman was a woman who could signify a sale, a fruitful exchange. A chorus of women, flaunting their reproductive bodies, dance about on stage dressed as a host of happy dollar signs upon a bursting cash register.

While such physiological and gendered interpretations of economy may seem passé, the female body (and female fashion) is still, to an extent, perceived as a barometer of economic stability. There is a

13. A rather comic embodiment of Spencer's analogous logic between the flow of blood and the circulation of commodities is exemplified in a famous 1896 London trial. Mrs. Castle, a wealthy American accused of shoplifting, was set free on the grounds that she was suffering from kleptomania, a disease that psychological medicine had traced back to the effects of "suppressed menstruation." The hoarding of blood (obstructed menstrual flow) was paralleled to a desire to hoard material goods, throwing into disorder the legitimate circuit of the free-flowing monetary economy (Shuttleworth 1990, 65).

popular adage that when the economy is good, the length of women's dresses get fashionably shorter. During the Carter 1970s, the length of skirts were lower than they had been for decades. In the 1980s, skirts got shorter and shorter, supposedly reflecting the economic "prosperity" of the Reagan era. Of course, this alleged prosperity can be viewed as a celebration of bigotry wherein American citizens were encouraged to exploit the poor, get rich, and not feel guilty about it. Blatant racism and sexism, noncompliance with affirmative action, homophobia, the aesthetic repression of the NEA, and the license to make serious bucks—let's binge, spend, squander the taxpayers' money (as in the Savings and Loans scandals)—left the American public paying for the indiscretions of the rich and trickle-down economics. By the early 1990s we were in a recession, a time to purge; thus longer skirts once again camouflaged the woman who represents the economic "scene," bearing symptoms of perverted free enterprise. With the following recession-free years of the Clinton administration, skirt lengths diminished once again.

Another popular correlate between economic conditions and female indexes claims that when women are proactive in the public sphere, the anorexic look and the incumbent medical problems of female starvation and/or purging becomes fashionable. What correspondences between the female body and the social body are being staged here? Kate Davy (1986, 23) suggests that the scourged look of anorexia and bulimia are stylishly inscribed on the female body to contrast women's increased visibility. As women enter the economic domain as potential partners in exchanges—when they buy and sell rather than get bought and sold—their potential leverage is aborted through an aesthetic counterattack. They are recirculated into material culture as immaterial specters (FIGURE 4.7). To ensure that her emptiness remains enticing, she is bestowed the air of a goddess. Just before being exiled out of sight, she emerges as an exquisite dream, a sacred object commanding veneration. The female is spirited away in order to offset the politics of her disembodiment and expulsion from symbolic and literal space. In her wake, she expels Pherómone, an odorous trace of herself, into the science fiction of advertising (FIGURE 4.8). With her corporeal departure secured, we are left with the likes of a Romeo Gigli commodity: "A perfume that reminds you of a woman who reminds you of a perfume."

The untenable partnership of female bodies and food in advertising similarly highlights Spencerian thought. First, the female body is

FIGURE 4.7 *Advertisement, Destiny (1990).*
Reprinted by permission of Marilyn Miglin Inc.

allied with the uncultivated bodyscape, raw territory to be claimed and processed. Earth Food Service advertises its bread with a naked woman cutting through a hearty dark loaf. The female body is equated with the bread itself, and the slicing of the knife foretells her own edibility and ultimate consumption. The woman cannot eat the bread she buys/is. She is instructed to consume only those edibles that will retain her appealing lo-cal figure. Women especially must eat and drink lite, must display no sign of profiting from intake. A woman must not obtain much weight (as in value), for her weight signals depreciation in his. She again epitomizes intake and expenditure, nutrition and waste. She must be a "smart cookie" (Fig Newtons)—that is, a "thin cookie"—no matter how many cookies she consumes, even if some are "richer than an OPEC nation" (Chips Ahoy). Women continue to be allied with the kitchen and food, yet no matter

FIGURE 4.8 *Advertisement, Pherómone (1991).*
Reprinted by permission of Marilyn Miglin Inc.

how much she devours, she must demonstrate that "looking good is a piece of cake" (Weight Watchers). She must be a consummate proto-type of an impossible resolution, negotiating every swallow with dis-gorging. An ad for Chiquita captures the hysterical dilemma: their ba-nana "puts a great deal back, but scarcely a thing on." The female form magically resolves another double-bind: according to Chiquita, it is the embodiment of "inconspicuous consumption."[14]

Advertising engages in mass visual hoarding, an obstruction in the free exchange of images. Employing Spencer's terminology to overturn his essentialist theories, one could say that ads indulge in uncontrolled male speculation. The anorexic response of women — including obstructed "flow," or cessation of menses — is perhaps a

14. See Veblen (1934) for his notion of conspicuous consumption, whereby an elite get fat off of the invisible labor of others. Advertising cul-ture disguises the politics of "conspicuous consumption" by restaging it as a problematic performance of the masses rather than of a privileged few.

mimicry of these nonflowing images. Ads reflect how society alternately binges upon the female body (consuming her as currency) and purges itself of her (exiling her into a holding tank of recyclable waste). The bulimic response of women—alternately binging and purging—is perhaps a mimicry of this ambivalent positing of the female body. The social body is responsible for what Spencer would have us attribute to female nature gone berserk. Her obstructed female economy is a symptom of a social economy obstructing her access to resources. Her hysteria is the failed but ostentatious attempt to redistribute the wealth.

5

Eat my face
a ritual journey

I. THE INITIATION

A slender and sanguine woman professes with an air of confidence: "When I get to a fork in the road, I eat." The visual message of this Virginia Slims ad suggests deprivation and mastery over temptation; the written message suggests gratification and lack of willpower. Virginia Slims ads have the dubious distinction of condensing inconsistencies and paradoxes into seamless resolutions. This ad epitomizes the miracle of female body-management: it reconciles the surrender to unrestrained consumption (I always eat) and the control over such self-absorption (I always remain slim).

Many ads invoke a real crisis, a moment of conflicted desire upon meeting a "fork in the road," and resolve the crisis. However, the resolution offered here blatantly refuses strife or ambivalence. Doubt is substituted with certainty, indecision is rendered comic. The Virginia Slims ad decrees whimsically that the solution is to simply consume. In popular ads, it is often women's *faces* that do this ambivalent consuming.

Symbolically, "face" represents the notion of reputation. To "keep face," one's appearance must be "fed," so to speak, with appropriately artificial food. At the same time, this face must also be "eaten"—exorcised of its defects, neediness, and stress. Any symptoms of the conflicted social body that might rupture the facade of seamlessness must be swallowed; she must swallow discord to gain face. To guarantee this double-performance of face, many ads promote the interchangeability of food and cosmetics: Estée Lauder, Yves Saint Laurent, and Aveda, to name only a few, serve women meals of paltry food and upright lipstick tubes (FIGURE 5.1).

Two ingredients essential to face food are wealth and beauty. Innumerable ads exhibit jewels and other extravagant assets, suspiciously approaching a woman's face (FIGURE 5.2). We must remember that the female's inner body has been constructed medically as

FIGURE 5.1 *Advertisement, Aveda lip colours (1990).*
Reprinted by permission of Aveda Corporation.

FIGURE 5.2 *Advertisement, "Multiple choice," Bijan (1991).*
Reprinted by permission of Bijan Fragrance.

out of control and impoverished, reflecting a phallocentric fear of losing control over the resources of others. The ingestion of wealth is intended to cancel the threat of impoverishment, perhaps just as the fetish, psychoanalytically speaking, is intended to cancel the threat of castration. By injesting diamonds and pearls, she symbolically assures the bourgeois macrobody (Crawford 1984) that deprivation and alienation will not come into visibility.

Wealth, although scarce, must appear abundant and easily accessed; it must seem as available as fast food. But such affluence is far more palatable when figured as "beautiful." One ad places a luscious, red cosmetic entrée—gobs of lipstick—upon a fork, while in another, a woman sips a velvety, expensive Moschino cologne through a straw. In merging the values of wealth and beauty, the deficient diet of industrial society is flushed out of consciousness.

Cosmetic products, as the Moschino ad reminds us, are "for external use only." They are to adorn the skin, the outside. As long as richness falls upon the face of things (in this case, literally on her face or, figuratively, upon the female body as the "face" of capitalism) there is no harm in caking it on. Hips and thighs, on the other hand, signal feared feminine reproductiveness. They cannot carry much literal or representational weight at all. In fact, it is in caricatures that mock femininity that these body parts are overweighted. The face is already inscribed as absolutely weightless; that is, it bears no gravity, no significance. Thus there is no concept of excess for eyelashes or lips, for all that is being fattened there is affectation. Max Factor offers 2000-calorie mascara—richness that transforms threatening fat into desired beauty. Christian Dior serves up Mascara Parfait. Superficial nourishment, no matter how much sits on your plate, no matter how much of it you devour, congeals into layers and layers of defense. The female face itself generates procreative power, propagating not only capitalist fantasies, but a legion of disguises for the living self beneath. Each face is remade more rich and beautiful, so overdetermined in its falsity that it comes to dissociate from the features beneath and project its own autonomous presence. "Face performance" has become so hypnotically streamlined that we forget it is a performance; after all, the raison d'être of cosmetic aides is to conceal something.[1]

There is more being eaten here than tokens of wealth and beauty. There is more than nourishment being refused women by reducing food to artifice. The female body of advertising undergoes a complex ritual of submission toward gaining face.

One of the preparatory stages of this ritual obliges her to show-and-tell the utensils that feed and autograph her facial canvas. She must be a salesperson for the commercial instruments to which she submits. Her skin looks placid but starved. She nibbles at the provisions, patiently awaiting the application of caky base, gummy lipsticks, precision liners, and powdered brushes that is to follow. In numerous ads, her face poses alongside these inanimate objects with an uncanny intimacy.

These early stages of the ritual process require that the female face

1. See Phelan (1993) for discussion of masquerade and "the paradox of using visibility to highlight invisibility" (96). See also Deleuze and Guattari (1988b).

and its provisions be publicly endorsed by science and certified by big business. Many commercial pitches for the beauty business (also known as the "prestige industry")—selling cleansing lotion, makeup base, or shampoo—employ medical and scientific terminology to give substance to the superficiality associated with beauty products. Cellulite beauty treatment is "formulated with technospheres that . . . break down and deliver Celluplex" (Elizabeth Arden). New Keri Anti-Aging moisturizing lotion comes from "Keri Laboratories" and "is rich in non-comedogenic moisturizers and formulated with active ingredients to protect your face and body from harmful U.V.A. and U.V.B. rays" (Keri). The desired result is to turn the fiction of makeup into an invincible fact. "Chanel . . . unveil[s] a uniquely personal color-coding system that takes the mystery out of the makeup at last." Estée Lauder and Max Factor have issued lines of makeup that emphasize "signature" and "definition," respectively. Cosmetic science bestows a truth function, a certifiable signature upon the charade of beautification.

Finally, advertising often goes one step further and disguises all signs of its techniques of puffery and spin in the very ads that rely upon them. For instance, a Nivea ad displays a full frontal view of a cosmeticized face framed by ad copy that states, "Isn't technology beautiful?" While we know that beauty is created by the subjective whims of media technologies, Nivea subsumes scientific technology into the mystifying and all-encompassing aura of Beauty.

The face is now ready to undergo its most critical phase in preparation for commercial marketability. Advertisers elude to that uncanny "something more" that commodities can do for us: L'Oréal mascara "does more than lengthen, separate and curl your lashes"; L'Oréal lipstick "does more than redden your lips." What is this mysterious more? It appears that these products not only prime the face for ritual infusion but actually execute a special initiatory penetration. From the tip of the red tube a resplendent discharge of light brightens the silhouetted darkness (FIGURES 5.3 and 5.4). Penetrating deep into the recesses of her skull, the shaft blazons a path for the wisdom of the macrobody. Borrowing ritual terminology, this red stick of insight is symbolically the knowledge of the "fathers" infusing her liminal status with all she must appear to be to pass as a useful and usable female member of society.

This edification bears a multiple, albeit fused, message. For one, it intimates enlightenment in the sense of male knowledge producing

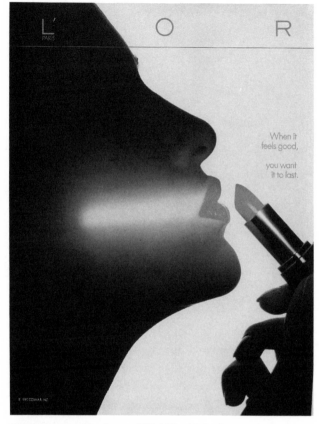

FIGURE 5.3 *Advertisement, L'Oréal lipstick (1990).*
Reprinted by permission of L'Oreal S.A.

light to heal perceived female darkness. The putting on of makeup, of pretense, is testimony to how patriarchal knowledge is defaced when it becomes hers; his wisdom becomes her beauty. An ad for Bonne Bell cosmetics features a close-up of a woman's face as she applies eyeliner. The ad copy reads: "Improve your EYE-Q. Eye-strokes are a streak of genius." Second, her market value is made a function of her ability to pass as white (racially). Third, the ray that gets through the facade connotes sexual penetration, a phallic entry transforming her face into a cavity, receptive to the particular matter about to be consumed. Sexually and racially marked, this face is the ceremonial mask a woman must wear and sell if she is to gain access to prevailing power. The canon (in the shape of a male sexual organ in the L'Oréal ads) comes with the purchased commodity whether you want it or not. Its absorption into the inner female economy is a

FIGURE 5.4 *Advertisement, L'Oréal mascara (1991). Reprinted by permission of L'Oreal S.A.*

requisite to beauty taking hold. As she applies her makeup—her artifice—she simultaneously swallows a whitewashing vision and the
cover girl is engendered in hysterical splendor.

Hysteria has been described by some medical practitioners as late
as the turn of the twentieth century as the consequence of a wandering womb in search of reproductive opportunities. As the myth
goes, the uterus, restless and overdetermined to gestate, travels, and
in so doing displaces other organs. Consequently, various hysterical
symptoms develop. According to advertising imagery (and, as we've
seen, to Freud as well), there is evidence of another interpretation
for such "disorders": there seems to be in symbolic male conduct, a
probing and wandering *phallus*. These enterprising male "members"
of the economy assert their control by masking themselves as indispensable products of beauty that will cure women of their systemic
illness. The phallus, advancing deep into the presumed terrain of the
female body, is contained *within* her face as she takes it into her.[2]

2. It is worth considering, as I have already indicated, that hysteria has always been a wandering phallus—wandering through the social body, through
the body of language—misread as a wandering womb. This would cast as hysterical the whole of Lacan's symbolic order in which signifiers of sexual difference wander about incomplete and obscured, encountering, culturally
speaking, a degree of privilege as well as limitation.

The cosmetic emission of whiteness into blackness, the upscaling of female reproductivity into male productivity, and the redemption of a dark mystery through enlightening science, are all evident in a contemporary ad for Kodak. The ad also reminds us of the photographic mission to capture an alluring angle on the masquerade and assign it truth value. The design of the ad illustrates how film undergoes a process very much like the L'Oréal face. An undeveloped negative of a woman's face cast downward is infused by a beam of light. In order for the image (the female neophyte) to be fully processed—made into a social positive that others will see—it/she acquiesces to and embodies the vision cast upon her. On the right side of the ad, we see the developed film of the woman's face, now uplifted.

What do the positive, developed, faces look like in advertising imagery? Many are sexualized close-ups, focusing in on one facial feature: a shut eye, framed by elongated lashes and darkly brushed brows, or big lips, fiery red, puckered and wet (FIGURES 5.5 and 5.6). Mascara-laden hairs become thick and furry pubic sheaths, intimating a jewel beneath the glimmering lid. The protruding scarlet moistness of lips signals heat and appetite, flaring labia in want of stimulation and satisfaction.

These lashes and lips do not only invite unrepressed consumptive behavior. Many close-ups simultaneously represent a need to curb

FIGURE 5.5 *Advertisement, Max Factor 2000 calorie mascara, Impact (1994). Reprinted by permission of Kenji Toma, photographer, and Procter & Gamble.*

FIGURE 5.6 *Advertisement, Max Factor lipstick, Impact (1994). Reprinted by permission of Kenji Toma, photographer, and Procter and Gamble.*

our consumptive frenzies. In Revlon's Ultima ads—Naked Eyes and Naked Lips—the lids, albeit soft and sensitive, are shut tight. The congealed redness of the lips are warning signs. Revlon offers its lipstick with the ad copy, "Color-lock: lock in a perfect lip line." The commodity does more than "hold the line against . . . feathering, bleeding and cornering"; it also appears to keep her mouth shut (FIGURE 5.7). These locked lips signify the hysterical tension between women's sexual desire and the cultural obstructions to its satisfaction. "When the earth moves, your lipstick shouldn't follow it" (Revlon). The unwavering redness puts a hold on verbal language as well as on appearance, equating feminine beauty with a guarantee of her speechlessness. An ad for Yves Saint Laurent blatantly captures the silencing effect of the commodity: a woman kisses an enlarged tube of lipstick which itself spawns a set of lips with which to return the woman's binding kiss. Several hysterical symptoms express through the face: locked jaw, atypical facial pains such as bruxism (grinding teeth), excessive yawning or shouting, inability to swallow, and fellation.

The beauty mask is created as a look that not only constrains but lasts, withstanding the "endurance test" (Coty) and "defy[ing] the advance of time" (Issima Eyesérum). Coty warns us of the dangers of masks that are vulnerable to life: "What good is color unless it

FIGURE 5.7 *Advertisement, Revlon Color-Lock (1991). Reprinted by permission of Revlon.*

can last longer than a passionate kiss, a romantic dinner, a double feature?" In fact, the more our faces "eat," the more binding our passion, the more controlled our romance, and the less flowing our emotions. A L'Oréal model with a single tear poised shamelessly on her cheek, declares: "I weep when I laugh. But my mascara never goes with the flow."

To flow or not to flow is one of the questions continually plaguing the hysteric, the advertisement-nourished female, and the medical practitioners who treat them. She must flow in terms of (1) her reproductive fertility as a biological object; (2) her dramatic versatility as a fashion object, and; (3) her representation of a healthy society enjoying nonobstructed consumerism. But she must not fall prey to the unpredictable vicissitudes of her flowing female nature.

Bound lips signal more than a celebration of female silence. They also indicate advertising's belle indifférence to historical change. According to an ad for *Allure*, a "little red lipstick" overcomes the "little red book," so millions of women bind their lips, stifle their voices, empty their minds, and forgo critical thinking (perhaps all thinking) in lieu of the power of painted lips—what Man Ray called the "Red Badge of Courage" (FIGURE 5.8).[3] *Allure* becomes "the revolutionary beauty"; lipstick (or nail polish, or panty hose, as the case may be) becomes political when it assumes a political body (in this case, a communist dissident). The lipstick wears a body of opposition, re-creating that opposition as intimate and safe. "Petrified beauty" suppresses change.[4]

This petrified and sexualized beauty spreads far beyond and independently of her body. It takes on an air of its own that replaces the female body and functions like an erotic floating signifier. These disembodied parts wear any number of cultural icons: a *New York Times* article, "When the Camera Lies" (Hochswender 1992, 8), features a sequence of sketches of the dislodged and slightly caricatured eyes of Mona Lisa, Marlene Dietrich, Marilyn Monroe, and Linda Evangelista, while the lips take on Joan Crawford, Garbo, Jean Harlow, and Julia Roberts. While they are presented to highlight the subtle differences between the parts, the effect is to subsume the different bodies, different people, into Eyes and Lips.

The relevance here of fashion photographer, Irving Penn, is two-fold: first, his "art" is comparable to the abstracted and sexualized eyes and lips that serve as floating signifiers of a disembodied femininity. In fact, Penn's designs for Clinique rely on his commanding ability to conjure the richness and power of this erotic mask without the woman's body at all. He creates poised compositions of upright mascara brushes and tubes, receptacles spilling their contents spotlessly, ingredients disarrayed in perfect order, inert yet dynamic fountains of gelatinous liquid, and lip brushes bathing in moist vermilion. Penn artfully capitalizes on disembodied, genitalized beauty.

3. The *Allure* image is an obvious re-creation of Man Ray's photograph titled "Red Badge of Courage," printed in *Bazaar* 1937. Both are printed as black-and-white photos with the lips signatured in bright red.

4. See Benjamin (1976, 1977) and Buck-Morss (1989) on the allegory of commodities that traces the disfiguration of all reality, followed by a remystification. According to Buck-Morss, human subjects strive for a fashionable ideal ("biological rigor mortis of eternal youth" [99]) that reinforces the always-the-sameness of the new, particularly regarding the potentially changing meaning of the female body within cultural currency. See Buci-Glucksmann (1987) for a feminist rendering of Benjamin's work, in which "petrified beauty" is, at once, a deformation and idealization of the female form, a beauty that absences the woman of expressivity (225).

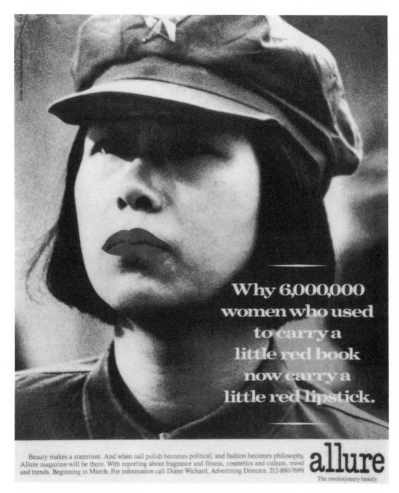

Why 6,000,000
women who used
to carry a
little red book
now carry a
little red lipstick.

Beauty makes a statement. And when nail polish becomes political, and fashion becomes philosophy, Allure magazine will be there. With reporting about fragrance and fitness, cosmetics and culture, travel and trends. Beginning in March. For information call Diane Wichard, Advertising Director, 212-880-7699.

allure

The revolutionary beauty.

FIGURE 5.8 *Advertisement, "Why 6,000,000 women," Allure (1990). Reprinted by permission of Condé Nast Publications, Inc.*

Second, Penn's decision to do Clinique ads was an attempt to escape, even remedy, the corrupted sensibility of commercial photography. He wanted to expose the depravity of this form that so crudely presents copies as though they were originals. Penn sought to treat modern society, suffering from the trauma of mass-produced forgeries, with the medicine of legitimate forgery: "art." But rather than transcending the limits of commercial photography, Penn, according to Krauss (1990), merely repressed the existence of the limits. His work became "art debauched by commerce" (27), and his still lifes inevitably incurred "the return of the repressed" (26). Psychosocially speaking, Penn did not succeed in making consumers (hysterics) any more able to live with their internalization of society's symptoms by presenting those symptoms as art instead of as copies. He merely reinscribed the illness within a frame less discernible as false. His art photography actually voided the difference between the two photographic traditions and normalized the violence all the more. The petrifying of subjectivity (hysteria) fostered by consumption of delusion remains a pathology however one defines it.

2. POST-INITIATION: ENVY, NARCISSISM, AND FACE POLITICS

Once the female is inducted into public currency, what does this sanctioned face get to say? In an Evolo ad for sneakers, a woman stares directly into the camera from behind a pensive gentleman. A shaft of light brands her eyes, recalling the penetrating phallic light that enters the faces of the L'Oréal women. Now that she is part of the inner sanctum, with authorized light absorbed into her face, she performs an attitude of self-possession, arrogance, and power. The ad copy declares: "CAPTURE THE ATTITUDE." Others can envy her as she envied him. She has crossed over and stands behind him in the camp of those who have, glaring with disdain at us, the readers, who have not (FIGURE 5.9).[5] Being envied is a form of reassurance, albeit a lonely one. Berger (1972) says it well:

> It depends upon not sharing your experience with those who envy you. You are observed with interest but you do not observe with interest—if you do, you will become less enviable. In this respect the envied are like bureaucrats; the more impersonal they are, the greater the illusion (for themselves and for others) of their power. The power of the glamorous resides in their supposed happiness: the power of the bureaucrat in his [and her] supposed authority. It is this which explains the absent, unfocused look of so many glamour images. They look out over the looks of envy which sustain them. (133)

The commercial interplay of envy and narcissism as gender-political subterfuge is critical here. As women in ads achieve the envied image, they share in the power that previously exploited them.

5. See the similarity in attitude in figure 3.7, Regnard's *Repugnance* from Charcot's iconography of hysteria.

FIGURE 5.9 *Advertisement, Inscription Rykiel (1990). Reprinted by permission of Sonia Rykiel.*

However, the woman's body still performs as an emblem of her own submission to authorities who continue to limit her access to power. The attitude with which she gazes at less-endowed others (uninitiated others), *is the same attitude with which she views herself.* She is the envied and the envious to herself. Her look of alienation is projected through advertising to read, paradoxically, as female narcissism. This suggests a Freudian reading whereby women have a privileged relation to narcissism in that they employ veils (modesty, charm, beauty, coquetry) to aid in covering up a "natural" deficiency.

An ad for Pantene hair products illustrates the warped link forged in advertising between envy and narcissism. A woman pleads (insincerely), "Don't hate me because I'm beautiful." The suggestion is that her newly inaugurated status in a man's world might appear a betrayal to her sister consumers who are *not* beautiful and thus *not* bestowed with postinitiation privileges. She is warding off hateful female envy.

Within the male Imaginary, as well, women are the envious potential castrators of his privilege and authority. The internalization of this "feminine evil" incurs a hysterical gender war within his own body. The deformed female of his imagination stands in his shoes and reflects his terror (of being the deformer/deformed) back at him. The image of the beautiful cover girl subdues the tension. Like a fetish, it substitutes for and binds the dissociated reaction to some recognition of the illegitimacy of his own social prerogatives. In the Pantene ad, a male-to-female interdiction (in which *he* says to *her*, "Don't hate me because I am unjustly powerful over you") is disguised as a female-to-female power struggle ("Don't hate me because I am beautiful").

Female narcissism is an agent of male narcissism, void of female ego. She masquerades as "beautiful" and in so doing invalidates her desire in order to satisfy his. Also, the specular distortion that women present pretends to hide what he does not want to see. Ironically, the primary thing he doesn't want to see, a representation of the phallus, isn't there anyway (Russo 1986, 223). Thus he *creates* the threat to his own narcissistic needs and then must dissolve them. Female hysteria assures him that what he fears, female variation and subjectivity challenging his own, is out of sight and therefore nonexistent. This confirms what Freud told us was true: narcissism for women signifies her being less differentiated than men and that her libidinal development has suffered some disturbance, as in perverts and homosexuals (Freud 1963b, 69).

Similarly, Freud (1961, 46–48) claimed that narcissism is not self-love but a form of self-preservation: an instinctual defense against death instincts and/or aggressive impulses. The narcissistic performances in fashion that we would popularly (and wrongly) identify as ego-based and female, seem to be symptoms of a phallic, self-preserving instinct. The exhibitionism of the phallus disguised as a cosmetic shrine becomes a parody (certainly male-narcissistic) in its excessive defense against female "lack" and its supposed loaning to women a look of power (FIGURE 5.10).[6]

6. Fromm (1962) and Lasch (1979) contribute to discussions of narcissism, but their analyses seem incomplete regarding issues of gender. Fromm deals with hostile individualism and narcissism as man's pride in seeing his reflection in his own godlike, technological advances. He fails, however, to ad-

FIGURE 5.10 *Editorial fashion feature, "Monumental Makeup" (1994). Reprinted by permission of Paul Taylor, photographer. © Paul Taylor.*

Does male narcissistic displacement encourage female hysteria? In an Elizabeth Arden ad, a nude female model faces halfway toward the camera with a vacant, somewhat disgusted look on her face, one hand perched stiffly on a hip, the other holding her bared breast. She embodies a contemptuous dominion over her own body that nullifies the very subjectivity she appears to possess, indicating the dissociative states that typify hysteria.

With enviable attitude firmly captured, the ultimate outcome of the ritualized woman is a very familiar commodity: the cover girl (FIGURE 5.11). It is evident that while she exhibits an attitude of in-

---

dress the unfulfillable envy of the consumer in the shadow of these mythic promises of grandeur. Lasch offers in-depth psychological definitions of narcissism, providing links between psychological behavior patterns and cultural expectations. For example, he defines narcissism as a defense against helpless dependency in early life manifesting as blind optimism and grandiose illusions of personal self-sufficiency. I cite Fromm and Lasch as each attempts to analyze cultural phenomena through the lens of psychological paradigms. My approach differs by focusing on gender specificity and in using hysteria to unveil the gender relations of late consumer capitalism. Deleuze and Guattari (1983) share some of my methodological approaches in employing a medical paradigm and a psychoanalytic figure (schizophrenia and Oedipus, respectively) to launch a dramatic political analysis of desire in, and sickness of, Western culture.

FIGURE 5.11 *Cover girl,* Cosmopolitan *(June 1990). Reprinted by permission of Hearst Corporation.*

solent self-satisfaction, she also looks like a rape victim. Her arms are crossed tightly over the chest, an air of impudence relaying either mockery or loathing. As she embraces herself firmly, she is nearly desperate, holding onto something she cannot afford to lose. Beneath the scorn are signs of terror; what she precariously possesses is not really hers, and just as it was given, it may at any moment be taken away. In a Christian Dior image that resembles this typical cover girl, she appears to be braving a compulsion to throw up. Perhaps, bulimia represents the inability to own—to "keep down"—the body images that a socially acceptable woman is expected to absorb.[7]

7. See anthropologist Michael Taussig's (1987) discussion of envy. Although Taussig is discussing the "envidia" of rural Venezuela, his insights further an understanding of the relationship between envy, narcissism, and hysteria. Taussig contends that envy produces evil effects by lodging within

Curiously, the anguished posture and facial expression in the Christian Dior ad—head thrust back, eyes closed—resembles Charcot's *Extase* (as seen in FIGURE 3.7), which supposedly captures a moment of pleasure, if not euphoria. In spite of Charcot's apparent empathy for his female patients, his interpretive labeling was perhaps misinformed.

Conceiving of envy in psychoanalytic terms, the hysteric's insatiable desire relays envy-in-extremis for the power she cannot have. Hysterics are notoriously seen as consuming, killing, and exhausting by their doctors. Mack (quoted in Chodoff 1982, 283) refers to this quality as "the stink of personality—hot house minds—no, not so much minds as appetites." Is it a vision that disfigures women in exchange for entry into the doctors' enviable world: prestige, the ability to name, and power over other's bodies? Do doctors arouse the unhealthy state of envy through the inappropriate narratives of "health" they sell their patients?

Cindy Sherman, a New York City–based visual artist, was commissioned by the now-defunct *7 Days* magazine to come up with her idea of a *Cosmopolitan* cover girl (FIGURE 5.12). What we can see in Sherman's self-portrait is the "stinking" stuff that lies swelling but concealed beneath the standard commercial fantasy: recycled alienation, repressed sexual rage and psychological trauma, vilified motherhood, and bulimic bile overcoming a half-animal/half-female body, exploding with the waste products of mass industrial production that femininity has been appointed to contain and reproduce.

Along with obscenity and ugliness, Sherman wants to splay monstrousness on the surface of wealth and beauty. Her image recodes the cover girl herself as a vision of the carnivalesque—what bourgeois culture identifies as bitch, trash, whore. Sherman makes visible, for a moment, a hysteric who can articulate (in a supposedly

---

bodies of those envied—in their stomach, head, chest, and lower back. This envy must be purged. "The envious person is dangerous, so aroused by envy that she or he will try to kill through magical means" (395). In the realm of advertising, what is envied is an illusion; the female consumer (the envious) learns to "kill," not so much the image (which only reincarnates over and over), but rather whatever obstructs her realization of this image—which is, of course, her own experienced subjectivity. She forgoes critical thought and difference for an impossible fusion; she is hysterical.

FIGURE 5.12 *Cindy Sherman,* Untitled *(1990). Commissioned portrait of* Cosmopolitian *cover girl by* 7 Days. *Reprinted by permission of the artist and Metro Pictures.*

worshiped body) the vulgarity her body channels. In that lucid moment, the cover girl we all want to be is an enraged and mistaken freak. Oppositions blur: the dreadful disease and the beautiful cure appear to be one and the same.

Hysteria, an ordinary aberration

Capitalism cannot thrive without certain human resources habitually depleted for the economic advantage of others. The depleted resource is relegated to the bearing of the freak: it must be visible (or it would be suspiciously absent) while simultaneously represented as either an outcast, a project for future renovation, or an already face-lifted sight. Over the course of history, the need for such a deviant class manifests in different forms, but all are obliged to monitor the power and meaning of certain threatening identities, dreams, and/or realities. In the 1960s, "freak" identified a user of narcotics and hallucinogens; by the 1980s the term—adopted by the freaks of the 1980s themselves—was popularly used to identify the general category of rebellious youth. Advertisements for Image Bank and Midori Melon Liqueur shamelessly label these rebellious youth, "other" and "slimeballs," respectively. They are figured as subhuman, graphically demonstrating that there is always something to be feared, something against which to be vigilant.

The female body frequently harbors this cultivated fear; it is conventionally employed to serve as an invariable blank slate upon which changeable definitions of deviance are overlaid. We could say that aberrations of several varieties, from criminal to clown, have worn the female body. But it is by impersonating commodities that women have most elaborately and extensively embodied a freakish terrain. Women have fused identities with perfume bottles, cash registers, wrist watches, and waffle irons. They have morphed into so many gadgets and creatures both sacred and forbidden, and so many combinations of things, that the female body is regarded as the fluid container into which any idea, fad, fantasy or phobia can be discharged.

Hysteria, as an aberration, not only fills the container but *is* the container, characterized by an exceptional knack for appropriating any and all mutating facades and fears. In appropriating the female body as site, the advertising industry has elevated hysteria to an ordinary and inescapable postmodern state of pathology. As an attribute of the social order, the very notion of pathology or disorder becomes moot. Hysteria is no longer something to be treated or cured. It is an everyday body of performative knowledge *and* the stage on which it plays; there is nowhere outside of hysteria.

There is, however, the promising opportunity to exploit it for its mimetic wisdom and subversive potential.

6

Representation is dead,
long live representation!

The most enduring aspect of the hysterical condition, regardless of its innumerable definitions and symptoms, is the inability to distinguish between truth and illusion. This inability was labeled by medical science as a sign of a pathological disorder linked with femininity. But in the realm of postmodern critique and popular culture, this same phenomenon (linked with the death of an original real) is celebrated; notions of authenticity and factuality are considered naive, while illusion (the fashioning of reality through representation) is hailed as the "essence" of reality itself, of contemporary consciousness, change, even resistance.

It is through the politics of duplicity and appropriation that hysteria is inculcated into cultural consciousness; hysteria mimics the politics of duplicity that it resists. How is it, then, that the immersion in these politics is envisioned as moorings of an emergent, even radical consciousness, while the hysterical, sociosomatic symptoms such an immersion engenders are still marked pathologically, bearing dismissive consequences for women in everyday life?[1] Why is there a

1. A similar inconsistency arises within certain arenas of anthropological research and analysis. Many ritual healing ceremonies (if not everyday belief systems) in places distant from the media-centers of cultural capitalism, feature possession, trance, convulsive fits, and magical or mythical thinking. See Katz (1982), Bramly (1977), and Feld (1990). Performatively speaking, they

postmodern valorization of advertising surface modalities and a simultaneous dismissal of the women who adopt them symptomatically? Perhaps hysteria too can be reenvisioned as an emergent, even radical consciousness. But what kind of recuperation is possible from a terrain that by definition erases subjectivity and replaces it with a hyperpresence that masks its own production? How can there be liberation where there is no reasonable expectation to distinguish clearly between truth and illusion? I believe the answer lies, in part, in re-viewing *how* popular images function as commentaries. Perhaps then, the very spectacle of hysteria can be performed as a critique that both accepts the inescapability of mediated postmodern culture (there is no abiding nonhysterical social condition) and still reclaims subjectivity for those whose experiences are seemingly erased within it (women are agents in the process of endowing meaning to the performances they play).

The crisis of representation

The crisis of representation—what I call the "hystericization of culture"—and how it is advanced through systematic techniques of displacement and substitution, blurs the subject-object distance necessary for rational and critical thinking. Consumers are captive within a universe of visual stimuli, exposed incessantly to clones. Ad images of women abound with twins, ghosts, echoes, and reflections that remind us we are never alone, we are split, forever sharing our consciousness with visions of our bodies transmuted into something both ideal and unrealizable (FIGURE 6.1). On some level we know we are cohabiting with versions of ourselves that are not ourselves. We come to understand our experience through the experience of representation itself. Photographic representation particularly promotes the fraudulent fact. When advertising's simulated reality reaches proportions whereby we can no longer

---

are quite comparable to hysterical attacks. They have come to be appropriated by anthropologists, New Ageists, spiritualists, and healers (in the Western Hemisphere) as indicators of healthy, interactive communities, albeit with all the attendant nostalgia and exotification. Meanwhile, much of the same behavior, when exhibited by (female) bargain shoppers, mental patients, artists, or political protestors of contemporary North America, is taken as evidence of a fixation or sickness, not a shamanic process or cure.

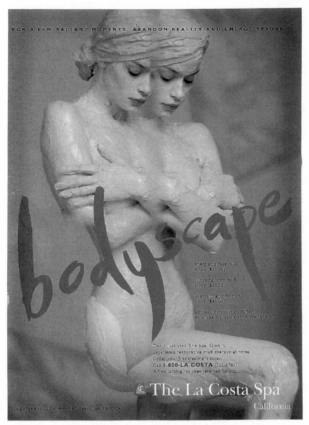

FOR A FEW RADIANT MOMENTS, ABANDON REALITY AND EMERGE REBORN

energizing face mud,
4.5 oz. ($25.00)

purifying body mud,
9.0 oz. ($32.50)

costorizing body mud,
5.0 oz ($40.00)

Limited Introductory Offer:
All three luxurious products ($75.00)

Don't just visit The Spa. Own it.
Experience restorative mud therapy at home.
Order your first treatment today.
Call 1-800-LA-COSTA (522-6782)
A free catalog has been reserved for you.

The La Costa Spa
California

LA COSTA PRODUCTS INTERNATIONAL, CARLSBAD, CA.

FIGURE 6.1 *Advertisement, "Bodyscape," The La Costa Spa (1992).*
Reprinted by permission of La Costa Products International.

trust our senses to tell us what is real, then we can say that collective consciousness is hysterical.

One dimension of the crisis of representation is that consumers experience the inability to read ideology apart from materiality. Two shifts occur simultaneously: the semiotic move from abstraction to object and a similar move from object to abstraction. Both that which is being represented and the representation itself can be either an abstraction or a tangible thing. The blur of reality and illusion is also a blur of objects and belief systems. Objects are as loaded and complex as are the systems of thinking that produce them. It is no longer possible to ask which comes first: experience or language, unconsciousness or consciousness, reality or representation, object or concept.

Another dimension of the crisis of representation is that the industry of reproduction is expanding into technologies capable of mutations beyond the usual photographic manipulations of light, framing, and exposures. Morphing, for example, is a computer process used in film and video, but most widely in advertising, whereby one thing is metamorphosed into another. Female models have been altered cosmetically and photographically for decades now; the beauty they advertise is unattainable in that the women who represent it *do not exist*. With morphing, the transformation is even more radical. Reproductive technology is able to generate sequences of resemblances, families of symbols. In an image produced by Industrial Light and Magic (the inventors of morphing, among other things), female lips and Toyotas share a symbolic intimacy. Notions of the real, already challenged by mass media, are thrust further into disorder.

Hysteria has been represented as frenzied rigidity. I have already posed the rhetorical question of how one lives such irreconcilable double-binds. As the hysterical contemporary female consumer merges the contradictions of her time into a vision that no longer knows that it is not itself, she embodies a profoundly sarcastic condition of truth. It is one that cannot articulate itself as a power politic. It is no more than a frantic sign, a contemptuous look of horror or disgust as she glances into the commercial mirror that has once again failed to transform her into her (dream) self. An ad for Memorex reads, "The mirror was not her friend, though I think she thought it was." Advertisers remind us incessantly that the mirror never lies. But they also produce a hall of mirrors; when we stare into it, we appear as our defects. Ads disown and re-present the doubt they create before we can name it, and use that implanted self-doubt as a weapon against us. Ads reinscribe our hysterical blindness and nourish that sarcastic inner province that is "true," but cannot see itself.

AUTOBIOGRAPHY OF A RADICAL FEMME, PART 1

What captivates me in the face of a joke is that something nonsensical is brought to my attention but is never fully disclosed. There is always that bit of sense one cannot get at. That is masked. The word "mask" comes from the Arabic word *maskharat*, meaning buffoon. And the word buffoon means "to puff."

I am the elusive puff, the defect in the mirror, that bit of sense one cannot get at. My foolishness makes a fool of the mirror, I am proof of its scam. My nonsense reveals common sense to be just another spectacle that has been determined without me, yet speaks for me.

But the becoming of a fool implies the abandonment of any consciousness of being one. The paradox cautions me: I become the joke that tor-
ments me; I am the phobia incarnate.

Portraits of duplicity: FacsiMommy and FacsiWife

Commodities generated a collective fantasy in the early twentieth
century, a fantasy that addressed the ambivalence of the growing
bourgeois class. The promise of commodity abundance became a
substitute for social revolution, assuaging discontent by seizing the
revolutionary ideas of Marx and Freud and subsuming them in a
capitalist scheme. Consumers experienced themselves performing in
the theater of purchases (Buck-Morss 1989, 216–34); they lost themselves in the spell-of-things. Meanwhile women, the primary site of
commodity culture, came to signify both the magician casting the
spell and the spellbound victim, sleepwalking through the exorcism
of her own subjectivity.

For such a captivating displacement to work, something theatrical
must be presented "hysterically," as if it were *not* fiction, *not* representation. In this way, the illusion loses its frame; the signifier that
says "this is theater" is dissolved, leaving fiction to be read as fact. It
is this making invisible the strategies of representation that inaugu-
rates representation as a hysterical medium.

The magic of advertising rests in denying its own theatricality.
Masters of illusion employ histrionic skills not to arouse doubts
about the authenticity of their illusions, but to heighten confidence
in the illusions' authenticity. In this way, they successfully manipulate
duped minds into resolved, though frantic, states of faith—at least
long enough to make a commodity purchase.[2]

An ad for FacsiMommy appeared in *New York Magazine* 20 November 1989. It exemplifies the kind of savvy manipulation that pre-
cipitates hysterical thought. Drill Laboratories, the manufacturers of

2. Every textbook I have seen on advertising declares that advertisers do
not create tastes, needs, or desires of the public, but merely give consumers
what they already want. Advertisers, in other words, portray themselves as
mimics (not fashioners) of consumer desire, with their ads merely manifesting in images what is already aesthetically popular. Advertisers' self-portraits
strike me as indicative of advertisers' tendency to absolve themselves of the
political biases of their representations.

FacsiMommy, open their narrative by intensifying feelings of inade-
quacy in mothers. I cite it at length here to convey its craftiness:

> Do you feel a little guilty every morning when you leave your
> child with its nanny or at the day-care center on your way to work?
> It's only human.
>
> Now Drill Laboratories has found a way to take the ambiva-
> lence out of ambition. Now you can go for that promotion *without*
> all that emotional commotion. . . . No, it's not exactly Mommy . . .
> it's FacsiMommy!
>
> Yes, a realistic life-size model of Mommy—dressed in Mom-
> my's clothes and wearing Mommy's "smell." Your child will never
> be far from a calming representation of yourself. What's more, at
> the flick of a switch, a built-in audiocassette player delivers some
> of Mommy's favorite prerecorded messages. So while you're
> downtown at the Dictaphone, you can still console your child
> thanks to FacsiMommy's realistic working mouth.
>
> And FacsiMommy is so lifelike that many children can't even
> tell the difference!
>
> All you have to do is visit a Drill Laboratories FacsiMommy
> Center and we'll measure you and make a facial mold. In no time,
> you'll be among the growing number of women who realize that
> two mommies *are* better than one. Especially when one's a Facsi-
> Mommy!
>
> Don't let your children say that you were never "there" for
> them. (45)

FacsiMommy works shrewdly to obliterate working mothers'
ability to answer the question, Is my child suffering from my being
out of the home? Does this ad merely name a fear that was already
unraveling contemporary women's self-confidence? Or might it in-
stigate the fear? If the fear was already there, was it based on aban-
doning her own passion for parental duty or on challenging the social role expected of her? And finally, regardless of cause for her
guilt, can such a facsimile actually pacify her obviously torn sense
of responsibility? This ad projects reactionary points of view: children need their mothers at home; women should not be in the
workplace; if a woman does not feel guilty about working, she's
not normal. It also projects that children's and parents' needs aren't
real, that they can be deceived into accepting the needs' satisfaction artificially.

The ad stages two kinds of doubling: first, through FacsiMommy herself (a literal stand-in) and second, by reproducing a historical moment for women (the hyperdomesticity of the 1950s, clearly referenced in the image of FacsiMommy) as an ongoing and universal condition. It is a technique of appropriation that reduces representation to reproduction, critical thought to hysterical thought.

A Virginia Slims advertisement employs similar tactics to render women and history hysterical. Working with the same notion of a cardboard stand-in—in this case a *FacsiWife*—the ad states that in 1904 "Mrs. George Hubbard found a clever way to sneak a cigarette while her husband still got the attention he demanded." The cardboard copy stands obediently beside him in the parlor as she steps outside for a smoke. We are seduced into believing that such mischievous reproductions of self were called for in 1904, but are no longer necessary. A far more modern and apparently "liberated" Virginia Slims woman can smoke wherever she pleases. Perhaps that's so. But the broader message is that the feminist struggle is passé, that women have "arrived," that their plight has changed irrevocably for the better. This is all metonymically deduced, of course, through her new relationship to cigarettes: today she can smoke (damage her health) in public or private. Meanwhile, the reality of extensive profit for the cigarette industry—an industry uninterested in anyone's health or freedom—is buried beneath the illusion of women's liberation. The Philip Morris image collapses historical fact (women are not free) into hysterical fact (women are represented as free) and thus obscures the visibility of women's continued oppression.[3]

Once we recognize this technique of conservative recuperation (representation that sustains status quo values) we find it in many ads and fashion spreads. Collections by French designers of slithery

3. Note the different Surgeon General's warnings on different cigarette ads. They tend to be chosen so that in relation to the image the gravity of the message is undermined. In one Virginia Slims ad, the warning reads: "Cigarette smoke contains carbon monoxide." A conceptual association is made between carbon monoxide and paint fumes, which are indirectly referenced in the ad. As we do not concern ourselves much with paint fumes, we are perhaps led to believe that carbon monoxide is equally innocuous. In another Virginia Slims ad (from the same campaign), the warning reads: "Smoking by pregnant women may result in fetal injury, premature birth, and low birth weight." Being that the model in the ad is clearly not pregnant, the message, once again, reads as immaterial.

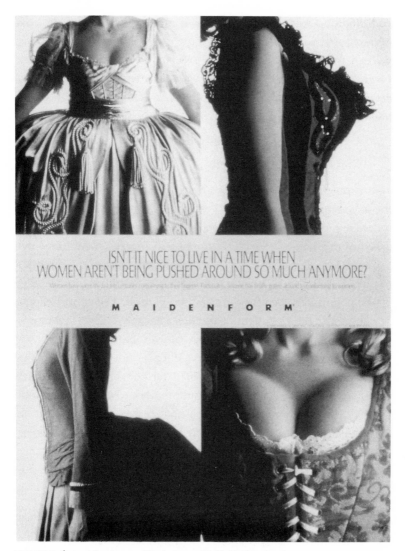

FIGURE 6.2 *Advertisement, "Pushed around," Maidenform (1992). Reprinted by permission of Maidenform, Inc.*

fuchsia sheaths and black velvet bustiers are labeled "The French Revolution." Another spread features female gun-toting Cuban revolutionaries with nails painted, hair in curlers, red lips, thick lashes, and lids lowered flirtatiously, illustrating "the classic expression of the conquistadora." An ad for La Choy Lite soy sauce sells its product with copy that says only "Revolutionary China—a radical idea." In yet another ad, four women leap off their feet for "Tribe, A Fragrance Uprising," advocating the *containment* of rebellion in a purchasable commodity, not an appreciation for women's sociopolitical uprising. Maidenform ads are some of the most cunning in congratulating women for radical progress that exceeds credibility (FIGURE 6.2). Over and over, advertising ideology and aesthetics give perfunctory homage to profound issues, and ambiguous acknowledgment to ethnicities, races, even whole nations, that must be seen but never heard.

Living in the look-machine

It is much easier to theorize critical interventions than perform them. The reason, in part, lies in the authority of the look. Everyday we are required to look at pictures of the things we consume before we consume them. These photographs and advertisements interpret products for us visually, label them with brand names, and direct us to precise locations where we can exchange our monies for the *look* of the commodity, not for the commodity itself. The commodity is nothing more than a functional medium for the deal we make with dominant culture. It does not exist without its representation; together they cross-corrupt and cross-adulate, most often upon the site of the female body. This narcissistic relationship that capital has with itself—in its double-form as commodity and representation of commodity—creates a hermetic seal that thrives on incorporating rebellious looks, uncanny looks, variegated looks, shattered looks, into a unified purchasable look, leading directly to consumerism.

Advertisers know it is all about looking. One frighteningly polemic ad reads as follows:

> *Look* at life in a new way. *Look* at what you've been doing. *Look* at how you've been acting. *Look* at yourself in the mirror. *Look* at your neighbor. *Look* at your partner. *Look* at your friends. *Look* at the world as your oyster. *Look* at what we're saying. *Look* at us. *Look* on the bright side. *Look* at your job. *Look* beyond the obvious. *Look* what matters in life. *Look* harder. *Look* who's talking. *Look* who's doing. *Look* who's making a difference. *Look*, no one said it would be easy. *Look* what the future has in store. *Look*, it's only your career. *Look* & Company Music. (emphasis in original)

While this ad might insinuate that there is more than what meets the eye, it stresses that this other realm is discernible through *Looking!* Many ads—such as those for Vitabath (as seen in FIGURES 3.5 and 3.6)—define how women feel inside by virtue of how she looks outside.[4] Experience is transformed by our looking at it. Sex, gender, and race are assessed—given a price tag—through the criterion of vision. Hysteria too is diagnosed by virtue of how a patient looks and/or performs, as is evident in Charcot's iconography and in contemporary readings of the histrionic personality. The patient who performs hysteria does not exist as a medical subject; she is viewed as an object through which pain performs; her relation to her symptoms is not part of the diagnosis.

In our attempt to recuperate hysteria as a critical analytic, we must reinsert subjectivity into the vacated subjectivity of hysteria. (Where this subjectivity is to come from is not obvious.) One approach is to ask ourselves why we, as women, feel the compulsion to repeat certain *looks*. Why have certain female postures survived not only in advertising and film, but in workplaces, on the streets, and in feminist critiques? Why the classic Monroe look or the porno/bulemic/cover girl look? What particular dialogue is going on between a woman and her body at the moment of these extolled arrests? Why do these arrests continue to have performative meaning for the women who perform them? What narratives accompany the repeated pain and poses? And finally, what is being expressed by the attention, or lack of attention, we confer on these bodily positions?

We can perhaps answer these questions (or at least better understand why we cannot) by understanding the nature of epidemic outbursts. Localized forms of collective delirium are spread through physical and visual proximity during states of excitement and susceptibility (Sirois 1982, 108). The hysterics in Charcot's care, for instance, had attacks only when housed with epileptics, who received much attention when in the throes of a fit. All forms of collective obsessive behavior are characterized by the "contagious, unorganized, uncontrolled nature of the process, which is recognized as spontaneous, unusual, odd, and which is *given neither support nor suppression by the whole community*" (103; my emphasis). This ambivalence is a function of displaced responsibility for the discontent and panic itself.

4. A prime example is the 1993 Nike campaign entitled "Love in Six Acts." Each act is an emotion (lust, fear, disgust, rage) embodied in full-page layout by a different female model. Various looks, or surface appearances, of race and class are woven problematically into the ad imagery. All the models are white and conspicuously upper-class.

The most important aspect is that tensions are unspoken and untold. Epidemic hysteria is thus used by society because it enables . . . people to displace or camouflage the real conflicts. Therefore the outbreaks become the focus where both the *individual and social conflicts are superimposed upon each other and cannot be distinguished* in so far as both are repressed out of consciousness. . . . There is a mirroring of the social conflict in the reality and the individual conflict in the fantasy, and the outbreak acquires the value of an *unconscious symbolic solution for the social situation.* (Sirois 1982, 109; my emphasis)[5]

The particular way in which women have carried in their bodies the "unconscious symbolic solution for the social situation," illuminates some of the obstacles that arise in trying to get a grip on critical vision. Why do women sustain the myths of femininity, including hysteria, that society prescribes? Does complicity suggest we enjoy our mythic roles, or that we are incapable of recognizing the inequality and thus deserve to suffer it? I submit that it is about as easy to fight systemic unconscious symbolism with conscious activism as it is to dictate the stuff of our dreams. Hysteria is a collective anxiety state; fear is preeminent and the real precipitating factors are obscured in commercial myths and fantasies. It is in the possibility of renting social conflict *out of the realm of her charge* (she is not individually culpable or sick) that begins to take the onus off her inevitable performance of these conflicts. When we recognize the forced intimacy between the female body and the social body, discernment between subject and object emerges; the visible and ruptured seam becomes part of women's subsequent performances. It is in the realm of performance *interfaced with this refocused spectatorship* that hysteria may assume critical power.

As women, as consumers, as live bodies, we are being appropriated but appropriating as well. If there were not continual stirrings of discontent and disapproval, however ambivalent or hysterical, what would advertisers be working so hard to quell? Interdependence is

5. Hysteria has been associated with hundreds of outbreaks since the fourteenth century over several continents, including the Loudon nuns of seventeenth-century England, the Barkers, Jumpers, and Shakers of late eighteenth-century Appalachia, and young girls in factories and prisons in Germany in the nineteenth century.

made explicit in a photograph, recirculated as postcard art, of a bill-board advertisement for Fiat overlaid with graffiti. In the ad, a woman lounges on the hood of the Fiat. The graffiti rebuttal reads, "When I'm not busy lying on cars I'm a brain surgeon." A typical body position assigned to women in ads—sexual ornamentation—is reconfigured here by including the discontent: I am more than a car accessory. Fiat suddenly loses its status as the hero of a commercial myth and becomes instead a sidekick, an amusing straight man, in a very different kind of cultural performance.

The notion of dialogue and intertextuality is at the heart of pho-tomontage, used by artists since the 1920s as a strategy of recom-posing bits of preexisting images to create other, more historically inclusive, oppositional images.[6] These montages refuse easy diges-tion of the image; their techniques reveal that mass-reproduced im-ages, no matter how seamless they appear, are in fact patchworks of incongruous "social-body-parts." They make visible to viewers the strategies of representation that are typically obscured.

Montage is used in all advertisements, and recently more and more ads overtly exhibit their cut-and-paste methods. As cultural critics, we have not addressed the complexities of inter-imagery, whether wielded by advertising designers or by those who challenge advertising's visual politics through the same medium. Cultural scholars frequently employ the theories of "con*text*," "decon*text*ual-ization," and "meta*text*" to offset our totalizing and ahistorical tradi-tions. While the notion of text has expanded to include visual and performative texts, we have not grown visually literate: we cannot discern subtle differences between images nor do we comprehend the complexities of how they confer meaning on each other. Images of Darwin beckon to replace Omar Sharif in Maidenform ads, Freud's presence haunts the images of Victoria's Secret, rayographs are family to Moschino and Irving Penn, the body positions of fash-ion babies shed light on ads for Virginia Slims, Charles Dana Gib-son's images enlighten those of Jordache. Consumers exhibit chronic hysterical symptoms—amblyopia, diplopia, and scopic allo-

6. John Heartfield and other dadaists infused popular print media with po-litically provocative counterimages during the rise of fascist power in Ger-many (1920s–1930s). Their work exemplifies the radical potential of pho-tomontage. See Kahn (1985) and Ades (1976).

aesthesia—in which sight is traumatized (blurred, doubled, reversed) but the cause cannot be traced to any intrinsic eye disease. A more sophisticated *looking* and juxtaposition of images as a constructed montage might "mind" these visual traumas.

Self-questioning our repeated body positions, critical witnessing, investigating montage techniques in relation to hysterical imagery— all introduce subjectivity or agency into the hysteria-induced body. But what I find particularly promising in the endeavor to engage hysteria within a feminist agenda, is how the spectacle of hysteria refuses a dualistic mode of us and them. Hysterical duplicity defies polar opposition; it honors, actually embodies, the idea that there is nowhere outside hysterical consumer culture to stand. This is the source of hysteria's bent for resistance. "Opposition" today must be one that knows hysteria well and that launches its performative attacks from slippery and borderless ground.

AUTOBIOGRAPHY OF A RADICAL FEMME, PART 2

I do not reject the images that consume me. I become them. I hesitate, thinking I will be taken for advocating some mindless, reactionary theory of the crude in which images critique structures of language and power. But what I feel inside these dramatically silent images is something not at all crude or simple. I am riddled with ambivalence. I am both the rule and its exception, the law and its outcast, the doctor and the hysteric, I cannot be one without the other. I visually reassemble thought so as to challenge its image of coherence. In so doing, I expose how bereft of vitality and meaning much of our thought is.

Playing hysteria: toward nonoppositional resistance

We live suspended between ourselves and our doubles, we lose the critical power of discretion in that blurred in-between space, and we fail to acknowledge the magical effects and meanings of what we consume daily. The culture of hysteria cannot be escaped, only reiterated and reframed. There is no way out of representation; we work and resist within its playground of ambivalence and sorcery. Benjamin (1976) tells us that the illusion of reality is inescapable; we wear the mask, we can't take it off, we shouldn't try to. We can, however, give the mask—through performance—any number of new expressions and denotations. Artists and activists engage duplicity as a tool of subversion. They duplicate the duplicity of advertising's power in order to expose it, revise it, and steal some of its power.[7]

The power and meaning of mimicry and repetition rest in the tension between challenging status quo politics and buttressing them. The case has been made by feminist theorists (Russo 1986; Butler 1990b; Kolbowski 1990; Diamond 1990–91) that the masked sites and apparatuses of rupture are weapons that women, very practiced in the art of subterfuge, have at their disposal. However, the attempt to reappropriate the aesthetics that ads construct as essential and requisite traits of femininity, runs the risk of reinstating the false essential. According to Butler (1990b), Spivak, as well as Kristeva, suggests that women use certain false and categorical attributes assigned them for purposes of resistance. Butler (1990b) paraphrases Spivak: "Feminists need to rely on an operational essentialism, a false ontology of women as a universal in order to advance a feminist political program. . . . The category of 'women' is not fully expressive . . . but . . . it could be used for strategic purposes" (280).

Similarly, Benjamin (1976) states that the power of transformation lies in how the object contains power. He suggests we must become objects in order to give them new meaning; we must enter the objects and make them act "abnormally." Employing this logic, women must enter the images fashioned by medicine and advertising and make *them* act abnormally. Given her inherited (and forced) intimacy with objects, she has privileged access to their meaning, subtleties, qualities, and capacities.

The insights of Benjamin, Spivak, and Butler can be employed to reenvision and reperform hysteria as a form of resistance, as a demand to be seen and heard when all other means fail.[8] It is precisely

7. Homi Bhabha's postulate of hybridity speaks to the enactment of colonialism rearticulated by the native as a parody. He states, "in the 'hybrid moment' what the native re-writes is not a copy of the colonialist original but a qualitatively different thing-in-itself, where misreadings and incongruities expose the uncertainties and ambivalences of the colonialist text and deny it an authorizing presence" (Bhabha, quoted in Parry 1987, 41–42). See also Bhabha (1984).

The hope here is that "colonial discourse, already disturbed at its source by a doubleness of enunciation, is further subverted . . . when the scenario written by colonialism is given a performance by the native that estranges and undermines the colonialist script" (Parry 1987, 42).

8. See Smith-Rosenberg's 1972 and 1985 discussions of hysteria as a form of resistance, albeit somatized.

because the hysteric embodies the social power politic of advertising and colonial power—the collapse of theatrics into truth—that hysterical performance can be garnered as an exemplary model for *critique* of that power politic. In the spectacle of hysterical symptomology, she implicates the appropriation of women's experience by medical science and the advertiser. She acts out the unseemly histrionics she has been subjected to (male hysteria) not only to expose its origins, but to give it another meaning.

AUTOBIOGRAPHY OF A RADICAL FEMME, PART 3

In embodying spectacle I assume presence, and this presence, even if marked lacking, adds subjectivity to that which is thought to be without it. I give subjectivity to the very spectacle that erases me. I am a female hysteric, a radical femme. I am acquiring my own untenable gait and enjoying it. This is possible only if I ignore the necessity of being a substantial person. Only if I dare for once to move before exhaustively consulting theory, method, and context. Only if I remain silent and overcome the premature urge to give expression to the unutterable. At least for this brief moment, the inevitable glut of analysis and self-indulgence is postponed. And I realize pleasure.

But finally, I feel ridiculous and I can't sustain the effort. I fear that my abandon to spectacle will betray me, appear as complicity with the very power structure I despise. Presence for the feminist critic is a dance with phobia.

The mockery the hysteric speaks will likely rearticulate woman as caricature and as fool. The potential problems of inaugurating a project of "performing hysteria" for resistant purposes are many. As we live a form of epidemic hysteria, the ability to access and then manipulate our blurred vision for purposes of effecting critical distance grows less and less viable. Efforts in this direction often feel exceptionally trivial within a mediated environment that rapidly transforms difference into sameness. Because of the form of the hysteric's protest and its century-old stigmatization as a personal, somatic, inarticulate, and feminized lack of control, the notion of *hysterical opposition* seems an oxymoron. The physicalized language in which hysteria ridicules power is conventionally read as a crude form of self-ridicule. A critique that emerges through hysterical performances will be obscured by the register in which the hysteric speaks.

So the question arises, What good is a protest, however critical its intentions may be, that reads culturally as affliction? If advertisers, doctors, and other popular power brokers succeed in representing signs of resistance as inconsequential (if not entirely indiscernible), then the notions of masquerade, mimicry, parody, and sarcasm, lose their transgressive potential. Do Cindy Sherman's visual commentaries as an avant-garde artist (such as her self-portrait of the blank-staring model strewn twisted and lifeless in a field, or her rendition of the cover girl as a contemptible and obscene prostitute) read critically amid images that convey embalmed and/or sexually objectified women? And if they do, for how long can they survive as representations that make a difference? How do consumers, glutted by visual stimulation and exposed to infinitesimal subtleties along the spectrum of representation, discern the differences of intention and meaning between images so visually similar? How does Barbara Kruger's image of a woman reflected in a shattered mirror—"You are not yourself"—provide any critical insight when juxtaposed with near-identical images that sell bitters for the treatment of neurasthenia in the 1890s and antiseptics for female acne in the 1990s? (FIGURES 6.3 and 6.4)?[9] Kruger's image could just as easily be an ad for ibuprofen's fast relief for PMS, or for New Freedom feminine pads promising desired comfort and peace of mind. Can we discern a difference between comedienne Sandra Bernhard's exaggerated sexual charades and grimaces, even lesbian overtones, in her supposedly tongue-in-cheek *Playboy* spread (Bernhard 1992), and the poses and countenances of more standard *Playboy* bunnies?[10]

It is with varying degrees of success that these and other artists use the politics of ambivalence to critique the ambivalent power structure that informs so much of advertising design. For instance, they use sarcasm (from the Greek *sarkazein*, "to tear flesh" or "to

9. Barbara Kruger was a graphic designer and photo editor with *Condé Nast* before she began creating her billboard-size "advertisements."

10. Several other images created by contemporary artists raise similar questions: David Lynch created a series of "postmodern heads" featuring women's whitewashed and balded heads with black metallic horns protruding from their scalps; Cindy Sherman's female-body-part sculptures appear to represent/reproduce Hans Bellmer's dismembered Poupées (dolls and figurines combined to suggest terrifying images of women); Todd Haynes's casting of Barbie dolls in his film about famous singer/anorexic Karen Carpenter, both challenges and reinserts the Barbie ideal.

FIGURE 6.3 *Trade card, Brown's Iron Bitters (1890–1895).*
Printer: A. Hoen & Co., Lith. Baltimore.

bite the lips in rage" [Skeat 1956, 534]) as a weapon to unveil the sarcasm that contaminates popular imagery. Similarly, the work of these artists is a kind of hysterical, sometimes electroshock, approach to hysteria itself. We feel it in Kruger's billboard-sized visual slaps and urgent declarations. It is evident in Cindy Sherman's multiple permutations of self and in her exhibit of pornographic poses of plastic dummies that uncomfortably interface pleasure and disgust. We recognize it in Kiki Smith's roomful of female nudes in humiliating poses that are "about the things that kill you. . . . [As an artist] you can stick it up in people's faces, cram it down their throats" (Smith, quoted in Nesbitt 1992, 78). All employ dominant techniques of representation of gender to implicate the rigging of gender, to satirize the look machinery and gaze police. They blur the lines between artifice and fact to demonstrate how the *media itself does it* as an act of vogueing, as compared to truth-saying. These artists inform us that fashion is always surreal. From their examples, we learn that performances of hysteria, enacted within a feminist agenda, cannot undo the hysterical script itself—the real will not be salvaged from the sham—but the script can be staged as a carnivalesque marvel, or a hysterical one-upping.

The more I live with popular ad images, the more I recognize that their written and visual texts are steeped in terror and laden with concealed vulnerability. The ads are as hysterical as we are, exhibiting symptoms ranging from the Calvin Klein detachment of la belle indifférence to the histrionic overexcitement of Crazy Eddie. In this awareness comes hope regarding efforts to recode the images we live with so intimately. I imagine hysteria offering insight toward nonoppositional resistance: a resistance that no longer refuses being polluted by that which is being resisted. Ads, equally hysterical, are neurological outlets we are irrevocably plugged into. An ad for Fantastik cleanser graphically displays how a commodity can create a symptom: the product, or "hero," wipes away language—erases mental exertion for its female consumers—as easily as a sponge

FIGURE 6.4 *Barbara Kruger,* Untitled *(You are not yourself) (1983). Reprinted by permission of Barbara Kruger.*

wipes away dirt (FIGURE 6.5). Is this empty presence not what the somatic symptom is? How might empty presence—from amnesia to seizure—be restaged to profit women, as it has profited so many commercial campaigns?

I am not suggesting that by restaging the various tropes of duplicity discussed in these pages—masquerade, ventriloquism, narrative, ritual, magic—women will necessarily reinvent the cultural experi-

FIGURE 6.5 *Advertisement, Fantastik (1989). Reprinted by permission of DowBrands L.P.*

ence of gender. Nor do I believe that hysteria, as it currently manifests itself as normalized consumer behavior, can be considered subversive (as does Smith-Rosenberg 1972), though I am enthralled by its latent potential. I do believe that the double-talking symptoms of hysteria can be strategically juxtaposed with what they displace, thus expressing the underlying stories of their creation.

Most intriguing, I imagine that through the repetition of the arrested body of hysteria, we are rehearsing an escape, not into fugue or dissociative states of pain, paralysis, or puerilism, but into the potential of spectacle and its oversignified mockery. The spectacle of hysteria is perfectly inappropriate, in part, because the inappropriateness captures the very paradox of spectacle-making. In assuming the only body we have—that of the hysteric—we embrace the absurd spectacle we are primed to resist; in becoming the mask itself we are particularly privy to, perhaps humbled by, what lies behind it.

It is by now evident that the commodity of consumer capitalism, the female body in advertising, and the hysteric within the arena of medical science, are mediums for commerce between the apparent and the hidden. What I hope is increasingly evident is how visual intelligence, bodily exclamations, and silent spectacles manage to stage a viable critique of the complex and the corrupt—how silence undoes dominant narratives, how image critiques ideology.

AUTOBIOGRAPHY OF A RADICAL FEMME, PART 4

I am suspicious of the angry woman. I am weary of the discourse of female pretense as power when delivered in progressively verbose waves of new feminisms. I'm bored with futile attempts to redeem vapid, anticommittal, postmodern ambiguity and obscurity from its entertaining but safe epistemological theories. Instead, I let speculation riddle my body and I fly precariously through the air in impossible postures, hanging precipitously over empty space. I walk the spiked pickets of a white picket fence. Perhaps I've surrendered myself to the empty superlatives of popular entertainment but my own fleshy and exhilarated presence is undeniable. I disappear into the spectacle of power, power as excess; I stop resisting the spectacle of inappropriateness to which I am assigned, I indulge the dignity of inappropriateness, and in this disappearance, I am shamelessly full.

Hysteria knows abandon and yet this abandon is not nostalgic or neutral; it is present and partial. It teaches that pleasure and resistance are not mutually exclusive. In our performances of hysteria, we can engage the *desires* that hysterical symptoms have displaced. We can attend to and celebrate that which women are fighting for alongside that which women are fighting against.

Hysterical symptoms are all we've got. They are "the real thing" and they lead the dramatic cry: "Representation is dead, long live representation!"

Bibliography

Abse, Wilfred D. 1982. "Multiple Personality." In *Hysteria*, edited by Alec Roy. New York: John Wiley and Sons.

———. 1987. *Hysteria and Related Mental Disorders: An Approach to Psychological Medicine*. Bristol, Great Britain: Wright.

Ades, Dawn. 1976. *Photomontage*. London: Thames and Hudson.

Althusser, Louis. 1971. "Ideology and Ideological State Apparatuses." In *Lenin and Philosophy, and Other Essays*, translated by Ben Brewster. New York: Monthly Review Press.

American Psychiatric Association. 1987. *Diagnostic and Statistical Manual of Mental Disorders: DSM-III-R*. 3d ed., rev. Washington, D.C.: American Psychiatric Association.

Anthony, E. James. 1982. "Hysteria in Childhood." In *Hysteria*, edited by Alec Roy. New York: John Wiley and Sons.

Apter, Emily, and William Pietz, eds. 1993. *Fetishism as Cultural Discourse*. Ithaca: Cornell University Press.

Ascher, Carol. 1987. "Selling to Ms. Consumer." In *American Media and Mass Culture: Left Perspectives*, edited by Donald Lazere. Berkeley and Los Angles: University of California Press.

Bakhtin, Mikhail. 1984. *Rabelais and His World*. Translated by Hélène Iswolsky. Bloomington: Indiana University Press.

Barthes, Roland. 1977a. "The Photographic Message." In *Image, Music, Text*, translated by Stephen Heath. New York: Noonday.

———. 1977b. "Rhetoric of the Image." In *Image, Music, Text*, translated by Stephen Heath. New York: Noonday.

———. 1981. *Camera Lucida: Reflections on Photography*. Translated by Richard Howard. New York: Noonday.

———. 1983. *The Fashion System*, translated by Matthew Ward and Richard Howard. New York: Hill and Wang.

——— 1987[1957]. *Mythologies*. Translated by Annette Lavers. New York: Hill and Wang.

Baudrillard, Jean. 1975. *The Mirror of Production*. Translated by Mark Poster. St. Louis: Telos.

———. 1983. *Simulations*. Translated by Paul Foss, Paul Patton, and Philip Beitchman. New York: Semiotext(e).

———. 1984. "The Precession of Simulacra." In *Art After Modernism: Rethinking Representation*, edited by Brian Wallis. New York: New Museum of Contemporary Art.

———. 1990a [1983]. *Fatal Strategies*. Edited by Jim Fleming and Philip Beitchman. Translated by W. G. J. Niesluchowski. New York: Semiotext(e).

———. 1990b [1979]. *Seduction*. Translated by Brian Singer. New York: St. Martin's.

Benjamin, Walter. 1969a. "Theses on the Philosophy of History." In *Illuminations*, edited by Hannah Arendt, translated by Harry Zohn. New York: Schocken Books.

———. 1969b. "The Work of Art in the Age of Mechanical Reproduction." In *Illuminations*, edited by Hannah Arendt, translated by Harry Zohn. New York: Schocken Books.

———. 1976. *Charles Baudelaire: A Lyric Poet in the Era of High Capitalism*. Translated by Harry Zohn. London: Verso.

———. 1977. *The Origin of German Tragic Drama*. Translated by John Osborne. London: NLB.

———. 1984. "Theoretics of Knowledge; Theory of Progress." *The Philosophical Forum* 15, nos. 1–2 (Fall–Winter 1983–84): 1–39.

———. 1986. "On the Mimetic Faculty." In *Reflections: Essays, Aphorisms, Autobiographical Writings*, translated by Edmund Jephcott. New York: Schocken Books.

Bensimon, Gilles. 1990. "Girls Will Be Boys." *Elle* (October): 292.

———. 1991. "Basic Black Unleashed." *Elle* (March): 137.

———. 1993. "The Natural Resources." *Elle* (January): 74.

Berger, John. 1972. *Ways of Seeing*. London: British Broadcasting Corporation.

Bernays, Edward L. 1928. *Propaganda*. New York: Horace Liveright.

Bernhard, Sandra. 1992. "Not Just Another Pretty Face." *Playboy* (September): 70–77.

Bernheimer, Charles, and Claire Kahane, eds. 1985. *In Dora's Case: Freud, Hysteria, Feminism*. New York: Columbia University Press.

Bhabha, Homi. 1984. "Of Mimicry and Men: The Ambivalence of Colonial Discourse." *October* 28 (Spring): 125–33.

Bobo, Jacqueline. 1988. "The *Color Purple*: Black Women as Cultural Readers. In *Female Spectators: Looking at Film and Television*, edited by Deidre Pribram. New York: Verso.

Bordo, Susan. 1990. "Reading the Slender Body." In *Body/Politics: Women and the Discourses of Science*, edited by Mary Jacobus, Evelyn Fox Keller, and Sally Shuttleworth. New York: Routledge.

——. 1993. *Unbearable Weight: Feminism, Western Culture, and the Body*. Berkeley and Los Angeles: University of California Press.

Bourneville, D. M., and P. Regnard. 1877–80. *Iconographie Photographique de la Salpêtrière*. Paris, vol. 1, 1877; vol. 2, 1878; vol. 3, 1879–80.

Bramly, Serge. 1977. *Macumba: The Teachings of Maria-José, Mother of the Gods*. New York: Avon Books.

Breuer, Josef, and Sigmund Freud. 1955 [1893]. *Studies on Hysteria*. Translated by and edited by James Strachey. New York: Basic Books.

Buck-Morss, Susan. 1989. *Dialectics of Seeing: Walter Benjamin and the Arcades Project*. Cambridge, Mass.: MIT Press.

Buci-Glucksmann, Christine. 1987. "Catastrophic Utopia: The Feminine as Allegory of the Modern." In *The Making of the Modern Body: Sexuality and Society in the Nineteenth Century*, edited by Catherine Gallagher and Thomas Laqueur. Berkeley and Los Angeles: University of California Press.

Butler, Judith. 1990a. *Gender Trouble: Feminism and the Subversion of Identity*. New York: Routledge.

——. 1990b. "Performative Acts and Gender Constitution: An Essay in Phenomenology and Feminist Theory." In *Performing Feminisms: Feminist Critical Theory and Theatre,* edited by Sue Ellen Case. Baltimore: Johns Hopkins University Press.

——. 1993. *Bodies That Matter: On the Discursive Limits of "Sex."* New York and London: Routledge.

Buzzi, Giancarlo. 1968. *Advertising: Its Cultural and Political Effects*. Translated by B. David Garmize. Minneapolis: University of Minnesota Press.

Cardinal, M. 1984. *The Words to Say It*. Translated by P. Goodhart. London: Picador/Pan Books.

Charcot, Jean-Martin. 1962 [1881]. *Lectures on the Disease of The Nervous System*. 2d ser. Translated by and edited by George Sigerson. New York: Hafner.

Chernin, Kim. 1985. *The Hungry Self: Women, Eating and Identity*. New York: Harper and Row.

Chodoff, Paul. 1982. "The Hysterical Personality Disorder: A Psychotherapeutic Approach." In *Hysteria*, edited by Alec Roy. New York: John Wiley and Sons.

Cixous, Hélène, and Catherine Clément. 1975. *The Newly Born Woman*.

Translated by Betsy Wing. Theory and History of Literature 24. Minneapolis: University of Minnesota Press.

Clark, Eric. 1989. *The Wantmakers: The World of Advertising: How They Make You Buy*. New York: Viking.

Copjec, Joan. 1981. "Flavit et Dissipati Sunt." *October* 18 (Fall): 22–40.

———. 1991. "Vampires, Breast-Feeding, and Anxiety," *October* 58 (Fall): 25–43.

Cox, G. Robert, and Edward J. McGee. 1990. *The Ad Game: Playing to Win*. Englewood Cliffs, N.J.: Prentice Hall.

Crawford, Robert. 1984. "A Cultural Account of 'Health': Control, Release, and the Social Body." In *Issues in the Political Economy of Health Care*, edited by John B. McKinlay. New York: Tavistock.

David-Menard, Monique. 1989. *Hysteria from Freud to Lacan: Body and Language in Psychoanalysis*. Translated by Catherine Porter. Ithaca: Cornell University Press.

Davy, Kate. 1986. "Buying and Selling the Look." *Parachute* (Summer): 21–24.

Deleuze, Gilles, and Felix Guattari. 1983. *Anti-Oedipus: Capitalism and Schizophrenia*. Translated by Robert Hurley, Mark Seem, and Helen R. Lane. Minneapolis: University of Minnesota Press.

———. 1988a. "1730: Becoming-Intense, Becoming-Animal, Becoming . . . Imperceptible . . ." In *A Thousand Plateaus: Capitalism and Schizophrenia*, translated by Brian Massumi. Minneapolis: University of Minnesota Press.

———. 1988b. "Year Zero: Faciality." In *A Thousand Plateaus: Capitalism and Schizophrenia*, translated by Brian Massumi. Minneapolis: University of Minnesota Press.

Diamond, Elin. 1989. "Mimesis, Mimicry, and the 'True-Real.'" *Modern Drama* 32, no. 1 (March): 58–72.

———. 1990–91. "Realism and Hysteria: Toward a Feminist Mimesis." *Discourse* 13, no. 1 (Fall–Winter): 59–92.

———. 1997. *Unmaking Mimesis: Essays on Feminism and Theater*. London: Routledge.

Doane, Mary Ann. 1991a. "Dark Continents: Epistemologies of Racial and Sexual Difference in Psychoanalysis and the Cinema." In *Femmes Fatales: Feminism, Film Theory, Psychoanalysis*. New York: Routledge.

———. 1991b. "Masquerade Reconsidered: Further Thoughts on the Female Spectator." In *Femmes Fatales: Feminism, Film Theory, Psychoanalysis*. New York: Routledge.

Dresser, Norine. 1989. *American Vampires: Fans, Victims, Practitioners*. New York: Vintage Books.

Edwards, Owen. 1990. "The Zen of Things." *American Photo* (November–December): 64–117.

Ehrenreich, Barbara, and Deidre English. 1973. *Complaints and Disorders: The Politics of Sickness.* Old Westbury, N.Y.: Feminist Press.

———. 1978. *For Her Own Good: 150 Years of the Experts' Advice to Women.* Garden City, N.Y.: Anchor.

Evans, Martha Noel. 1989a. "Corsets and Convulsions: Controlling Women's Bodies in Late Nineteenth Century France." Presented at the conference on Theatre of the Female Body, Hartford, Connecticut.

———. 1989b. "Hysteria and the Seduction of Theory." In *Seduction and Theory: Readings of Gender, Representation, and Rhetoric,* edited by Dianne Hunter. Chicago: University of Illinois Press.

Ewart, Gavin. 1985. "The Joys of Surgery." In *The Young Pobble's Guide to His Toes.* London: Hutchinson.

Ewen, Stuart. 1976. *Captains of Consciousness: Advertising and the Social Roots of the Consumer Culture.* New York: McGraw-Hill.

———. 1988. *All Consuming Images: The Politics of Style in Contemporary Culture.* New York: Basic Books.

Ewen, Stuart, and Elizabeth Ewen. 1982. *Channels of Desire: Mass Images and the Shaping of American Consciousness.* New York: McGraw-Hill.

Ey, Henri. 1982. "History and Analysis of the Concept." In *Hysteria,* edited by Alec Roy. New York: John Wiley and Sons.

Eysenck, H. J. 1982. "A Psychological Theory of Hysteria" In *Hysteria,* edited by Alec Roy. New York: John Wiley and Sons.

Faludi, Susan. 1991. *Backlash: The Undeclared War Against American Women.* New York: Doubleday.

Feld, Steven. 1990. *Sound and Sentiment: Birds, Weeping, Poetics, and Song in Kaluli Expression.* Philadelphia: University of Pennsylvania Press.

Fenton, George W. 1982. "Hysterical Alterations of Consciousness." In *Hysteria,* edited by Alec Roy. New York: John Wiley and Sons.

Fleming, Anne Taylor. 1991. "Living Dolls." *Allure* (March): 129–33.

Foucault, Michel. 1967. *Madness and Civilization: A History of Insanity in the Age of Reason.* Translated by Richard Howard. London: Tavistock.

———. 1979. *Discipline and Punish: The Birth of the Prison.* Translated by Alan Sheridan. New York: Vintage Books.

———. 1980. *The History of Sexuality.* Vol. 1, *An Introduction.* Translated by Robert Hurley. New York: Vintage Books.

Fox, Charles D. 1913. *Psychopathology of Hysteria.* Boston: Gorham.

Fox, Sally. 1987. *The Victorian Woman: A Book of Days.* Boston: Little, Brown.

Fox, Stephen. 1984. *The Mirror Makers: A History of American Advertising and Its Creators.* New York: William Morrow.

Frederick, Christine. 1929. *Selling Mrs. Consumer.* New York: Business Bourse.

Freud, Sigmund. 1953 [1897]. "Extracts from the Fliess Papers." In *The Standard Edition of the Complete Psychological Works of Sigmund Freud,* vol. 1, edited and translated by James Strachey. London: Hogarth, 1953–1974.

——. 1957a [1917]. "Mourning and Melancholia." In *The Standard Edition of the Complete Psychological Works of Sigmund Freud*, vol. 14, edited and translated by James Strachey. London: Hogarth, 1953–74.

——. 1957b [1926]. "The Question of Lay Analysis." In *The Standard Edition of the Complete Psychological Works of Sigmund Freud*, vol. 22, edited and translated by James Strachey. London: Hogarth, 1953–74.

——. 1957c [1917–19]. "The 'Uncanny.'" In *The Standard Edition of the Complete Psychological Works of Sigmund Freud*, vol. 17, edited and translated by James Strachey. London: Hogarth, 1953–74.

——. 1959 [1927]. "Fetishism." In *Collected Papers*, vol. 5, edited by James Strachey. New York: Basic Books.

——. 1961 [1920]. *Beyond the Pleasure Principle*. Translated by James Strachey. New York: Norton.

——. 1962 [1905]. *Three Essays on the Theory of Sexuality*. Translated by James Strachey. New York: Basic Books.

——. 1963a [1905]. *Dora: An Analysis of a Case of Hysteria*. New York: Collier.

——. 1963b [1914]. "On Narcissism: An Introduction." In *General Psychological Theory: Papers on Metapsychology*. New York: Collier.

——. 1965 [1933]. "Femininity." In *New Introductory Lectures on Psychoanalysis*, edited by and translated by James Strachey. New York: Norton.

Fromm, Erich. 1962. *Beyond the Chains of Illusion: My Encounter with Marx and Freud*. New York: Simon and Schuster.

Fuss, Diana. 1989. *Essentially Speaking: Feminism, Nature and Difference*. New York: Routledge.

——. 1992. "Fashion and the Homospectatorial Look," *Critical Inquiry* (Summer): 713–37.

Gallagher, Catherine. 1987. *The Making of the Modern Body: Sexuality and Society in the Nineteenth Century*. Berkeley and Los Angeles: University of California Press.

Gilbert, Sandra M., and Susan Gubar. 1979. *The Madwoman in the Attic: The Woman Writer and the Nineteenth Century Imagination*. New Haven: Yale University Press.

Gilman, Charlotte Perkins. 1980 [1892]. "The Yellow Wallpaper." In *The Charlotte Perkins Gilman Reader: "The Yellow Wallpaper" and Other Fiction*, edited by Ann J. Lane. New York: Pantheon.

Gilman, Sander L., ed. 1976. *The Face of Madness: Hugh W. Diamond and the Origins of Psychiatric Photography*. New York: Brunner-Mazel.

——. 1985a. "Black Bodies, White Bodies: Toward an Iconography of Female Sexuality in Late Nineteenth-Century Art, Medicine, and Literature." *Critical Inquiry* 12 (Autumn): 204–42.

——. 1985b. *Difference and Pathology: Stereotypes of Sexuality, Race, and Madness*. Ithaca: Cornell University Press.

———. 1991. *The Jew's Body*. New York: Routledge.

Glass, James M. 1993. *Shattered Selves: Multiple Personality in a Postmodern World*. Ithaca: Cornell University Press.

Goffman, Erving. 1979. *Gender Advertisements*. Cambridge, Mass.: Harvard University Press.

Gold, Arthur, and Robert Kizdale. 1991. *The Divine Sarah: A Life of Sarah Bernhardt*. New York: Knopf.

Graham, Dan. 1982. "The End of Liberalism (Part II)." In *The Unnecessary Image*, edited by Peter D'Agostino and Antonio Muntadas. New York: Tanam.

Griggors, Camilla. 1997. "The Despotic Face of White Femininity." In *Becoming-Woman*. Minneapolis: University of Minnesota Press.

Grundberg, Andy. 1990. "The Unnatural Coupling of Surrealism and Photography." In *The Critical Image: Essays on Contempory Photography*, edited by Carol Squiers. Seattle: Bay Press.

Haraway, Donna. 1991. *Simians, Cyborgs, and Women: The Reinvention of Nature*. New York: Routledge.

Hebdige, Dick. 1988. *Hiding in the Light: On Images and Things*. London: Routledge.

Hirschmuller, Albrecht. 1978. *The Life and Work of Josef Breuer*. New York: New York University Press.

Hochswender, Woody. 1992. "When the Camera Lies." *New York Times*, 21 June, section 9, 8.

hooks, bell. 1992. *Black Looks: Race and Representation*. Boston: South End.

Huyssen, Andreas. 1986. "Mass Culture as Woman: Modernism's Other." *In After the Great Divide: Modernism, Mass Culture, Postmodernism*. Bloomington: Indiana University Press.

Irigaray, Luce. 1985a. *Speculum of the Other Woman*. Translated by Gillian C. Gill. Ithaca: Cornell University Press.

———. 1985b. *This Sex Which Is Not One*. Translated by Catherine Porter. Ithaca: Cornell University Press.

Jacobus, Mary, E. Fox Keller, and Sally Shuttleworth, eds. 1990. *Body/Politics: Women and the Discourses of Science*. New York: Routledge.

James, Stanlie M., and Busia, Abena P. A., eds. 1993. *Theorizing Black Feminisms: The Visionary Pragmatism of Black Women*. New York: Routledge.

Janet, P. 1920. *The Major Symptoms of Hysteria*, 2d ed. New York: Macmillan.

Jardine, Alice. 1987. "Of Bodies and Technologies." In *Discussions in Contemporary Culture 1*, edited by Hal Foster. Seattle: Bay Press.

Jaspers, K. 1963. *General Psychopathology*. Translated by J. Hoenig and M. W. Hamilton. Chicago: University of Chicago Press.

Jastrow, Robert, ed. 1984. *The Essential Darwin*. Boston: Little, Brown.

Jones, Ernest. 1953. *The Life and Work of Sigmund Freud*. New York: Basic Books.

Jordanova, Ludmilla. 1980. "Natural Facts: A Historical Perspective on Science and Sexuality." In *Nature, Culture and Gender*, edited by Carol P. MacCormack and Marilyn Strathern. Cambridge: Cambridge University Press.

———. 1989. *Sexual Visions: Images of Gender in Science and Medicine between the Eighteenth and Twentieth Centuries*. Madison: University of Wisconsin Press.

Kahn, Douglas. 1985. *John Heartfield: Art and Mass Media*. New York: Tanam.

Kaplan, Ann. 1983a. "Is the Gaze Male?" In *Powers of Desire: The Politics of Sexuality*, edited by Ann Snitow, Christine Stansell, and Sharon Thompson. New York: Monthly Review Press.

———. 1983b. "Theories of Melodrama: A Feminist Perspective." *Women and Performance* 1:40–48.

Katz, Richard. 1982. *Boiling Energy: Community Healing among the Kalahari Kung*. Cambridge, Mass: Harvard University Press.

Kaye, Elizabeth. 1993. "So Weak, So Powerful." *New York Times*, Styles Section, 6 June, 1.

Keller, Evelyn Fox. 1985. *Reflections on Gender and Science*. New Haven: Yale University Press.

Kendell, R. E. 1982. "A New Look at Hysteria." In *Hysteria*, edited by Alec Roy. New York: John Wiley and Sons.

Klerman, Gerald L. 1982. "Hysteria and Depression." In *Hysteria*, edited by Alec Roy. New York: John Wiley and Sons.

Kolbowski, Silvia. 1990. "Playing with Dolls." In *The Critical Image: Essays on Contemporary Photography*, edited by Carol Squiers. Seattle: Bay Press.

Krauss, Rosalind. 1990. "A Note on Photography and the Simulacral." In *The Critical Image*, edited by Carol Squiers. Seattle: Bay Press.

———. 1993. *The Optical Unconscious*. Cambridge, Mass.: MIT Press.

Krauss, Rosalind, and Jane Livingston, eds. 1985a. "Corpus Delicti." In *L'Amour Fou*. Washington, D.C., and New York: Corcoran Gallery of Art and Abbeville Press.

———. 1985b. "Photography in the Service of Surrealism." In *L'Amour Fou*. Washington, D.C., and New York: Corcoran Gallery of Art and Abbeville Press.

Kretschmer, Ernst. 1960. *Hysteria, Reflex and Instinct*. New York: Philosophical Library.

Kristeva, Julia. 1986. "The True-Real." In *The Kristeva Reader*, edited by Toril Moi. New York: Columbia University Press.

———. 1987. "Freud and Love: Treatment and Its Discontents." In *Tales of Love*. New York: Columbia University Press.

———. 1995. "Countertransference: A Revived Hysteria." In *New Maladies of the Soul*, translated by Ross Guberman. New York: Columbia University Press.

Krohn, Alan. 1978. *Hysteria: The Elusive Neurosis*. Vol. 12, nos. 1–2. Monograph 45–46. New York: International Universities Press.

Kroker, Arthur, Marilouise Kroker, and David Cook. 1989. *Panic Encyclopedia: The Defininitive Guide to the Postmodern Scene.* New York: St. Martin's.

Kunzle, David. 1982. *Fashion and Fetishism: A Social History of the Corset, Tight-Lacing, and Other Forms of Body-Sculpture in the West.* Totowa, N.J.: Rowman and Littlefield.

Lacan, Jacques. 1968. "The Function of Language in Psychoanalysis." In *The Language of the Self: The Function of Language in Psychoanalysis,* edited and translated by Anthony Wilden. Baltimore: Johns Hopkins University Press.

Lane, Ann J., ed. 1980. *The Charlotte Perkins Gilman Reader: "The Yellow Wallpaper and Other Fiction.* New York: Pantheon.

Larkin, Alile Sharon. 1988. "Black Women Film-makers Defining Ourselves: Feminism in Our Own Voice." In *Female Spectators: Looking at Film and Television,* edited by Deidre Pribram. New York: Verso.

Lasch, Christopher. 1979. *The Culture of Narcissism: American Life in an Age of Diminishing Expectations.* New York: Warner Books.

Lears, Jackson. 1994. *Fables of Abundance: A Cultural History of Advertising in America.* New York: Basic Books.

Lerner, Harriet E. 1981. "The Hysterical Personality: A 'Woman's Disease.' " In *Women and Mental Health,* edited by Elizabeth Howell and Marjorie Bayes. New York: Basic Books.

Lewis, Helen B. 1981. "Madness in Women." In *Women and Mental Health,* edited by Elizabeth Howell and Marjorie Bayes. New York: Basic Books.

Logan, Peter. 1993. "Reading and Writing Hysteria: Thomas Trotter and William Godwin." Unpublished paper, presented at the Modern Language Association, New York City 1993.

Lombroso, Cesare, and William Ferrero. 1920. *The Female Offender.* New York: D. Appleton.

Marcuse, Herbert. 1964. *One-Dimensional Man: Studies in the Ideology of Advanced Industrial Society.* Boston: Beacon.

Marx, Karl. 1993 [1867]. *Capital.* Provo, Utah: Regal Publications.

McCarren, Felicia. 1995. "The 'Symptomatic Act' Circa 1900: Hysteria, Hypnosis, Electricity, Dance." *Critical Inquiry* 21 (Summer): 748–74.

McClintock, Anne. 1995. *Imperial Leather: Race, Gender and Sexuality in the Colonial Context.* New York: Routledge.

Merskey, Harold. 1982. "Hysterical Mechanisms and Pain." In *Hysteria,* edited by Alec Roy. New York: John Wiley and Sons.

Metter, Bert. 1990. "Advertising in the Age of Spin." *Ad Age* (October): 36.

Metz, Christian. 1990. "Photography and Fetish." In *The Critical Image,* edited by Carol Squiers. Seattle: Bay Press.

Meyers, William. 1984. *The Image-Makers: Power and Persuasion on Madison Avenue.* New York: Times Books.

Mitchell, S. Weir. 1972 [1887]. *Doctor and Patient.* New York: Arno.

Modleski, Tania. 1982. *Loving With a Vengeance: Mass-Produced Fantasies for Women*. Hamden, Conn.: Archon.

——. 1986a. "Femininity as Mas(s)querade: A Feminist Approach to Mass Culture." In *High Theory, Low Culture*, edited by Colin McCabe. Manchester: University of Manchester Press.

——. 1986b. *Studies in Entertainment: Critical Approaches to Mass Culture*, edited by Tania Modleski. Bloomington: Indiana University Press.

——. 1987. "The Search for Tomorrow in Today's Soap Operas." In *American Media and Mass Culture: Left Perspectives*, edited by Donald Lazere. Berkeley and Los Angeles: University of California Press.

Morrison, Toni, ed. 1992. *Race-ing Justice, En-gendering Power*. New York: Pantheon Books.

Mulvey, Laura. 1975. "Visual Pleasure and Narrative Cinema." *Screen* 16, no. 3 (Autumn): 412–28.

Myerson, Abraham. 1920. *The Nervous Housewife*. Boston: Little, Brown.

Nesbitt, Lois. 1992. "Shock of the Nasty: Art's Bad Girls." *Elle* (December): 78.

Ogilvy, David. 1988 [1963]. *Confessions of an Advertising Man*. New York: Atheneum.

Orvell, Miles. 1989. *The Real Thing: Imitation and Authenticity in American Culture, 1880–1940*. Chapel Hill: University of North Carolina Press.

Owens, Craig. 1983. "Medusa Effect, or The Specular Ruse." In *We Won't Play Nature to Your Culture/Barbara Kruger*. London: Institute of Contemporary Arts.

Packard, Vance. 1957. *The Hidden Persuaders*. New York: David McKay.

——. 1961. *The Status Seekers*. New York: Penguin.

Parry, Benita. 1987. "Problems in Current Theories of Colonial Discourse." *Oxford Literary Review* 9, nos. 1–2: 27–58.

Phelan, Peggy. 1993. *Unmarked: The Politics of Performance*. London: Routledge.

Pietz, William. 1993. "Fetishism and Materialism: The Limits of Theory in Marx." In *Fetishism as Cultural Discourse*, edited by Emily Apter and William Pietz. Ithaca: Cornell University Press.

Pincus, Jonathan. 1982. *Hysteria Presenting to the Neurologist*, edited by Alec Roy. New York: John Wiley and Sons.

Preston, Ivan L. 1975. *The Great American Blow-Up: Puffery in Advertising and Selling*. Madison: University of Wisconsin Press.

Ricoeur, Paul. 1970. *Freud and Philosophy: An Essay on Interpretation*. New Haven: Yale University Press.

Ries, Al, and Jack Trout. 1986. *Marketing Warfare*. New York: New American Library.

Riviere, Joan. 1929. "Womanliness as a Masquerade." *International Journal of Psychoanalysis*, 10: 303–13.

Roy, Alec. 1982. "Hysterical Neurosis." In *Hysteria*, edited by Alec Roy. New York: John Wiley and Sons.

Rubin, Gayle. 1975. "The Traffic in Women: Notes on the 'Political Economy' of Sex." In *Toward an Anthropology of Women*, edited by Rayna R. Reiter. New York: Monthly Review Press.

Ruse, Michael. 1979. *The Darwinian Revolution: Science Red in Tooth and Claw*. Chicago: University of Chicago Press.

Russett, Cynthia Eagle. 1989. *Sexual Science: The Victorian Construction of Womanhood*. Cambridge, Mass.: Harvard University Press.

Russo, Mary. 1986. "Female Grotesques: Carnival and Theory." In *Feminist Studies/Critical Studies*, edited by Teresa de Lauretis. Bloomington: Indiana University Press.

Russell, Thomas J., and Ronald Lane. 1990. *Kleppner's Advertising Procedure*. 11th ed. Englewood Cliffs, N.J.: Prentice Hall.

Schneider, Rebecca. 1997. *The Explicit Body in Performance*. London: Routledge.

Schudson, Michael. 1984. *Advertising, The Uneasy Persuasion: Its Dubious Impact on American Society*. New York: Basic Books.

Schulz-Keil, Helena, ed. 1988. *Hystoria*. Lacan Study Notes, special issue, nos. 6–9. New York: New York Lacan Study Group.

Schutzman, Mady. 1990. "Dr. Charcot's Hysteria Show." *Women and Performance: A Journal of Feminist Theory* 5, no. 1: 183–89.

———. 1998. "A Fool's Discourse: The Buffoonery Syndrome." In *The Ends of Performance*, edited by Peggy Phelan and Jill Lane. New York: New York University Press.

Selzer, Richard. 1976. *Mortal Lessons: Notes on the Art of Surgery*. New York: Simon and Schuster.

Shapere, D. 1980. "The Meaning of the Evolutionary Synthesis." In *The Evolutionary Synthesis: Perspectives on the Unification of Biology,* edited by Ernst Mayr and William B. Provine. Cambridge, Mass.: Harvard University Press.

Shipley, Joseph T. 1984. *The Origins of English Words: A Discursive Dictionary of Indo-European Roots*. Baltimore: Johns Hopkins University Press.

Showalter, Elaine. 1985a. *The Female Malady: Women, Madness and English Culture, 1830–1980*. New York: Pantheon.

———. 1985b. *New Feminist Criticism: Essays on Women, Literature and Theory*. New York: Pantheon.

———. 1993. "On Hysterical Narrative." *Narrative* 1, no. 1 (January): 24–35.

———. 1997. *Hystories: Hysterical Epidemics and Modern Media*. New York: Columbia University Press.

Shuttleworth, Sally. 1990. "Female Circulation: Medical Discourse and Popular Advertising in the Mid-Victorian Era." In *Body/Politics: Women and the Discourses of Science*, edited by Mary Jacobus, Evelyn Fox Keller, and Sally Shuttleworth. New York: Routledge.

Silverman, Kaja. 1986. "Fragments of a Fashionable Discourse." In *Studies in Entertainment: Critical Approaches to Mass Culture*, edited by Tania Modleski. Bloomington: Indiana University Press.

———. 1992. Introduction to *Male Subjectivity at the Margins*. New York: Routledge.

Sim, Myre. 1982. "The Management of Hysteria." In *Hysteria*, edited by Alec Roy. New York: John Wiley and Sons.

Sirois, Francois. 1982. "Epidemic Hysteria." In *Hysteria*, edited by Alec Roy. New York: John Wiley and Sons.

Skal, David J. 1990. *Hollywood Gothic: The Tangled Web of Dracula from Stage to Scream*. New York: Norton.

Skeat, Walter W. 1956. *An Etymological Dictionary of the English Language*. London: Oxford University Press.

Slater, Eliot. 1982. "What is Hysteria?" In *Hysteria*, edited by Alec Roy. New York: John Wiley and Sons.

Smith, Protheroe. 1845. *Lancet* 1.

Smith-Rosenberg, Carroll. 1972. "The Hysterical Woman: Sex Roles and Role Conflict in 19th-Century America." *Social Research* 39, no. 4 (Spring): 652–78.

———. 1985. *Disorderly Conduct: Visions of Gender in Victorian America*. New York: Knopf.

———. 1989. "The Body Politic." In *Coming to Terms: Feminism, Theory, Politics*, edited by Elizabeth Weed. New York: Routledge.

Sontag, Susan. 1977. *On Photography*. New York: Anchor Books.

Squiers, Carol. 1989. "Jan Groover: The Still Life Seen in an Enigmatic Light." *American Photographer* (March): 38–43.

———, ed. 1990. *The Critical Image: Essays on Contemporary Photography*. Seattle: Bay Press.

Stallybrass, Peter, and Allon White. 1986. "Bourgeois Hysteria and the Carnivalesque." In *The Politics and Poetics of Transgression*. Ithaca: Cornell University Press.

Strouse, Jean. 1980. *Alice James, A Biography*. Boston: Houghton Mifflin.

Suleiman, Susan Rubin. 1990. *Subversive Intent: Gender, Politics, and the Avant-Garde*. Cambridge, Mass.: Harvard University Press.

Taussig, Michael. 1980. "Reification and the Consciousness of the Patient." *Social Science and Medicine* 14B: 3–13.

———. 1987. *Shamanism, Colonialism, and the Wild Man: A Study in Terror and Healing*. Chicago: University of Chicago Press.

———. 1992. *The Nervous System*. London: Routledge.

———. 1993. *Mimesis and Alterity: A Particular History of the Senses*. New York: Routledge.

Traweek, Sharon. 1995. "Bodies of Evidence: Law and Order, Sexy Machines, and the Erotics of Fieldwork among Physicists." In

Choreographing History, edited by Susan Leigh Foster. Bloomington: Indiana University Press.

Valenzuela, Luisa. 1986. "A Legacy of Poets and Cannibals: Literature Revives in Argentina," *New York Times Book Review* (16 March): 3.

Veblen, Thorstein. 1934. *The Theory of the Leisure Class: An Economic Study of Institutions*. New York: Modern Library.

Veith, Ilza. 1963. *Hysteria: The History of a Disease*. Chicago: University of Chicago Press.

Wajeman, Gerard. 1988. "The Hysteric's Discourse." *Hystoria* 6–9, special issue. New York: New York Lacan Study Group.

Wallace, Michele. 1990. *Invisibility: From Pop to Theory*. London: Verso.

Ward, Montgomery. 1895. *Montgomery Ward & Co. Catalogue and Buyer's Guide*, no. 57, Spring and Summer. New York: Dover.

Webster, Frank. 1980. *The New Photography: Responsibility in Visual Communication*. London: John Calder.

Weekley, Ernest. 1921. *An Etymological Dictionary of Modern English*. London: J. Murray.

Weiss, Allen S. 1989. "L'Amour Fou, L'Amour Unique." In *The Aesthetics of Excess*. Albany: State University of New York Press.

Whitlock, F. A. 1982. "The Ganser Syndrome and Hysterical Pseudo-Dementia." In *Hysteria*, edited by Alec Roy. New York: John Wiley and Sons.

Wicke, Jennifer A. 1988. *Advertising Fictions: Literature, Advertisement, and Social Reading*. New York: Columbia University Press.

Wilden, Anthony. 1968. "Lacan and the Discourse of the Other." In *The Language of the Self*, translated by Anthony Wilden. Baltimore: Johns Hopkins University Press.

Williams, Rosalind, H. 1982. *Dream Worlds: Mass Consumption in Late-Nineteenth Century France*. Berkeley and Los Angeles: University of California Press.

Williamson, Judith. 1978. *Decoding Advertisements: Ideology and Meaning in Advertising*. New York: Marion Boyars.

——. 1986a. *Consuming Passions: The Dynamics of Popular Culture*. New York: Marion Boyars.

——. 1986b. "Woman Is an Island: Femininity and Colonization." In *Studies in Entertainment: Critical Approaches to Mass Culture*, edited by Tania Modleski. Bloomington: Indiana University Press.

Willis, Susan. 1987. "Gender as Commodity." *South Atlantic Quarterly* 86, no. 4 (Fall): 403–421.

——. 1991. "I Want the Black One: Is There a Place for Afro-American Culture in Commodity Culture?" In *A Primer for Daily Life*. London: Routledge.

Woodruff, Robert A., Donald W. Goodwin, and Samuel B. Guze. 1982.

"Hysteria (Briquet's Syndrome)." In *Hysteria*, edited by Alec Roy. New York: John Wiley and Sons.

Yeazell, Ruth Bernard, ed. 1981. *The Death and Letters of Alice James: Selected Correspondence*. With a Biographical Essay by Ruth Bernard Yeazell. Berkeley and Los Angeles: University of California Press.

Index

Note: Page numbers in **bold** type refer to illustrations.

Edwards, Owen, 72

Egoiste perfume advertising, 122

El Camino advertising, 93

Elizabeth Arden advertising, 38, 156, 167

Elle, advertising in, 137–38, 143–44

Elle Decor advertisement, 146

The English Malady (Cheyne), 103n19

Enigmatic female in advertising, 119–20, **120**, 125

Envy: disguises in advertising, 164–66, **165**; and hysteria, 167–69, 168n7

Erotisme (Charcot), 85, **88**

ESPIRIT advertisement, 61, **63**

Essence/all-body condition, 103–105

Estée Lauder advertising, 48, 144, 156

Eve cigarette advertising, 18

Everlast advertisement, 61

Evolo advertisement, 164

Ewart, Gavin, 50–51, 51n3

!ex'cla.ma'tion advertisement, 105

EXP advertisement, **101**

Extase (Charcot), 85, **86**, 169

Face food, social function of, 152–54. *See also* Cosmetic advertising

FacsiMommy advertisement, 176–78

FacsiWife advertisement, 178

The Farmers Friend, 92

Fasen psychosis, 107

Fashion babies, 61

Fashion photography: premise, 70; still life reality, 71–72; surrealistic approach, 70–71. *See also* Advertising themes

Female domestication: advertising images, 24, 127; cultural sanctions, 127–28, 127n4

Femaleness. *See* Feminine attributes

Female sexuality: animality associa-

tions, 137–39; Freud's acknowledgment of mystery, 134–35; race associations, 139–40. *See also* Fetish, commodity as

Feminine attributes: biology and social constructs, 27; and child-woman role, 29–30; effects of social changeability, 7–8; Gibson Girl as model, 23–24; and growth of industrial capitalism, 19; photography as judge, 35–36, 55–56; surgical search for, 49–52; nineteenth-century medical lore, 17–18, 19, 20n2, 41; upper-class manner as prototype, 17, 19

Fetish, commodity as: female body as accessory, 141–42; female role in male psyche, 130–33; gender blurring, 142–45; invisibility of profitmaking intent, 128–29, 133; Marx's theory, 129–30; uncanny effects in advertising, 133, 134, 135. *See also* Woman as commodity

Fig Newton advertising, 149

Fleming, Anne Taylor, on Barbie, 44, 45

Food/female body partnering, 148–50. *See also* Face food, social function of

Frederick, Christine, 126

Freud, Sigmund: Anna O. case, 121n2; and Charcot, 33, 81; Dora's treatment, 123–24, 127n4; forces of disgust, 111–12; grief displays, 101; responsibility for symptoms, 64n8; influence on surrealism, 67–68; "little man" characterization, 25; mystery of female sexuality, 134–35; narcissism, 136n7, 166; repetition compulsion theory, 97; and S. Bernhardt, 33; *Studies in Hysteria,* 122, 123; and symbolic symptoms,

UNIVERSITY PRESS OF NEW ENGLAND publishes books under its own imprint and is the publisher for Brandeis University Press, Dartmouth College, Middlebury College Press, University of New Hampshire, Tufts University, and Wesleyan University Press.

About the author
Mady Schutzman teaches in the School of Critical Studies at California Institute of the Arts. She is the coeditor of *Playing Boal: Theatre, Therapy, Activism* (Routledge, 1994). Her work has been published in *The Ends of Performance*, edited by Peggy Phelan and Jill Lane (NYU Press, 1998) and in *The Contaminating Theater,* edited by Jill MacDougall (Northwestern U Press, 1998).

Library of Congress Cataloging-in-Publication Data
Schutzman, Mady, 1950–
    The real thing : performance, hysteria, and advertising / Mady Schutzman.
        p.   cm.
    Includes bibliographical references and index.
     ISBN 0–8195–6367–6 (alk. paper). — ISBN 0–8195–6370–6 (pbk. : alk. paper)
      1. Advertising—Psychological aspects.   2. Hysteria (Social psychology) I. Title.
HF5822.S289   1999
659.1'042—dc21   98-50170